AS

Psychology

Erika Cox

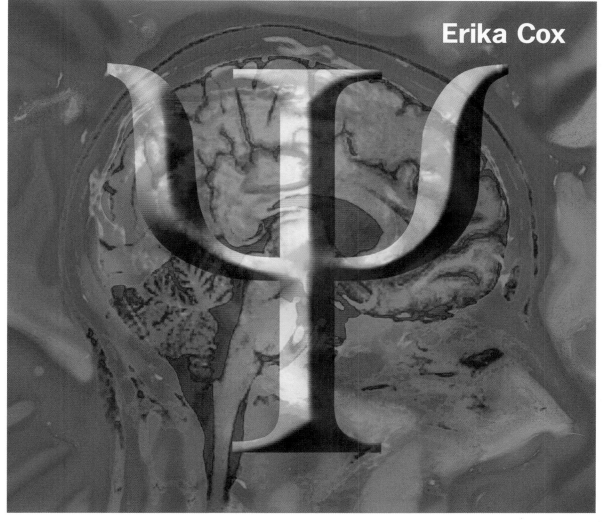

Philip Allan Updates, an imprint of Hodder Education, part of Hachette Livre UK, Market Place, Deddington, Oxfordshire OX15 0SE

Orders

Bookpoint Ltd, 130 Milton Park, Abingdon, Oxfordshire OX14 4SB
tel: 01235 827720   fax: 01235 400454

e-mail: uk.orders@bookpoint.co.uk

Lines are open 9.00 a.m.–5.00 p.m., Monday to Saturday, with a 24-hour message answering service. You can also order through the Philip Allan Updates website: www.philipallan.co.uk

ISBN 978-1-84489-614-1

First printed 2008
Impression number   5   4   3   2   1
Year   2013   2012   2011   2010   2009   2008

Design by Juha Sorsa
Printed in Italy

Hachette Livre UK's policy is to use papers that are natural, renewable and recyclable products and made from wood grown in sustainable forests. The logging and manufacturing processes are expected to conform to the environmental regulations of the country of origin.

Contents

Unit 2: Biological psychology, social psychology and individual differences

Introduction

About this book

This textbook has been written to meet the requirements of the 2008 AQA (A) Psychology specification. It provides comprehensive, accessible and up-to-date coverage of all the topic areas covered in the specification. However, you may find it interesting to follow up some of the topics covered, and learn something about other areas of psychology, by reading around the subject — for example, you might be interested in subscribing to *Psychology Review*, a quarterly magazine aimed at A-level psychology students.

This book starts with a chapter entitled 'Introducing psychology', as for many students this will be the first time that they learn about the subject, and no previous knowledge of psychology is expected for the AS course. The aim of this chapter is to provide some guidance on the kinds of topics in which psychology is interested, together with some background material about different approaches and major theories in psychology, which will be useful when you come to study the topics prescribed in the specification.

The remaining chapters follow the order of the AS specification, which is divided into two units. Unit 1 (PSYA1) covers topics in Cognitive Psychology (memory) and Developmental Psychology (attachment), together with Research Methods. Unit 2 (PSYA2) covers topics in Biological Psychology (stress), Social Psychology (social influence) and Individual Differences (abnormality).

You will find that there are quite a lot of specialised terms in psychology. These are usually defined in the text on the first occasion that they appear, but occasionally are instead included in a glossary at the end of each chapter. Psychology is also very much research-based, so you will find a large number of studies in the book. These include classical studies, carried out some time ago, but which are still regarded as important today, but also some very recent research that has provided useful insight into psychological issues.

About the exam

Assessment objectives

The exam has three assessment objectives:
- AO1 — knowledge and understanding of psychological theories and research
- AO2 — analysis and evaluation of psychological material, and the ability to apply psychological knowledge to unfamiliar situations

- AO3 — description and understanding of the various methods used in psychological research, and the understanding and application of ethical principles in research

These assessment objectives are weighted differently, with all three being given equal weighting in Unit 1, but with rather more weighting given to AO1 and AO2, compared with AO3, in Unit 2. To achieve the highest grades, you will need to do well on all three objectives.

The unit tests

Each unit is tested in a $1\frac{1}{2}$-hour exam, which consists of short-answer questions, questions requiring responses to stimulus material and questions requiring extended writing, in which the quality of written communication (QWC) will be assessed along with the content of the answer. All the questions are compulsory.

Exam answers are written in allocated spaces on the question paper, which gives some indication of how much you are expected to write. There may be occasions when you cannot fit your answer into the space provided, in which case you will need to alert the examiner to the page where your answer will be concluded. However, this should not happen very often, because if you are writing an overly lengthy answer to one question, you are likely to be taking time from other answers.

How much you should write is also indicated by the number of marks allotted to each question, which is shown on the question paper. As each paper is worth 72 marks, and each exam lasts for 90 minutes, you should aim to spend about 5 minutes writing n answer to a 4-mark question, 15 minutes on a 12-mark question that requires extended writing, and adjust the time in proportion for questions that are allotted different amounts of marks. If a question is worth very few marks, you will not get credit for writing an unnecessarily detailed answer. On the other hand, you will not gain many marks if you write only two or three lines in answer to a 12-mark question.

You may find it useful to get a copy of the specification. Your teacher may be able to give you one, or a copy can be downloaded from www.aqa.org.uk. The specification is useful in that it tells you exactly what you need to know for the exam. For example, if a theorist or a piece of research is not named in the specification, then you cannot be asked a question in the exam that relates explicitly to that theorist/research.

Understanding exam questions

Process words in exam questions are those that tell you how to approach each question. It is important to pay attention to these words, as well as the topic a question addresses, so that you focus your answer in the way required. For example, if a question only requires AO1 skills, you will not gain any marks for including AO2 material.

Process words include the following:

Outline — this requires you to give brief information. It can be an AO1 term (see 'Assessment objectives', above), as it does not ask for any evaluation. However, it could also relate to AO2 marks where the question asks you to apply psychological knowledge to a vignette, i.e. a description of a situation.

Identify — this is also an AO1 term, and requires very brief information. It is used with questions that are worth only 1 or 2 marks and can be answered in two or three words, or that ask you to match items to different headings.

Discuss — this requires you to give information and comment on it, i.e. to outline and evaluate, so it is a term that covers both AO1 and AO2 skills. The AO2 aspect could include commenting on the strengths and limitations of a theory, and/or positive and negative criticisms of research studies.

Explain — this is an AO2 term, elaborating on the information you provide. An example could be explaining the differences between two competing theories that seek to explain a particular phenomenon.

Evaluate — this is also an AO2 term, which covers such skills as commenting on the strengths and limitations of a theory, and/or positive and negative criticisms of research studies.

Revision tips

- Organise your notes into the different topics covered in the exam so that they are easy to use when you come to revise.
- Use the specification to check that you have notes on everything on which you can be asked questions.
- Plan your revision time. Be realistic about how much time can be spent on revision, and allow for time off to relax.
- Make sure you continue to take exercise, eat healthily and get enough sleep during the revision period. It is difficult to revise and sit exams when you are feeling under the weather.
- Try to think positively about the exams, i.e. as a way of demonstrating what you know, rather than a hurdle to be crossed. Changing the way we think about something so that we take a more positive view is called cognitive restructuring, and can contribute to reducing stress. It may help to know that examiners use positive marking; they are looking for something for which they can give credit, rather than for points that you have got wrong, which they ignore.
- Revising for short periods of half an hour or so with breaks in between is more effective than attempting to revise for a longer period, for example 2 hours at a time, without a break.
- Reading and re-reading information in a textbook and class notes is useful, but memory research has demonstrated that we remember more when we actively engage with material, compared with the more passive activity of reading. One way to do this is to try answering past questions. There are samples on the AQA website, and further exam-type questions in this book. You can always try making up your own questions using these as a guide.

- Remember to revise not only basic information about theories and research, but also evaluation of this material. This will be needed to gain high AO2 marks, but is often overlooked in revision. A lot of evaluation is contained in this book, and you may also think of additional points yourself.
- Practise writing timed answers under exam conditions. This will help you to get a feel for the time that you should allow for each question, so you are less likely to get your timing wrong in the exam. Remembering to focus on what precisely the question is asking may also help you to answer in the exam the question that has been set, and not a question that you hoped would be there.
- Drawing up a detailed colour-coded revision timetable does not count as revision, however pretty it is. In psychology, this is known as displacement activity, where we put off doing something important that we are not very keen to do by doing something unimportant instead.

Chapter

Introducing psychology

In this chapter, we will be looking at:
- what is psychology?
- the history of psychology
- perspectives in psychology:
  - psychodynamic
  - behaviourist
  - physiological
  - cognitive
  - humanistic

What is psychology?

Psychology is generally defined as 'the science of mind and behaviour'. However, although this gives a general idea of what psychology is about, it can be rather misleading. There are many different kinds of psychology, not all of which would fit tidily into this definition.

As we will see, not all branches of psychology agree that psychology should be a science, following the same principles as traditional and well-established sciences, such as physics or chemistry. The term 'mind' refers to internal mental processes, such as thinking, problem solving and memory, but some psychologists prefer to concentrate on observable phenomena, i.e. behaviour, rather than speculate — as they see it — on unobservable processes. In contrast, other psychologists place greater weight on internal processes — thinking and feeling — than on behaviour.

There are six main topic areas within psychology. **Cognitive psychologists** are interested in the ways in which we process information, so their research focuses on topics like memory, decision making and problem solving.

Developmental psychologists are mainly interested in how children develop, for example, how children's thinking differs from that of an adult, how personality develops, or how attachments are formed in infancy and how the nature and quality of these attachments may affect later development. Their area of research may also cover development not only in childhood but across the life span; for example, they may be interested in the psychological changes that are associated with old age.

Physiological psychologists (or **biopsychologists**) are interested in how the body functions, and in making links between physiological processes and psychological experience and behaviour. For example, they may investigate how brain damage affects memory, or how a chemical imbalance can be linked to mental disorders, such as depression or schizophrenia.

These topic areas are concerned with principles that can be applied to people in general. However, some psychologists are interested in **individual differences**, for example, why people have different personalities, or different levels of intelligence, or why some people develop a mental disorder while others do not.

People are social creatures, so much of their experience and behaviour is affected by other people. This is the area in which **social psychologists** work. For example, they may look at reasons why people obey orders given by others, or factors that lead them not to do so. In the area of relationships, they may look at factors that influence our choice of partner, or reasons why relationships break down.

Finally, **comparative psychologists** study animal behaviour — for example, innate behaviour patterns such as avoiding predators that help animals to survive and flourish within their environment. This is not only because the study of animal behaviour is interesting in its own right, but also because an understanding of animal behaviour may help to establish general principles that could also apply to people.

To give you a general overview of psychology, this course will be looking at topics with examples drawn from each of the first five areas above.

However, psychology is not only interested in establishing the principles that explain how people function. It is also interested in **applications** — for example, suggesting how we can improve memory — an important topic for exams! — or how we may best cope with stress. We will be looking at these and other examples in this course.

It has been argued that psychology is really no more than common sense. After all, most of us try to make sense of what is going on around us, understand what people are like and explain why they behave as they do. Some psychological research has indeed confirmed common-sense ideas — for example, that people are likely to choose a partner with whom they share some interests. However, our everyday common-sense ideas are based on a limited number of observations and may not always apply to people in different cultures and in situations that we have not experienced. For example, from a Western viewpoint, we might assume that people are naturally competitive, but in some cultures (such as North Korea), the well-being and success of the group is more important than that of the individual. Psychological research can provide evidence, collected in a structured and systematic way, for common-sense ideas, or it can challenge them.

Furthermore, some of the scope of psychological research is outside the experience of a common-sense approach. An obvious example is the information gathered using brain scanning techniques. Unless we are trained psychologists, common sense can only tell us in a general way about the effects of brain damage on behaviour, whereas a systematic study of the brain would give us much more detailed information.

Finally, common sense can be wrong. For example, it tells us that if you punish someone for a behaviour, they will not do it again. Yet this is in spite of prisons being full of people who have re-offended! As we will see, behaviourist research has shown that punishment is not the best way of eliminating undesired behaviour, and has suggested more effective methods.

Nonetheless, common sense is not without its uses. It has suggested ideas that can be tested in a rigorous and objective fashion, and psychological research has often been able to confirm common-sense viewpoints. However, psychology can organise and extend our understanding beyond common sense.

Summary

- Psychology is hard to define as there are many different kinds of psychologist.
- There are six main topic areas: **cognitive** psychology, **developmental** psychology, **biopsychology**, **individual differences**, **social** psychology and **comparative** psychology.
- Psychologists are interested not only in gathering information but also in possible **applications**.
- Psychology goes beyond **common sense**, investigating ideas in a systematic way and providing information not available through casual observation.

The history of psychology

Psychology as a defined subject in its own right is relatively new, going back little more than 100 years. However, it has its roots in the **philosophy** of the ancient Greeks, and some of their ideas are still relevant to psychology today.

For example, Plato argued that we are born with ideas and knowledge. Learning and development are therefore not so much the result of experience, but rather the process of revealing to ourselves what we already know; the unfolding, as a result of maturation, of innate knowledge and understanding. This approach is known as **rationalism** or **nativism**, and has echoes in some current psychological theories. For example, Chomsky argues that since children develop the effective use of language so quickly, there must be some innate knowledge about the general structure of language that enables them to do so.

North Wind Picture Archives/Alamy

Aristotle

Aristotle was a pupil of Plato. In contrast to his master, he argued that very little is innate and that all learning must come from experience. We learn through making links between different aspects of the world that occur together. This approach is known as **associationism**. It was taken up by seventeenth-century philosophers, in particular Hobbes, Locke and Hume, who claimed that experience is the basis of all knowledge of the world. They are known as **empiricists**, 'empiricism' deriving from the Latin word that means 'experience'. This approach is also represented in modern psychology, most notably in the learning theory of Watson and Skinner, which will be examined later in this chapter.

A further philosophical tradition that has influenced psychology is that of **constructivism**. In *Critique of Pure Reason* (1781), the philosopher Immanuel Kant brought together the ideas of nativists and empiricists. He argued that experience is necessary for learning and development, but that at the same time we must be born with something present in the mind if we are to make sense of reality. He suggested that we have an innate rule-forming capacity that allows us to make sense of experience and so construct models of reality.

The theories of the Swiss developmental psychologist Jean Piaget (1896–1980) are an important example of this approach in modern psychology. Piaget was interested in the development of children's thinking. He proposed that the thinking of a young child is quite different from that of an adult and develops through stages. Development comes about as the result of the child's interaction with his/her environment (an empiricist view), and children are born with the intrinsic motivation to act on their environment and to develop their understanding as a result of this interaction (a nativist view). Children, therefore, construct their own understanding.

The beginnings of modern psychology as we know it came with the opening by Wilhelm Wundt of the first psychology laboratory at the University of Leipzig in Germany in 1879. The earlier philosophical approaches involved speculation about the nature of the mind, but Wundt aimed to analyse the mind in a more structured way. Participants were exposed to a standard stimulus, for example the sound of a metronome or a light, and were asked to report their sensations. Asking people to report their experiences in this way is known as **introspection**. Wundt and his co-workers aimed to record these introspections and analyse them in terms of their component elements, in the same way as a chemist might analyse a chemical compound and thus uncover the underlying structure. For this reason, Wundt's approach is known as **structuralism**.

Other psychologists were also investigating mental experience at around the same time. In America, William James published *The Principles of Psychology* in 1890.

Unlike Wundt, he believed that psychology should aim to study mental experience as a whole, rather than try to break it down into its component elements. However, like Wundt, he also used the method of introspection. James had some interesting ideas about a large range of topics — for example, the development of identity, human instincts and emotion — and many of these have influenced more modern theories.

A rather different approach to psychology was taken by the German psychologist Hermann Ebbinghaus (1850–1909), who published *Concerning Memory* in 1885. He can be placed within the tradition of introspection, but he also took a carefully controlled experimental approach in his research into the nature of memory. His work and the contribution that he made to the study of memory will be examined in a little more detail in Chapter 2.

It is important to note that the method of introspection raises certain problems. The researcher has to depend on the skill, and indeed the willingness and honesty, of the person reporting his or her experiences. Wundt provided training for the people that he tested in this way, but his research nonetheless depended on their level of awareness of their experiences and their skill in reporting them accurately. Reporting a sensation while it is occurring may interfere with the sensation, but if it is reported afterwards it may be less accurate. With simple sensations, accurate reporting may not be too difficult, but it is likely to be more problematic as the stimuli to which the respondent is exposed become more complex. The key issue here is that introspection is essentially **subjective**. Only the person concerned can observe and report on internal processes, and there is no way of checking whether the report is accurate, as it does not lend itself to measurement and precise analysis.

Because of these kinds of problems, John Watson (1878–1958) suggested that psychology should take a different approach. He proposed that psychology should be considered a science, and like any other science it should adopt scientific methods and, in particular, collect objective data — unlike the subjective data produced by introspection.

As you will know from your study of biology, chemistry or physics, the scientific method involves the observation of a phenomenon, and the development of a general theory to explain it, leading to a specific, testable hypothesis. An experiment is then set up to test this hypothesis, isolating the factor in which you are interested, and controlling for other factors that are not relevant but which may influence the outcome. Information (data) must be collected, which is objective, so that others running a similar experiment could check their results against those of your experiment. The data are then analysed, so that conclusions can be drawn from the results, either supporting the hypothesis or leading to a new hypothesis being developed.

Watson believed that this was an appropriate model for psychology and that behaviour was the appropriate form of data. He founded the school of thought called **behaviourism**, which will be looked at in more detail later in this chapter. He believed that all human functioning could be studied in this way, even claiming — mistakenly — that thinking is expressed in tiny movements of the vocal cords.

Mary Evans Picture Library/Alamy

Sigmund Freud

However, not all psychologists embraced this approach. Sigmund Freud (1856–1939) started to develop his **psychodynamic theory** around 1900, giving a lot of weight to unconscious processes in the mind. Unconscious factors can sometimes be inferred from behaviour, but the methods that Freud adopted depended heavily on talking to patients and interpreting what they said to him. Freud used the **case-study method**, where an individual or a small group of individuals is studied in detail. Up to a point, it can be considered as scientific, in that it involves the careful collection and analysis of information, and Freud saw himself as a scientist. However, his methods are far removed from those of the behaviourists.

The experimental method has long been the dominant tradition within psychology, involving the careful collection and statistical analysis of objective and quantifiable data, but other methods have become more widely used in recent years. Many psychologists now believe that more subjective methods may also have a valuable contribution to make.

Summary

- Psychology has its roots in the **philosophy** of ancient Greece, many ideas of which can be linked to psychological issues.
- Modern psychology began with researchers like Wundt, whose methods relied on **introspection**.
- Watson argued that psychology should be approached like any other science and so should aim to gather objective data. He started the movement known as **behaviourism**.
- Not all psychologists accept that strictly scientific methods are the most appropriate .way of carrying out psychological research.

Perspectives in psychology

It should now be apparent that psychology is an extremely diverse subject. Psychologists vary in terms of the basic beliefs they have about the nature of people, the questions they think are important to address in order to extend our understanding and knowledge, and the methods they think are most appropriate to further their research aims. These different perspectives can be summarised under five main headings: psychodynamic, behaviourist, physiological, cognitive and humanistic. Each of these will be looked at briefly in turn.

The psychodynamic perspective

The psychodynamic or psychoanalytic perspective was developed by **Freud**. His theory has been extremely influential, and although some of his views are controversial, he nonetheless put forward ideas relating to many areas of psychology, for example aggression, mental disorders, personality and moral development.

One of Freud's basic ideas was the concept of **psychological determinism**. He explained that all our behaviour is motivated: it is not random, but has an underlying cause. He also laid great stress on the importance of **unconscious processes** and believed that **childhood** was a crucial time in terms of determining adult characteristics and behaviour.

The unconscious

Freud proposed that all behaviour has an underlying cause and that the reasons why we behave as we do are often unconscious. An example of this is what came to be known as a Freudian slip, or **parapraxis**, where we say or do something that we had not consciously intended. For example, you may 'forget' a dentist's appointment, as you unconsciously wish to avoid the possible pain and discomfort that going to the dentist may involve. Freud gave an example from one of his patients:

> A young man, rather cautious about commitment, finally proposed to his girlfriend and was happy when she accepted him. He took her home, and then got on a tram to go home himself. He asked for two tickets. Six months after his marriage, he was not entirely happy. He did not get on well with his parents-in-law and missed time spent with his friends. One evening, after fetching his wife from her parents' house, he got on a tram and asked for one ticket.
>
> Sigmund Freud, *The Interpretation of Dreams*, 1900

Freud suggested that on the first occasion, asking for two tickets expressed the young man's wish that his girlfriend were with him. On the second occasion, he unconsciously wished that she were *not* there as he was unhappy with his marriage, and so he only asked for one ticket.

Freud's view of the unconscious is perhaps his most important contribution to psychology. The existence of the unconscious had been recognised before Freud, but it was generally regarded as a store for information that is no longer of any importance. For Freud, on the other hand, the unconscious is dynamic; an active force that motivates much of our behaviour. A great deal of the material in our unconscious is there because it is painful and is therefore kept out of consciousness to protect us. The unconscious can be contrasted with the **conscious**, i.e. the ideas of which we are currently aware (such as the information that you are reading now), and the **preconscious**, i.e. material that can easily be brought to consciousness (such as what you ate for lunch yesterday).

The concept of **unconscious conflict** plays a major part in Freud's theory. It can be seen in parapraxes, in disturbing emotional states and also in dreams, which Freud believed expressed symbolically underlying conflict.

Unconscious conflict can also be related to the **structure of the mind**. Freud proposed that the mind has three parts: the id, the ego and the superego. This is a theoretical division rather than an anatomical one — there is no suggestion that these different parts of the mind correspond to different parts of the brain.

The **id** is present at birth. It is unconscious and the seat of our instincts. It operates on the **pleasure principle**, i.e. seeking pleasure and avoiding pain. It is also the source of the psychic energy that Freud called the **libido**.

As children get older, the **ego** develops from the id, as they realise that instant gratification is not always possible and that pain cannot always be avoided. The ego therefore operates on the **reality principle**. It takes the desires of the id into account, but must decide how they may best be satisfied.

The **superego** develops at around the age of 5 years. This is the moral part of the mind, i.e. the conscience and the ego ideal: what the child would like to be.

There is often conflict between the impulses of the id and the requirements of the superego, and Freud believed that the way in which this conflict is resolved is crucial to personality development. Ideally, we are governed by the ego. People who are governed by the id would in extreme cases be termed sociopaths, with no concern for anyone or anything except gratifying their own desires. On the other hand, those who are dominated by the superego are likely to be neurotic, and dominated by feelings of guilt and shame.

It is the job of the ego to try to balance the desires of the id with what is realistically possible and the demands of the superego. For example, the id may wish to punch the traffic warden who has just put a ticket on your car, while the superego would find such aggression socially unacceptable. The ego would need to find a way of acknowledging the impulse of the id, but express the frustration in a more

A driver expresses her frustration at receiving a parking ticket in a socially acceptable way

Digital Vision/Alamy

socially acceptable way to appease the superego, perhaps by slamming the car door rather more sharply than necessary.

One role of the ego is to protect us from the anxiety associated with unconscious conflict. Freud suggested that we use unconscious **ego defence mechanisms**, coping mechanisms that allow id impulses to be expressed and that are quite effective, especially in the short term. There are a number of these, and three examples are displacement, repression and sublimation. The traffic warden example shows **displacement**, where feelings that cannot be expressed directly towards their real targets are instead expressed towards a substitute object, in this case the car door rather than the traffic warden. **Repression** is motivated forgetting. For example, it has been claimed that people can 'forget' being abused as a child: the memory is so distressing that they are no longer consciously aware of it ever having happened. **Sublimation** is the only defence mechanism that is effective in the long term. Here, unacceptable impulses are expressed in a socially acceptable way. For example, you might play a game of rugby to re-channel aggressive impulses or inappropriate sexual impulses that cannot be expressed directly. We do not choose the defence mechanisms that we use, but those we do use contribute to our personalities.

Childhood

Freud believed that childhood is an extremely important part of life, in that experiences during this period form the basis of adult personality. He believed that the child has instinctual needs — hunger, thirst, sex — that are important sources of motivation. However, society puts constraints on the expression of these instincts, and this also represents a crucial factor in children's development.

Freud proposed that children go through a series of psycho-sexual stages, always in the same order, in each of which there is a focus on pleasure obtained from a different **erotogenic** (i.e. pleasure-giving) part of the body.

The **oral stage** lasts from birth till about the age of 1 year, and the source of pleasure here is the mouth. Children of this age obtain pleasure from sucking when they are fed, and seem to enjoy putting any new object into their mouths.

After this, the child enters the **anal stage**, where the child experiences pleasure in expelling or holding in faeces. During this stage, the child learns that there are restrictions as to when and where defecating is acceptable, and that there are implications, in terms of pleasing parents (or not), related to this activity.

At around the age of 5 years, the child enters the **phallic stage**, where pleasure is obtained from the genitals. This stage is experienced differently by boys and by girls. The boy goes through the crisis that Freud called the **Oedipus complex**, during which he develops unconscious sexual feelings towards his mother. As these feelings are unacceptable, he fears they

Young children enjoy putting new objects into their mouths

will be punished by castration by his father, and so develops castration anxiety. To resolve this issue, the boy identifies with his father — symbolically 'becomes' his father — taking in his father's beliefs and values. According to Freud, this is the basis of the development of the superego, and thus a sense of morality. Girls go through a similar crisis, though rather less precisely described, which Freud called the **Electra complex**. According to Freud, girls blame their mother for their lack of a penis, and so transfer their affections to their father. This fades away with time as they come to realise they can never possess their father, but because they do not face the same threat of castration as boys, there is not the same pressure to identify with the moral standards of the mother. Freud believed, therefore, that girls have a less well-developed sense of morality than boys.

The **latency period** lasts from the age of 5 years until puberty. The child turns aside from his or her sexuality and concentrates instead on social and intellectual development. At adolescence, the child then moves into the **genital stage**, during which adult sexual feelings are experienced, and mature love is possible.

Freud believed that it is possible for an individual to become **fixated** in one of these stages, either through over-gratification of the pleasure-giving activities associated with it, or the frustration of these activities. This would lead to adult characteristics symbolic of the stage in which the individual was fixated. For example, fixation in the anal stage could be demonstrated in an adult who is particularly mean: the child who derived pleasure from holding on to his faeces is now an adult who symbolically continues to do so, by being unwilling to part with money or possessions. The child who derived pleasure from expelling faeces might express this symbolically as an adult by being over-generous. Fixations can be caused by the intense pleasure associated with taboos, such as smearing faeces. This could be expressed by the adult being exceedingly untidy and messy, or becoming a potter: as the child enjoyed smearing faeces, the adult expresses this symbolically by smearing clay.

According to Freud, adult personality is therefore determined not only by the balance between id, ego and superego, together with the use of particular defence mechanisms, but also by childhood experiences during the psychosexual stages.

Psychoanalysis

Freud's theory has practical application within the associated therapy of **psychoanalysis**. Freud originally developed his theory thanks to the work he did with his patients, which helped him to realise that the sources of psychological problems often lie in childhood experience, and are unconscious. The therapy aims to uncover these unconscious experiences, so that the issues to which they relate can be dealt with, or 'worked through'.

In order to access the unconscious, Freud developed a number of special techniques. For example, he believed that in sleep, the unconscious is closer to the surface and therefore potentially more easily accessible. By analysing and interpreting dreams, he uncovered the unconscious fears and wishes expressed symbolically in his patients' dreams. Psychoanalysis will be examined in more detail in the final chapter of this book.

Commentary

There are many criticisms to be made of Freud's theory. He claimed that it applied universally, but it was developed on the basis of therapy sessions he conducted with patients who were mostly middle-aged, middle-class Viennese women, a limited group from which to generalise. Moreover, his use of case studies means that his interpretations were subjective and did not produce the kinds of objective data necessary to a science, so his ideas are difficult to test in an objective way. His emphasis on sexuality has also been questioned.

At the same time, the psychodynamic perspective has been extremely influential, and many later theorists within it have built on and developed Freud's ideas. For example, Erik Erikson (1902–94) developed the theory to recognise development across the life span, not just in childhood, and gave more weight to social than to sexual influences. Freud was also the first person to develop a systematic theory of personality, and his emphasis on the importance of the unconscious is widely recognised.

Summary

- In the **psychodynamic perspective**, the 'model of the person' is one through which behaviour and experience are shaped by **unconscious** processes.
- In Freud's theory, the idea of **conflict** is central. There is conflict between the different structures of the mind: **id, ego** and **superego**.
- **Ego defence mechanisms** protect us from the anxiety created by unconscious conflict and contribute towards our personality.
- Personality is also shaped by our experience of the **psychosexual stages** in childhood, and possible **fixation** in one stage.
- The theory has the associated therapy of **psychoanalysis**.
- While there are criticisms of the psychodynamic perspective, it has put forward some widely accepted ideas and has been extremely influential.

The behaviourist perspective

As discussed earlier, the behaviourist perspective developed as a result of the ideas put forward by John Watson. He proposed that psychology should adopt scientific methods in order to achieve acceptance as a science. He rejected internal processes, such as thoughts and feelings, as potential sources of data, as they could neither be directly accessed nor objectively measured. He saw behaviour as the only acceptable form of data.

Within this perspective, the behaviour of **non-human animals** is often studied. Darwin's theories of evolution had suggested that there is a continuity between animals and humans, so carrying out experiments with animals could help to establish general laws of behaviour that might then be relevant to explaining human behaviour.

The use of animals has other advantages. They can be bred for laboratory experiments, so that they are genetically identical and the experiments can be replicated, and their life experience before taking part in a study can be controlled.

This means that possible confounding variables, which might affect the behaviour of *human* participants, can be eliminated. Animals are also less likely than humans to be affected by **demand characteristics**, i.e. aspects of the study that may lead participants to guess — rightly or wrongly — the purpose of the research and so change their behaviour. Many of the animals used in research, such as rats and pigeons, also have a much shorter life span than humans, allowing changes across the life span (for example in memory) to be tested more easily. A further advantage is that animals can be treated in ways that would be unacceptable for human participants — for example, being kept hungry so that hunger is a motivator. Of course, this does not mean that experimenters can treat animals in whatever ways they think appropriate. Guidelines, which must be strictly adhered to, have been laid down in the UK in the *Animals (Scientific Procedures) Act* (1986). Experimenters also need a licence from the Home Office to carry out research with animals, and have to justify their proposed study in terms of the scientific contribution that they expect it to make.

Classical conditioning

In proposing what the nature of a scientific study of psychology should be, Watson was particularly interested in the link between an event in the environment (a **stimulus**), such as touching something hot or hearing your name being called out, and the behaviour that follows (a **response**), in this case moving your hand or turning your head in the direction of the voice. Behaviourism is therefore sometimes known as **S-R (stimulus-response)** psychology. Watson believed that learning was a process of associating a stimulus with a response. These ideas were taken up by others interested in this approach, and their theories are grouped together as **learning theory**.

Jupiter Images/Banana Stock/Alamy

Dogs respond to the sight of food by salivating in expectation

Watson's ideas tied in to research being carried out by **Ivan Pavlov** (1849–1936), a Russian physiologist who was interested in the digestive processes of dogs and, in particular, the salivation reflex, the in-built response to food that is the first stage of the digestive process. In the course of his research, Pavlov noticed that the dogs not only salivated in response to the taste of food, but also when they could only see it. He carried out a series of studies to investigate whether this response could also be triggered by other stimuli (see Box 1.1).

With the dog salivating to the sound of the bell, there is an objectively measurable change in behaviour, so the dog can be said to have learned to salivate to the sound of the bell. This kind of learning, associating a stimulus and a response, is called **classical conditioning**.

Watson saw Pavlov's work as a good example of the scientific approach that he wanted to see in psychology and carried out studies using this method with human participants (see Box 1.2).

Box 1.1 Pavlov (1927)

Aims: To investigate the possibility of a dog learning to associate a novel stimulus with the salivation reflex.

Procedure: A dog was held in a harness to restrict movement. A bell was rung, which the dog had not heard before, to check that the dog did not automatically salivate to this sound. The experimenter then rang the bell and immediately afterwards presented food to the dog. This was repeated several times. Finally, the bell was rung on its own.

Results: When the bell had been rung and the food presented very close together in time, the reflex response of salivation was shown. After this procedure, when the bell was rung on its own, salivation was produced.

Conclusions: As a result of the repeated pairings of bell and food, an association between the stimulus of the bell and the response of salivation had been formed.

NS (bell)	⟶	No particular response
UCS (food)	⟶	UCR (salivation)
NS (bell) ⎫ UCS (food) ⎭	⟶	UCR (salivation)
CS (bell)	⟶	CR (salivation)

Key

NS = Neutral stimulus, so called because it does not lead to any particular response.

UCS/UCR = Unconditional stimulus/response. The UCS is always automatically followed by the UCR; there are no conditions to be met for this to happen.

CS/CR = Conditioned stimulus/response. The CS only produces the CR *on condition* that it has previously been paired several times with the NS.

Box 1.2 Watson and Rayner (1920)

Aims: To investigate classical conditioning with a human participant.

Procedure: This study was carried out with an 11-month-old infant known as Little Albert. Before the study, Albert was tested for possible reactions to a range of stimuli, including a white rat, a rabbit, various other animals, cotton wool and burning newspapers. He did not show any fear to any of these stimuli. However, he did show a fear response — not surprisingly — when a loud noise was made behind him: a hammer hitting an iron bar. The experimenters made this noise several times, on each occasion presenting him with the white rat at the same time. The white rat was then presented on its own.

Results: After the pairings of noise and rat, Little Albert developed a fear response to the white rat. This response diminished over time, but was still evident a month later.

Conclusions: Humans can be classically conditioned in the same way as non-human animals. This is an example of a **conditioned emotional response** and could be a way of explaining fear responses. It is possible that people develop phobias through forming this kind of S-R association.

There are clearly some ethical problems here, in that the whole experience was extremely distressing to the child, whereas psychologists have a duty to protect participants from short-term stress and longer-term harm. It is also not clear whether the child's mother was given full information about what the study would involve. However, it does demonstrate that the principles of classical conditioning can be applied to humans. Psychologists have made use of this in several ways, in particular in devising effective therapies. In Chapter 7, classical conditioning will be examined again, in the context of abnormality.

Operant conditioning

Operant conditioning is another example of the behaviourist perspective, and is associated with **B. F. Skinner** (1904–90). In common with classical conditioning it emphasises observable behaviour. It is concerned with learning, and sees learning as a process of association. However, unlike classical conditioning, it does not see learning as an association between stimulus and response, but between behaviour and the consequences of that behaviour. The basic principle behind Skinner's theory is that behaviour is shaped and maintained by its consequences. While classical conditioning relates only to reflex behaviour, operant conditioning relates to all behaviour.

B. F. Skinner demontrating a Skinner box in his Harvard laboratory

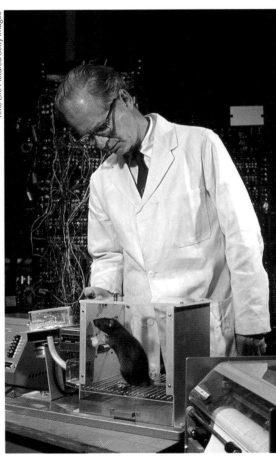

Time Life Pictures/Getty Images

Skinner believed that all behaviour is learned, apart from the reflexes with which we are born. He also claimed that an animal can learn to produce any behaviour of which it is physically capable if appropriate techniques are used. The key ideas in the theory are **reinforcement** and **shaping**. Reinforcement refers to the positive outcome of a behaviour that makes it more likely to be repeated. Shaping refers to gradually modifying behaviour, using reinforcement, as the behaviour produced becomes more like the target behaviour.

This can be illustrated by Skinner's experiments in training a rat to press a lever for food in a 'Skinner box'. The rat was kept hungry so food represented a reinforcer. When the rat was first put in the box, it would be reinforced with food for approaching the lever. Once it was reliably in this area of the box, it would be reinforced only when it touched the lever with any part of its body. Once this behaviour was established, it would be reinforced only when it touched the lever with a paw, and then finally only when it pressed the lever. Using this method, Skinner even taught pigeons to play table tennis. Skinner carried out a lot of his work on rats and pigeons, but his work also has relevance to human learning.

Skinner made a distinction between **positive reinforcement** (where there is a positive outcome to behaviour), **negative reinforcement** (when the outcome of a behaviour is 'that something unpleasant stops'), and **punishment** (where the outcome of a behaviour is either 'that something positive stops' or 'that something negative occurs'). Table 1.1 shows this distinction and provides examples of outcomes.

Table 1.1	Reinforcement and punishment			
Term	**What happens**	**Effect**	**Example**
Positive reinforcement	Something pleasurable is added to a situation	Behaviour is strengthened	Praise; food if hungry
Negative reinforcement	Something unpleasant is removed from a situation	Behaviour is strengthened	Pain stops
Punishment	Something pleasurable is removed or something unpleasant is added to a situation	Behaviour is weakened	An expected treat is taken away; physical punishment

Skinner believed that the best way to change behaviour reliably is with the use of positive reinforcement. While punishment may be necessary to put an immediate stop to dangerous behaviour — for example, a child putting his or her fingers in an electric socket, it should otherwise be avoided, for several reasons:

■ Punishment is unpleasant and is likely to change behaviour only in the short term, as the behaviour is likely to come back.
■ Punishment gives no indication of what the desired behaviour would be.
■ Punishment may also have undesirable effects — for example, if a child is always slapped by the mother for undesired behaviour, he or she may (through classical conditioning) come to associate the mother with pain and distress.

The principles of operant conditioning have been applied in a range of situations, for example to help children with learning difficulties acquire skills, and improve behaviour management in the classroom. The use of star charts and stickers in primary schools is now quite common.

Social learning theory (SLT)

Social learning theory developed out of operant conditioning. Like operant conditioning, it accepts that all behaviour (including social behaviour) is learned and that positive reinforcement brings about learning. However, it also suggests that we can learn not only through the outcomes of our own behaviour, but also by observing the behaviour of others and the outcomes of their behaviour.

Albert Bandura (b. 1925) is one of the foremost theorists in this area. He used the term '**observational learning**' to describe learning through the observation of others' behaviour and its outcome. If the outcome is positive, we may then produce this behaviour ourselves; he called this **modelling**. Modelling is not just copying what we see, but rather learning the general rules and principles underlying the behaviour and its outcome, such as focusing on relevant aspects of the behaviour being observed and remembering its critical features so that they can be reproduced. Bandura therefore introduced an element of cognition into learning, and so moved away from the traditional behaviourist stance that internal and unobservable behaviours are not a focus for the study of psychology.

Bandura believed that there are three sources of models:
■ the family
■ the sub-culture (the people with whom we mix outside the immediate family)
■ the mass media

He demonstrated modelling in a series of experiments that he carried out with children (see Box 1.3).

The conclusions to be drawn were refined in a later study, in 1965 (see Box 1.4).

Box 1.3 Bandura et al. (1963)

Aims: To investigate the effects of observing aggression in an adult model.

Procedure: In a playroom containing a range of toys, children watched an adult attacking a large inflatable Bobo doll in unusual ways, e.g. hitting it with a hammer, and saying 'Pow!' The adult then left the playroom and the behaviour of the children was observed. A control group of children did not see the adult attack the Bobo doll. Their behaviour in the playroom was also observed.

Results: The children who had observed the adult attacked the Bobo doll in similar ways to the adult. The children who had not observed the adult did not.

Conclusions: Children learned particular behaviours towards the Bobo doll through observational learning, and then modelled the behaviour when given the opportunity.

Box 1.4 Bandura (1965)

Aims: To observe the effects on modelling by children of seeing a model reinforced or punished for a behaviour.

Procedure: The procedure was similar to the previous study, except that one group of children saw the model being rewarded for aggressive behaviour, a second group saw the model being punished, and a third control group went straight into the playroom after observing the model. The children in the group that saw the model being punished were later offered a reward if they could reproduce the behaviour they had observed.

Results: There was little difference between the first and third groups in the number of imitated aggressive behaviours, but initially there were significantly fewer in the group who had seen the model punished (the second group). However, when the children in the second group were offered a reward, the number of imitated aggressive behaviours in this group rose to a level similar to those of the other two groups.

Conclusions: Observation is enough for behaviour to be learned, but reinforcement is necessary for the behaviour to be modelled.

Commentary

The behaviourist perspective has been criticised for its failure to include mental processes, which are arguably central to what makes us distinctively human, and the use of animals in research has been condemned for similar reasons. However, behaviourism has been influential in attempting to make psychology a science, using careful observation and measurement. It also has many applications, in therapies for people with mental health problems and more widely.

Summary

- Behaviourist approaches can be grouped together as **learning theory**. This approach proposes that all behaviour (except reflexes) is learned and that we learn by **association**. It often carries out studies using animals. The data are **behaviour**.
- In **classical conditioning**, an association is formed between a stimulus and a response: **S-R learning**. Some therapies are based on this approach.
- In **operant conditioning**, an association is formed between **behaviour** and its **consequences**. The key ideas in bringing about behaviour change are **shaping** and **reinforcement**. Positive reinforcement is the most effective way of changing a behaviour. The principles have been widely applied, particularly in education.
- **Social learning theory (SLT)** developed out of operant conditioning. Behaviour is acquired through **observational learning** and **modelling**. Unlike classical and operant conditioning, there is an element of **cognition** in this account. Observation is sufficient for a behaviour to be learned, but **reinforcement** is necessary for it to be modelled.
- Behaviourism has been criticised for restricting the area of study to behaviour. However, it has been influential in making psychology take a more scientific approach to research, and it has wide practical applications.

The physiological perspective

Psychology is concerned with behaviour and experience, but these must have their basis within the physical body. The physiological perspective therefore focuses on making links between how the body works and psychological functioning. Animal experiments can sometimes be a starting point for research in this area.

The study of the **brain** is an essential component of research in physiological psychology. One area of interest is **localisation of function**, i.e. how different parts of the brain can be linked to specific behaviours and experience. The development of brain scanning techniques has played

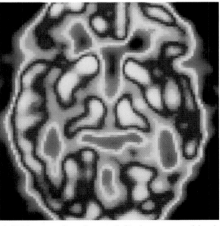

A PET scan showing activity in a normal brain

an important role in this field. **Positron emission tomography (PET) scans** show which areas of the brain are active while carrying out psychological tasks. For example, we will see in the chapter on memory (Chapter 2) that these scans have lent support to the proposal that there are different functions within working memory. The effects of **brain damage** can also be informative. Again in Chapter 2, we will see how damage to a structure called the hippocampus has demonstrated its involvement in long-term memory.

Psychologists are also interested in biochemical processes. **Neurotransmitters** are chemical messengers that allow neurones (nerve cells) to communicate with each other. It has been suggested that psychological disorders may be caused by an imbalance of neurotransmitters. For example, depression has been linked with low levels of serotonin, and schizophrenia with high levels of dopamine. This has applications in the area of mental health with respect to the use of medication to correct an imbalance and so manage these disorders.

Hormones are another kind of biochemical, produced by the endocrine system and carried to other parts of the body in the blood. For example, the hormone ACTH (adrenocorticotrophic hormone) is associated with the physical response to stress, which again suggests that the use of drugs to adjust hormone levels can be a useful way of helping people who experience stress. We will be looking at these ideas in more detail in the chapter on stress (Chapter 5).

Genetics is another area of interest. Physical characteristics, such as eye colour, and some physical disorders, such as cystic fibrosis, are passed on through the genes from parent to child. Psychologists taking the physiological perspective are interested in whether psychological characteristics, for example, temperament and intelligence, are also transmitted in this way. As we will see in Chapter 7, there is some evidence that some mental illnesses may be at least in part genetic.

In this area of research, **twin studies** are often carried out. Twins can be monozygotic (MZ), i.e. they develop from the same fertilised egg and are therefore genetically identical. They can also be dizygotic (DZ), i.e. they develop from two fertilised eggs and therefore only have approximately 50% of their genes in common, just like other brothers and sisters. Research also compares MZ and DZ twins. The reasoning here is that twins share the same environment and therefore any differences between them cannot be due to environmental influences. If there is a genetic component to the characteristic being studied, MZ twins should therefore be more similar than DZ twins. This kind of approach will be examined in more detail in the chapter on explaining psychological abnormality (Chapter 7).

Evolutionary psychology is another approach that investigates the effect of genes. Darwin's theory of evolution proposes that there are variations within a species — for example, humans vary in height. Where a particular variation is **adaptive**, i.e. makes an individual better suited to a particular environment, it increases the chances that an individual with genes coding for this variation will survive long enough to reproduce and pass them on to the next generation. The genes of other individuals, who do not survive long enough to reproduce, will be lost to the gene pool.

This theory has been used to explain both physical and psychological characteristics. Evolutionary psychologists aim to make sense of psychological characteristics, for example phobias (irrational fears that are out of all proportion to the danger that an object or situation poses), in terms of how they would have been **adaptive** in our evolutionary past. For instance, they might explain acrophobia, which is a fear of heights, in this way. If we go back thousands of years in our evolutionary past, individuals who had a strong fear of high places (which present the danger of being harmed or killed by falling) and so kept away from them, would have been more likely to survive long enough to reproduce and pass on their genes, including those that code for fear of heights, to the next and future generations.

Most of the approaches within the physiological perspective adopt a scientific method, testing hypotheses in ways that involve careful measurement and the control of possible confounding variables. Evolutionary psychology, however, uses the rather different method of **reverse engineering** (sometimes called **functional analysis**). It draws on the principles of evolutionary theory and our knowledge of past environmental conditions to explain why a particular characteristic might have promoted survival and reproduction, and therefore the passing on of particular genes. This can be thought of as rather like using mechanical principles and the observations of how a car works to deduce why it was designed in that way. This method has been criticised for being speculative and impossible to test, but has nonetheless produced some interesting ideas.

Commentary
Physical factors are an important influence on psychological functioning, so physiological psychology has a lot to offer. However, social and cultural factors are also of great significance, so this perspective can only give a partial picture.

Summary

- The **physiological perspective** links physiological functioning to psychological functioning.
- It is interested in the functioning of the normal **brain** and the effects of brain damage.
- Links are made between the biochemical systems of **neurotransmitters** and **hormones**, and psychological characteristics.
- Psychological characteristics may be the result of **genetic inheritance**.
- **Evolutionary psychology** explains psychological characteristics in terms of their adaptiveness in our evolutionary past.
- Most research in this area takes a **scientific** approach, though evolutionary psychology uses the more speculative approach of **reverse engineering**.
- An understanding of physiological factors is essential in psychology, but social and cultural factors are also important.

The cognitive perspective

Even though the behaviourist perspective was popular in the 1940s and 1950s, many psychologists criticised it for giving no role to internal mental processes, pointing out that thoughts and feelings are important in many areas of human functioning and therefore should have a place in psychology. As mentioned above, behaviourists do not claim that mental processes do not exist, but rather do not consider them an appropriate focus of study, because they are not directly observable or measurable. However, psychologists from other schools of thought believe that focusing only on observable behaviour and ignoring the mental processes leading to that behaviour provides an extremely limited account of psychological functioning. For example, it is almost always impossible to tell what someone is thinking. We can ask them to describe their thought processes, but this has all the drawbacks of introspection, which was discussed earlier.

Cognitive psychologists are particularly interested in the mental processes involved in perception, attention, memory, language and thinking, such as problem solving and decision making. An analogy can be drawn between these mental processes and the way a computer works: information is fed into the computer, it is processed in some way, and there is then an output. In the same way, the model of the person proposed by cognitive psychologists is of an **information processor**: information is fed in from the outside world, we process it, and the result of this processing is behaviour and experience.

Although we cannot observe and measure cognitive processes directly, we can access them indirectly by looking at the results of processing. Most of the research in this area has therefore taken an **experimental approach**. For example, in some of the research described in Chapter 2, people were asked to carry out memory tasks under controlled conditions, leading to some kind of measurable results, such as the number of words remembered from a word list, or the levels of activity in particular parts of the brain. Similar methods are used in other areas of cognition, such as research into perception. Occasionally, however, more interpretative methods are employed, for example **discourse analysis**, which analyses pieces of text such as newspaper reports.

In recent years, this perspective has been strongly influenced by the use of computers. **Artificial intelligence** (AI) combines cognitive psychology and computer science. Researchers have developed computer programmes that can carry out the kinds of complex cognitive tasks associated with human functioning, and which may therefore shed light on human cognition. An influential theoretical framework in this area is **connectionism**. For example, Plunkett and Juola (1999) used computational modelling to investigate the processes by which children progress to using grammatically accurate forms of irregular verbs, such as 'go' and 'come'.

Commentary

The cognitive approach is limited in that it focuses on only one aspect of human functioning, not taking into account the influence of factors such as emotions. Some psychologists also see the use of computational modelling as artificial and far removed from the richness of what people experience in the real world.

At the same time, the study of cognition is necessary to bridge the gap in behaviourism between stimulus and response if we are to have a more complete understanding of how humans function. The cognitive perspective has also been influential in developing therapies for people with mental disorders, an aspect that will be examined more closely in the chapter on abnormality (Chapter 7).

- The **cognitive perspective** has a model of the person as an **information processor**.
- This perspective usually uses **scientific methods**, with the data being the results of cognition.
- **Computational modelling** is often used.
- Though somewhat limited in scope, the cognitive perspective is an important area in psychology, which has made a valuable contribution to **therapeutic interventions**.

The humanistic perspective

This perspective developed during the 1960s, as a result of dissatisfaction with the dominant perspectives of psychodynamics and behaviourism. In particular, some psychologists were unhappy with the somewhat pessimistic view of the psycho-dynamic perspective, which sees people as constrained by unconscious forces over which they have no control, and with the lack of weight given by behaviourists to conscious awareness. For these reasons, the humanistic perspective is sometimes known as the **third force**, emerging in response to the dominance of psycho-dynamics and behaviourism.

The humanistic perspective emphasises the importance of **conscious awareness** and the ability of people to make choices and control their lives. This approach also questions the appropriateness of scientific methods in psychology, its proponents believing instead that what is important is the individual's experience of being a person. They therefore often use the case-study method and value the insights that they believe introspection can give.

An early theorist within this general perspective was Abraham Maslow (1908–70), who in 1954 proposed a theory of motivation, which suggested that humans have a hierarchy of needs (see Figure 1.1).

At the bottom are the most basic physiological needs necessary for survival, such as food and sleep. Next come safety needs, i.e. a reasonable level of protection from harm. Above that are the needs for love and belonging: we need contact with other people and acceptance from them. The fourth level is esteem: we need others to recognise our qualities and abilities, and to be able to respect ourselves. These four groups of needs are **deficiency needs**, in that they can be met. They are distinguished from the highest level of the hierarchy: the need for **self-actualisation**, which Maslow defined as 'to become everything that one is capable of becoming'. How this need is addressed will vary from person to person. It could be expressed in

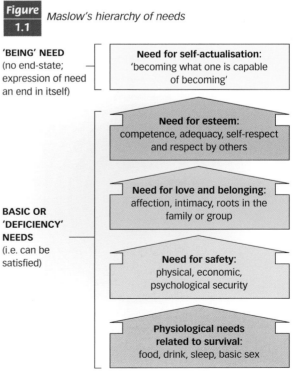

Figure 1.1 Maslow's hierarchy of needs

'BEING' NEED (no end-state; expression of need an end in itself)

Need for self-actualisation: 'becoming what one is capable of becoming'

Need for esteem: competence, adequacy, self-respect and respect by others

Need for love and belonging: affection, intimacy, roots in the family or group

BASIC OR 'DEFICIENCY' NEEDS (i.e. can be satisfied)

Need for safety: physical, economic, psychological security

Physiological needs related to survival: food, drink, sleep, basic sex creativity, in athletic prowess, or in being a good mother or friend. This is a '**being**' **need**, in that it can never be achieved in the same way as the needs lower down the hierarchy. Expression of this need is an end in itself.

Maslow explored what would make a healthy and fulfilled personality. His ideas have been built on by Carl Rogers (1902–87), who is regarded as the main figure within humanistic psychology. There are three basic principles underlying his approach. First, it is a **phenomenological approach**, which means that people's individual subjective experiences are important. For this reason, the term 'experiential' is sometimes used to describe it. Instead of analysing people and their behaviour in an objective way, the emphasis is on subjectivity — a person's own sense of being themselves and their awareness of their own existence as individuals, moving through life towards old age and death. Although Rogers recognised unconscious influences, he believed that the most valuable source of knowledge about a person comes from his or her conscious awareness.

The second principle of Rogers's approach is his belief in the fact that we all have a tendency towards **self-actualisation** or **personal growth**: we are capable of making choices and bringing about changes in our lives, and in most situations we are aware of having choices. This is not to say that our choices are unlimited — quite often they are restricted by social constraints. We may not always be aware of the possibilities that are open to us, and we may indeed be afraid to make particular choices, but we do have choices and the potential to change. Humanistic psychologists believe that people can be helped to change and lead more fulfilling lives by becoming as aware as possible of their feelings and motivations, and the influences upon them.

The third principle refers to our **sense of self**, which has two sources: our own experience, and the evaluations that others make of us, particularly our parents and other significant people in our lives. Problems can arise, particularly in childhood, when the evaluations of others are conditional. If parents put across the message that children are loved only when they behave in a certain way, development becomes distorted. The fear of losing love causes the child to become the person that the parent values, rather than truly becoming the person that he/she wishes to become. In this way, personal growth is blocked.

The aims of humanistic psychology are to explore the experience of the individual and to facilitate personal growth. This is often carried out through **person-centred counselling**, to help clients become aware of how they really feel and how they wish to be. The therapist offers **unconditional positive regard**, showing a warmth towards and respect for his/her clients, regardless of what they say or do. The therapy is non-directive, in that clients are encouraged to explore and express their feelings, rather than respond to suggestions from the therapist. From this, clients will develop a more consistent sense of self, with no need to shut off any of their feelings. They should develop a closer consistency between how they see themselves and the ideal self, the person that they would like to be. The aim is to allow clients to explore the possibilities of change and open themselves up to experiences and situations that previously would have been threatening, a process that Rogers calls 'becoming a person'.

Commentary

With its focus on individual experience, the humanistic perspective is quite different from other perspectives. It has been criticised for its lack of scientific rigour, and for its belief that a scientific approach is not appropriate for the study of people. It has also been accused of not giving enough weight to the influence of social and cultural forces, and of reflecting Western values and attitudes, and therefore not being readily applicable to other cultures. However, it has been extremely influential — in particular, in terms of the development of therapies that are based on the general principles that it proposes.

Summary

- The **humanistic perspective** developed as a result of dissatisfaction with the dominant perspectives of **psychodynamics** and **behaviourism**.
- **Maslow** suggested that our highest need is for **self-actualisation**; developing our potential as much as possible.
- **Rogers** believed that the richest source of information about a person comes from his or her **subjective experience**. We have the capacity for **personal growth**, but development may be blocked by the evaluations of others.
- **Person-centred counselling** encourages individuals to explore their sense of self and the choices open to them in becoming the person that they want to become, in a **non-directive** and **non-judgemental** situation.
- The humanistic perspective has been criticised for reflecting the values of a particular culture and for the methods that it uses. However, it has been influential in the development of **counselling** and related therapies.

Terms explained

associationism (or empiricism): the philosophical position reflected in some areas of psychology, in particular the behaviourist perspective, that development depends on learning through experience, with very little being present at birth. This is the 'nurture' aspect of the nature-nurture debate.

behaviourism: a perspective in psychology that is concerned only with the study of directly observable behaviour. Thoughts and feelings are therefore not taken into account as they can only be accessed by subjective reporting (introspection).

case study: an in-depth study of an individual or a small group of individuals, usually carried out because they are unusual in some way. For example, it has been used to assess the psychological effects of brain damage, and to investigate the characteristics of an individual with a phenomenal memory.

classical conditioning: learning through the association of a stimulus and a response. It was shown originally with dogs by Pavlov, but can apply also to people, e.g. in the study of Little Albert, carried out by Watson and Rayner. It is the basis of some therapies, such as systematic desensitisation.

cognitive psychology: the branch of psychology that investigates how we process information, and the factors that influence processing. It covers topics such as attention, memory, decision making, perception and problem solving.

comparative psychology: the branch of psychology that investigates animal behaviour, on the basis that this may help to establish general principles that may also apply to people.

connectionism: theories that model brain function using computers. A connectionist network accepts input, makes various computations, and produces an output, and so is used as a model of human information processing.

constructivism: the philosophical position reflected in some areas of psychology, in particular Piaget's theory of cognitive development and Bartlett's account of memory, which claims that development is constructed through the interaction of innate characteristics and experience.

developmental psychology: the branch of psychology that focuses in particular on the development of children, but also, more broadly, development across the lifespan.

discourse analysis: a qualitative method of analysing written or spoken material, such as interviews, conversations, and newspaper reports. It examines what language is used, and how it is used to construct a particular meaning. For example, the terms 'terrorist' and 'freedom fighter' can be used to represent the same person in very different ways.

introspection: literally 'looking inside'; asking people to report their experiences. It was the main method used in early psychology, but was then largely replaced by more objective methods. However, it is now becoming more widely used, because it can provide rich and detailed data.

operant conditioning: learning through the association of behaviour and its consequences. It was shown originally with rats and pigeons by Skinner, but can also apply to people. It has been applied in behaviour modification programmes, for example to change the way children behave in a classroom.

PET scan: a person inhales, or is injected with, a radioactive tracer. More active areas of the brain take up more of this substance, and so give off more radioactivity, which shows up on the scan. This method allows links to be made between particular areas of the brain and specific activities.

physiological psychology (or biopsychology): the branch of psychology that is interested in making links between our physical make-up and physiological processes and psychological experience and behaviour. Examples include the possible genetic basis of mental illness and the effect of hormones on the experience of stress.

psychodynamic perspective: a perspective initially developed by Sigmund Freud (1856–1939), which stresses the importance of childhood experience, the influence of unconscious processes and the role of psychic conflict in experience and development.

rationalism (or nativism): the philosophical position, reflected in some areas of psychology, which claims that everything necessary for development is present at birth, with development depending on maturation. This is the 'nature' aspect of the nature-nurture debate.

social learning theory (SLT): a development of operant conditioning, which suggests that we learn not only through the consequences of our own behaviour, but also through observing the behaviour of others, and its consequences.

social psychology: the branch of psychology that investigates the influence of other people on our psychological functioning and behaviour.

AQA (A) AS Psychology

Unit 1:

Cognitive psychology, developmental psychology and research methods

Chapter

Memory

In this chapter, we will be looking at:

- early memory research
- short-term memory (STM) and long-term memory (LTM)
- the multi-store model of memory
- research relating to the multi-store model, and criticisms of it
- the working memory model of memory
- research relating to the working memory model, and criticisms of it
- the effects of the wording of questions and misleading information on eyewitness testimony (EWT)
- the effects of age and anxiety on the accuracy of EWT
- the use of the cognitive interview in EWT
- strategies for memory improvement

Memory is crucial to every aspect of our lives. Without it, you would not be able to read a book, write an essay, be able to find things when you need them, use a knife and fork or a computer, recognise friends and family or, more generally, learn from experience. The study of memory is therefore relevant to our daily lives. The ultimate aim of research in this area, apart from establishing the general principles underlying memory, is to apply the findings to practical problems. For example, knowing how memory works could suggest ways in which people could be helped to develop a more efficient memory, and could help police interviewers increase the amount of useful information provided by eyewitnesses to crimes. These applications will be examined later in the chapter.

Memory is thought of in terms of three processes:

- **Registration** refers to taking in information through the sense organs, and putting it into the memory system.
- **Storage** is the process through which information is held in the system.
- **Retrieval** is the process of recall, i.e. bringing memories into consciousness.

Early memory research

The experimental study of memory began more than 100 years ago, with research done by Hermann Ebbinghaus (1850–1909). He carried out an extensive series of studies, with the aim of establishing the general principles of how memory works.

His work was unusual in a number of ways. Firstly, all his studies were done with himself as the only participant. Secondly, the material that he used was lists of nonsense syllables; sets of three letters known as **CVCs** (consonant-vowel-consonant), such as KED or WUG, which are not meaningful words.

Ebbinghaus took an **associationist** approach, believing that memory rests on the association of ideas. Learning a list of items was therefore seen as the result of forming associations between the items on the list. An example of his research is shown in Box 2.1.

The research of Ebbinghaus was important in determining some of the basic principles of how memory works. He was the first to suggest that memory consists of more than one system or store: a short-term system and a long-term system, later referred to by James (1890) as **primary memory** and **secondary memory**. The terms now used for this distinction are **short-term memory (STM)** and **long-term memory (LTM)**. Many of Ebbinghaus's findings have been replicated numerous times. For example, he established that we are more likely to remember items near the start of a list (the **primacy effect**) and near the end (the **recency effect**) than those in the middle.

| Box 2.1 | Ebbinghaus (1885) |

Aims: To establish how quickly information is forgotten over time.

Procedure: Ebbinghaus prepared a long list of nonsense syllables, read them through at a steady pace, and then tried to recall them. He noted how many items he could remember, then repeated the procedure until he could recall the complete list. He then looked at how quickly items were forgotten.

Results: At first, quite a lot of items were forgotten, but with successive trials, the rate of forgetting decreased.

Conclusions: The immediate forgetting at the start of the process is the loss of material from a short-term memory store. The more gradual forgetting over repeated trials is the loss of material from a long-term store.

However, several criticisms can be made of Ebbinghaus's approach. This kind of research, if done today, would test a number of participants, rather than just one. While there is no reason to suppose that Ebbinghaus's memory was in any way unusual, there is no guarantee that one person is representative of the population as a whole, so it would be impossible to generalise the findings reliably. It may also be that carrying out research on oneself might introduce an element of bias, with the participant unconsciously influencing the results to fit in with his or her expectations.

Perhaps even more importantly, the use of CVCs could be questioned. Ebbinghaus wanted to investigate what he thought of as 'pure' memory, uncontaminated (as he saw it) by meaning. CVCs have the advantage that they are not in any way distinctive, so memory would not be influenced by meaning. However, we remember things because they are meaningful to us, so studies using CVCs could be seen as having low **ecological validity** because they do not relate well to real-life memory.

The research could also be criticised in terms of the ecological validity of using lists. While lists are still sometimes used in memory experiments, we seldom need to remember lists in real-life situations.

In his book, *Remembering* (1932), Frederick Bartlett (1886–1969) challenged the associationist standpoint. He took a **constructivist** approach, seeing memories not as an exact copy of material that has been remembered, but rather as a *reconstruction* of the original information, which might therefore not be entirely accurate. He also stressed that memory should be investigated using meaningful material, and so set the pattern for later memory research. His ideas will be examined more closely later in the chapter.

Summary

- Memory involves the three processes of **registration**, **storage** and **retrieval**.
- The early work of **Ebbinghaus** established some of the basic principles of how memory works, but is open to criticism.
- His **associationist** approach was criticised by **Bartlett**, who emphasised the importance of meaning in memory, which he saw as a **reconstructive** process.

Short-term and long-term memory

Short-term memory (STM) and long-term memory (LTM) can be distinguished in several ways. First, they differ in terms of **capacity**, i.e. how much information they can hold. The capacity of STM is thought to be 7 ± 2, that is between five and nine pieces of information. For example, if a person is given a list of words to remember, he/she is likely to remember between five and nine of them, whatever the size of the list. The capacity of LTM is unlimited; we are always able to take in and remember new information.

A second difference between the two stores is their **duration**. Information in STM can be held for up to 30 seconds, though this can be extended by rehearsal (i.e. repeating the information to yourself to keep it within STM). Information in LTM can be held indefinitely, though some of the information in LTM will be lost. For example, you can probably remember a number of incidents from your childhood, but are likely to have forgotten many more.

The stores also differ in terms of **encoding**, i.e. the way in which information is put into each store. In STM, information is usually encoded **acoustically**: when you repeat in your head a telephone number that you wish to remember only long enough to dial it, it is the *sound* of the number that is being held in STM. In LTM, encoding is mainly **semantic**: information is processed by its meaning. However, LTM encoding may also be **visual** — for example, when you bring to mind what your house looks like, or **acoustic**, when you remember pieces of music.

An example of repeating information to feed short-term memory involves children learning multiplication tables at school

There is quite a lot of research evidence to support these differences between STM and LTM, and this will be the focus of the next sections in this chapter.

Short-term memory (STM)

Capacity

Span measure is used to establish the capacity of STM, i.e. the number of items in a list that can be repeated back immediately and in the correct order.

This was investigated in a classic paper by **Miller** (1956), 'The magical number seven, plus or minus two: some limits on our capacity for processing information'. The paper reviewed existing research in this area and found that most people could only repeat back 7 ± 2 items (i.e. between five and nine). This was the case whether the items were numbers, letters, words or tones with different pitches.

Miller used the term '**chunking**' to explain how the capacity of STM can be increased. Chunking refers to putting two or more pieces of information together to form one unit of information. For example, an unrelated sequence of letters such as CSEG is four separate pieces of information. However, the sequence GCSE forms a meaningful unit if you are familiar with the English education system: the four separate pieces of information can be combined to form one larger unit. Miller therefore claimed that the capacity of STM is 7 ± 2 *chunks*, rather than 7 ± 2 individual pieces of information.

Duration

The duration of STM has been tested using the **Brown-Peterson technique** (see Box 2.2).

Box 2.2 | **Peterson and Peterson (1959)**

Aims: To establish the duration of STM when rehearsal is prevented.

Procedure: Participants heard a **trigram** — a random group of three letters — such as HGW. They were asked to recall immediately what they had heard, or to recall only after a set retention interval: 3, 6, 9, 12, 15 or 18 seconds. During the period before recall, they were asked to count backwards in 3s from a specified number. The aim of the counting was to prevent **maintenance rehearsal**, i.e. repeating the trigram to themselves to hold it in STM.

Results: After the 3-second delay, recall of the trigram was very high, but decreased steadily as the retention interval lengthened.

Conclusions: Without rehearsal, the duration of STM is only a few seconds.

Encoding

Research has shown that information is put into STM in an **acoustic** form (see Box 2.3). However, **visual** encoding in STM is also possible. For example, images such as abstract pictures, which would be impossible to translate into an acoustic code, can be held in STM for brief periods of time, as investigated by Conrad in 1964.

Box 2.3 | **Conrad (1964)**

Aims: To establish the form in which information is encoded into STM.

Procedure: Participants were shown a sequence of six letters from B C F M N P S T V and X. They were asked to write them down as they appeared, but the presentation was too fast for them to keep up, so they had to be held in STM. The errors that they made were analysed.

Results: Participants often made **acoustic confusion** errors, where the letters that they had seen were replaced by those with a similar sound. For example, P was written instead of B or V. There were almost no errors where letters with different sounds were confused, e.g. S for P.

Conclusions: Even when information is presented visually, encoding is acoustic.

Long-term memory (LTM)

LTM is seen as a relatively permanent store. The **capacity** of LTM is not known, and it seems likely that there is no upper limit to the amount of information that can be stored. The **duration** of LTM can be anything from 30 seconds (the proposed duration of STM) to a lifetime. For example, you are unlikely ever to forget your name, but may well have forgotten what you had for lunch last Tuesday.

Encoding in LTM appears to be largely **semantic**. This means that information is put into LTM in terms of its meaning, as investigated by Baddeley in 1966 (Box 2.4).

Box 2.4 Baddeley (1966)

Aims: To establish and compare the forms of encoding of information into STM and LTM.

Procedure: Participants were given short lists of words to recall. These included:
- words that were acoustically similar, e.g. 'mad', 'can', 'man'
- words that were semantically similar, e.g. 'huge', 'big', 'long'

There were also control lists that were either acoustically or semantically dissimilar. Participants were asked to recall the lists either immediately, i.e. from STM, or later, i.e. from LTM.

Results: For immediate recall, there was confusion between acoustically similar words, but not for semantically similar words. For later recall, there was confusion between semantically similar words, but not for acoustically similar words.

Conclusions: The confusion between acoustically similar words when recall was immediate supports the idea that encoding in STM is acoustic. The confusion between semantically similar words when recall was delayed supports the idea that encoding in LTM is semantic.

Summary

- **Short-term memory (STM)** and **long-term memory (LTM)** differ in capacity, duration and encoding.
- The **capacity** of STM is 7 ± 2 items of information, which can be increased by **chunking**. LTM appears to have no upper limit.
- The **duration** of STM is up to 30 seconds, which can be increased by **rehearsal**. The duration of LTM is anything from 30 seconds to a lifetime.
- **Encoding** in STM is mainly acoustic. In LTM it is mainly semantic, but can also be visual or acoustic.

Models of memory

The multi-store model of memory (MSM)

In psychology, models are sometimes developed as a way of representing psychological processes, such as perception or memory. The aim of a model is to provide a framework of the way such processes work, within which research can take place. The multi-store model of memory and the working memory model are two of the models that have been developed to explain memory processes. These will now be examined in detail.

The multi-store model was developed by Atkinson and Shiffrin (1968 and 1971). This model is sometimes known as the 'modal model' (i.e. the most frequently occurring one), because in many ways it is similar to other models that were created at around the same time. It is also sometimes known as the 'two-process model', as a result of its emphasis on the two memory stores of short-term memory (STM) and long-term memory (LTM).

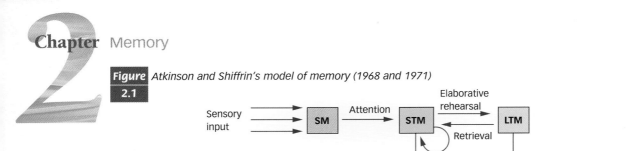

Figure 2.1 Atkinson and Shiffrin's model of memory (1968 and 1971)

The model describes the structural components of memory in terms of three stores: sensory memory (SM), STM and LTM. It also describes the processes involved in memory. Memory is seen in terms of information flowing through a system. Information reaching our sense organs enters the SM. A lot of information reaches the sense organs, most of which does not reach conscious awareness. However, if we pay attention to sensory information, it enters the STM, while the information that we do not attend to is lost. Information can be held briefly in STM, and rather longer if we rehearse it. If it is not rehearsed, this information is also lost after a few seconds. If information is rehearsed further, it is moved into LTM, where it can remain indefinitely, though much information in this store is also forgotten. Information in LTM can also be retrieved to STM when it is needed to carry out a task in STM. These processes are shown in Figure 2.1 and Table 2.1. The model suggests that all information must pass through the stores in order and that it differentiates between the stores in terms of capacity, duration and encoding.

Table 2.1 Comparing SM, STM and LTM

	SM	STM	LTM
Capacity	Small	7 ± 2 items	Unlimited
Duration	0.25–2 seconds	Up to 30 seconds	Indefinite period of time
Encoding	Modality specific	Mainly acoustic	Semantic/visual/acoustic

The kind of rehearsal used to keep information in STM differs from the rehearsal that moves information from STM to LTM. For example, if you need to keep a telephone number in your head long enough to dial it, you repeat it over and over to yourself in your head. This is acoustic rehearsal, i.e. it uses the sound of the number, and this is enough to maintain the information in STM. Craik and Watkins (1973) called this kind of rehearsal **maintenance rehearsal**. However, to move information from STM to LTM, what Craik and Watkins call **elaborative rehearsal** is used. This kind of rehearsal is semantic, i.e. it processes the information using its meaning. For example, you might remember the PIN number 4823 by thinking 'Uncle Jim is 48 and lives at number 23'.

Evidence supporting the MSM

As noted earlier, there is some support for the idea of the two distinct stores of STM and LTM, for example in the different kinds of encoding used. Further evidence comes from the **serial position effect** (see Box 2.5): the position of a word in a list influences how likely it is to be recalled (see Figure 2.2), a phenomenon first observed by Ebbinghaus (see page 27).

Box 2.5 Murdock (1962)

Aims: To compare recall for words in different positions in a list.

Procedure: Participants were presented with a list of words, at the rate of one per second. They were then asked to remember as many words from the list as they could, in any order.

Results: Words at the beginning of the list were more likely to be recalled than those in the middle (the **primacy effect**). Similarly, those at the end of the list were also more likely to be recalled than those in the middle (the **recency effect**). Murdock called this difference in recall depending on the position of the words in a list the **serial position effect**.

Conclusions: Rehearsal of the words near the beginning has moved them into LTM, from which they have been recalled, while those near the end are still in STM, and are recalled from there. This supports the idea that there are two distinct memory stores of STM and LTM.

Further support for the serial position effect comes from Glanzer and Cunitz (1966). In a variation of the Murdock study, they asked participants to count backwards in 3s as soon as the presentation of the list of words was completed (the Brown-Peterson technique — see Box 2.2, page 30). While the primacy effect remained, the recency effect disappeared. Presumably, the first words in the list had been processed into LTM during the presentation of the list, but those near the end were affected by the counting task and so did not remain in STM.

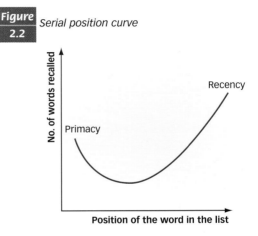

Figure 2.2 *Serial position curve*

Studies of amnesics — people whose memory has been impaired, typically because of brain damage — also support the distinction between STM and LTM (see Box 2.6).

Box 2.6 Milner (1966)

Milner carried out a case study of HM, a man who had frequent major epileptic fits. Drastic brain surgery was carried out to cure his epilepsy, involving the removal of a structure in the brain called the hippocampus. Although his epilepsy was cured, he suffered from severe **anterograde amnesia**, i.e. extreme difficulty in forming new memories. His memory was normal for everything from *before* the surgery, but was seriously impaired for anything *after* the surgery.

HM's short-term memory remained relatively normal, in that he could remember events for several seconds, and longer with rehearsal. However, he was not able to transfer information to long-term memory. For example, he would read a magazine without realising that he had already read it, and had no idea what the time was unless he had just looked at a clock. Although he could remember people he had known before the surgery, he could not remember people he had met since then, even when he had met them many times.

Cognitive psychology

In a similar case, brain damage was caused by a rare brain infection (see Box 2.7).

Box 2.7 **Blakemore (1988)**

Clive Wearing was a musician and a world expert on Renaissance music. A brain infection destroyed his hippocampus, together with other parts of the brain. Like HM, his short-term memory was relatively unaffected, but his long-term memory, even for events *before* the brain damage, was also impaired. He, too, was incapable of transferring to LTM memories from after the infection. For example, each time his wife came into his hospital room, he believed that it was the first time she had visited him, even though she might have been in several times that morning.

Both these case studies support the idea that STM and LTM are different systems. HM and Clive Wearing appeared to have normal STM, as measured by digit span, but severe deficits in LTM.

Further evidence of this kind comes from an exactly opposite pattern of deficit. Shallice and Warrington (1972) carried out a study of KF, who suffered damage to the left hemisphere of his brain as a result of a motorcycle accident. His LTM appeared to be unaffected, but his STM, as measured by digit span, was only one or two items, instead of the expected 7 ± 2 items.

Criticisms of the MSM

The multi-store model has been particularly useful in drawing a distinction between the structures of memory — the different stores — and the processes involved. However, there are a number of criticisms that can be made.

One major problem is that the MSM sees both STM and LTM as unitary stores, while there is a good deal of evidence that each is **fractionated**, i.e. made up of several components. Tulving (1972) suggested that there are two separate systems within LTM: **semantic memory** and **episodic memory**.

Semantic memory: memory for facts, e.g. that Paris is the capital of France and that an emu is a large, flightless bird.

Episodic memory: memory for personal and public experiences, e.g. where you went on holiday last year and the death of Princess Diana.

Tulving reported that when patients were asked to think about personal events (episodic memory) or information about a particular topic (semantic memory), brain scans showed different parts of the brain as being active, with the frontal cortex being more active during episodic memory, and areas towards the back of the cortex showing more activity during semantic memory.

However, these systems are closely related. For example, general knowledge about France (semantic memory) would be related to your experiences while on holiday there (episodic memory). Since they are so closely related, Cohen and Squire (1980) grouped these two kinds of memories together as **declarative memory** and suggested that LTM can be divided into declarative memory ('knowing that') and **procedural memory** ('knowing how') — for example, how to ride a bicycle (see Figure 2.3).

Figure 2.3 *Declarative and procedural memory*

There is evidence that the two separate systems of declarative memory and procedural memory exist in LTM from the case studies of HM and Clive Wearing (see Box 2.8).

Box 2.8 HM and Clive Wearing

HM
Although HM (see Box 2.6) could remember a lot from before his operation, after surgery he could not remember anything about recent current events (semantic memory), find his way back to his room in the hospital or recognise medical staff. He did not remember that his father had died (episodic memory). This suggests that declarative memory had been damaged. However, he remembered how to read and write, and was able to learn new motor skills, such as the pursuit rotor task (a task that involves keeping a stylus in contact with a moving target). He gradually improved on this task, which suggests that new procedural memories had been established and that his procedural memory was still functional. However, he had to be reminded that he could carry out this task, as this information would be held in episodic memory, which was damaged.

Clive Wearing
After the brain damage caused by the virus, Clive Wearing (see Box 2.7) could not remember who wrote *Romeo and Juliet* (semantic memory) and could not recognise a picture of the Cambridge college that he had attended as an undergraduate (episodic memory). When shown pictures of Queen Elizabeth II and the Duke of Edinburgh, he thought that they were singers he had known from church (confusion between episodic and semantic memory). However, he could still read and conduct music, and play the organ. Like HM, he was able to learn new motor tasks, such as mirror reading, and he improved over time, suggesting that, like HM, his procedural memory still functioned well.

Although declarative memory covers both semantic and episodic memory, there is further evidence that they are, at least to some extent, separate systems (see Box 2.9, page 36).

There is evidence that STM is similarly fractionated. For example, in the study of KF by Shallice and Warrington (1972) (see page 34), while his STM for things that he heard (auditory stimuli) was poor, his memory for visual stimuli was much better. This suggests that there may be separate short-term stores for auditory and visual information. We will be looking at evidence for the fractionation of STM in more detail in relation to the **working memory model** in the next section.

| Box 2.9 | Butterworth (in Radford, 1992) |

Dr S., a neurologist, fell while skiing. When the people with whom he was skiing caught up with him, he was surprised to find that his wife looked extremely old and he failed to recognise some of his younger colleagues. The previous 25 years appeared to be a blank. This suggested that his episodic memory had been affected. He then skied to the bottom of the mountain, which demonstrated that his procedural memory was still functional, and he was taken to the local hospital. In hospital he asked for a brain scan and made a correct diagnosis of transient global amnesia when he saw the scan, which suggested that his semantic memory was also still functional, as this kind of brain scan was not in use prior to the 25 years that he appeared to have lost. He later recovered completely.

A further problem with the MSM is the implication that in order to reach LTM, information needs to pass from sensory memory to STM, and only then to LTM. The case of KF challenges this proposal, because his STM was damaged but he had no problem in establishing new long-term memories.

Another issue is that the MSM is only concerned with the *amount* of information being processed through the system, and not with the *nature* of that information. We know intuitively that whether we remember information depends to some extent on that nature of that information. For example, some people find it easy to remember football scores, but have great difficulty in remembering vocabulary in a foreign language, or dates in history.

These two issues are brought together in the phenomenon of **flashbulb memory**. This is a term coined by Brown and Kulick (1977) to describe memories that are particularly vivid and detailed, and are associated with strong emotions.

Flashbulb memories can relate to personal events. For example, you might have such a memory for the time you broke your arm when you were a child and had to go to hospital, or getting your first bicycle for your birthday. They can also relate to public events, particularly when the event is unexpected. For example, depending on their age, people may have vivid memories of the assassination of President Kennedy (1963), Mrs Thatcher's resignation as prime minister (1990), the death of Princess Diana (1997) or the terrorist attack on the World Trade Center on 11 September 2001. Shapiro (2006) found that people had vivid memories of the attack on the Twin Towers, with very little loss of detail, even after 2 years.

The key factors here are that events that lead to flashbulb memories are surprising, distinctive and associated with strong emotions, linking in to the idea that the nature of information is an important factor in memory. They also seem to go directly into LTM without the rehearsal from STM that the MSM suggests is necessary.

Summary

- The multi-store model (MSM) sees memory in terms of information flowing through separate stores, from sensory memory (SM) to STM and LTM.

- Each of these stores has its own characteristics.
- The MSM is supported by **experimental evidence** and by studies of **amnesia**.
- However, clinical evidence suggests that both STM and LTM are **fractionated** rather than being unitary stores.
- The MSM assumes that information must pass through the stores in order. It does not take into account the second assumption — the **nature of the information** to be remembered.
- Both these assumptions are challenged by the phenomenon of **flashbulb memory**.

The working memory (WM) model

The WM model was developed by Baddeley and Hitch (1974). In contrast to the MSM, it is concerned only with short-term memory and it focuses on the systems by which information is processed and the functions that it carries out, emphasising the idea of active processing — hence the name 'working' memory. This differs from the MSM, in which the stages are passive stores through which information flows.

The WM model sees short-term memory as fractionated, i.e. made up of different sub-systems. The **central executive** is the most important part of WM, as it controls three **slave systems**: the **visuo-spatial scratchpad** (sketchpad), the **articulatory loop** (also known as the phonological loop) and the **primary acoustic store**. It can be thought of as a limited-capacity workspace that can be used flexibly to control other parts of the system. It is modality-free, as it can process information from any of the senses. It is used when you are carrying out difficult mental tasks, such as problem solving. It acts as an attention system, deciding which information entering the sense organs should be attended to, and planning the allocation of resources to other parts of the STM and directing their work. It can also be used for the temporary storage of information, while another task in STM is being carried out. For example, if you mentally add two numbers such as 238 and 416, whichever method you adopt, the subtotals are held in the central executive while you work on the rest of the problem.

The visuo-spatial scratchpad, which is sometimes referred to as the **inner eye**, uses a visual code and processes visual and spatial information such as abstract patterns, which cannot easily be translated into an acoustic code. The articulatory loop, known as the **inner voice**, holds information in an auditory code. For example, in trying to remember a phone number for a long-enough period of time in order to dial it, you 'hear' the number being repeated in your head. Baddeley et al. (1975) established that the capacity of the articulatory loop equated to as much information as could be repeated in 2 seconds. For example, it could hold more words like 'cat', 'toe' and 'pink' than words like 'conservatory', 'kangaroo' and 'individual', which would take longer to say. The capacity of the articulatory loop is therefore limited by time rather than by the number of items.

The role of the articulatory loop has been demonstrated using the technique of **concurrent verbalisation**. If people are asked to repeat a phrase out loud and at the same time carry out another verbal task, such as learning a list of words or reading, performance on this second task is impaired. Repeating the phrase occupies the articulatory loop, making it unavailable for the second task. This is known as **articulatory suppression**.

The distinction in WM between the visuo-spatial scratchpad and the articulatory loop has been demonstrated experimentally in a study carried out by Den Heyer and Barrett (1971) (see Box 2.10 and Figure 2.4).

Box 2.10 **Den Heyer and Barrett (1971)**

Aims: To investigate the coding of material in STM, using a technique called **modality specific interference**.

Procedure: Participants were briefly shown a grid, similar to that in Figure 2.4, and asked to remember both the letters and where they were on the grid. They were then given an inter-ference task, intended to interfere either with the visual or the articulatory system of STM. This took the form of a **verbal task** (counting backwards aloud) or a **visual task** (pattern matching). They were then asked to complete the grids that they had seen. The results were scored in two ways: the number of letters correctly remembered, irrespective of where they had been put on the grid, and the number of correct positions occupied by a letter, even if the letter was incorrect.

Results: Recall of the letters was more disrupted by the verbal task, while position recall was more disrupted by the visual task.

Conclusions: The letters were encoded acoustically, because recall was more affected by the verbal task. The positions of the letters were encoded visually, because recall was more affected by the visual task. The findings support the idea that there are separate systems within STM: one dealing with visual information and one with acoustic information.

Figure 2.4 Den Heyer and Barrett grid

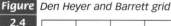

The concept of a **primary acoustic store**, or **inner ear**, is a later addition to the model. It is believed to receive information directly from the ears or via the articulatory loop and uses an acoustic code. The concept was added when it was found that information presented acoustically — unlike the silent tasks of list-learning or reading mentioned previously — was not affected by articulatory suppression.

Evaluation of the WM model

The WM model is supported by evidence that there are different sub-systems in STM, and that visual processing must be included in any model of STM, in contrast to the emphasis of the MSM on *acoustic* encoding.

It is also supported by evidence from positron emission tomography (PET) scan studies of brain activity, carried out by the Wellcome Foundation. This kind of scan shows a three-dimensional representation of the structures of the brain and the activity in its many areas while a person carries out different tasks. PET scans have shown different areas being activated when tasks using the different elements of WM are being carried out (see Figure 2.5).

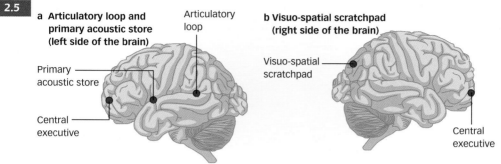

The WM model also has potential practical applications, for example in education. If children with normal intelligence are having difficulty in learning to read and they also have trouble in recognising rhyme, there may be a problem with the articulatory loop. Interventions focusing on the articulatory loop could well be a way of supporting children with this kind of problem.

However, this model is limited in that it only considers STM, and so only looks at one part of the memory system. Moreover, the model is still under development. For example, Baddeley (1996) has suggested that the central executive could itself be fractionated into four separate but related functions: allocating attention; switching retrieval strategies; coordinating performance on two different tasks; and providing processing capacity that is available to any of the slave systems. In support of this suggestion, Baddeley (1996) cites research demonstrating that people with Alzheimer's disease have difficulty in carrying out two tasks simultaneously, while normal ageing is associated with difficulty in focusing attention, two different aspects of the central executive.

Summary

- The **working memory (WM) model** is concerned only with **STM** and emphasises active processing of information.
- The **central executive** controls the **visuo-spatial scratchpad**, the **articulatory loop** and the **primary acoustic store**.
- The model is supported by **experimental evidence** and by **PET scans**. It may have practical applications.
- The model is **limited** by its focus on STM. It is still in the process of development.

Memory in everyday life

In contrast to the CVC studies carried out by Ebbinghaus (page 27), Bartlett (1932) argued that in order to establish how memory works, we need to carry out tests in which people are asked to recall *meaningful* material. He argued that material to be recalled is integrated with past experience, so memory is not only affected by the information with which we are presented, but also by our previous knowledge. He suggested that we create **schemas**, i.e. packets of information about people or events based on previous experience, which are used in processing new information. The use of schemas cuts down processing effort, but influences (and may distort) the processing of new information. What we recall is therefore not just a reproduction of information, but a **reconstruction**.

Bartlett's most famous study is one in which participants were asked to remember a Native American story (see Boxes 2.11 and 2.12).

Bartlett's idea of reconstruction implies that memory is often both incomplete and distorted. In everyday situations, this is unlikely to have far-reaching consequences. However, when witnesses give evidence in court, accurate recall of events can mean the difference between imprisonment and freedom. In the next section, we will look at factors that affect the reliability of eyewitness testimony.

Box 2.11   **Bartlett's 'War of the ghosts' (1932)**

One night, two young men from Egulac went down to the river to hunt seals, and while they were there it became foggy and calm. Then they heard war cries and they thought: 'Maybe this is a war party.' They escaped to the shore and hid behind a log. Now canoes came up, and they heard the noise of paddles and saw one canoe coming up to them. There were five men in the canoe and they said: 'What do you think? We wish to take you along. We are going up the river to make war on the people.' One of the young men said: 'I have no arrows.' 'Arrows are in the canoe,' they said. 'I will not go along. I might be killed. My relatives do not know where I have gone. But you,' he said, turning to the other, 'may go with them.' So one of the young men went, but the other returned home. And the warriors went on up the river to a town on the other side of Kalama. The people came down to the water and they began to fight, and many were killed. But presently, the young men heard one of the warriors say: 'Quick let us go home: that Indian has been hit.' Now he thought: 'Oh, they are ghosts.' He did not feel sick, but they said he had been shot. So the canoes went back to Egulac, and the young man went ashore to his house and made a fire. And he told everybody and said: 'Behold I accompanied the ghosts, and we went to fight. Many of our fellows were killed and many of those who attacked us were killed. They said I was hit, and I did not feel sick.' He told it all, and then he became quiet. When the sun rose, he fell down. Something black came out of his mouth. His face became contorted. The people jumped up and cried. He was dead.

Box 2.12   **Bartlett (1932)**

Aims: To investigate the effect of prior knowledge on memory for an unfamiliar story.

Procedure: Participants read a Native American story, 'The War of the ghosts' (see Box 2.11).

After 15 minutes, they were asked to write down as much of the story as they could remember, as accurately as possible. People's memory for the story was also tested over increasing periods of time, in one case after 10 years.

Results: Recall of the story was much shorter than the original, with large sections being omitted. Details were left out that were inconsistent with the participants' understanding of the story. Sometimes new material was introduced to make the story seem more logical, or one particular aspect, for example the idea of ghosts, given more prominence than it had in the original story. Recall was also affected by the participants' emotional reaction to the story, for example. 'something horrible came out of his mouth'.

Conclusions: Memory is an **active reconstruction** of material: a few facts are stored, from which the memory is reconstructed, fitting it within a framework of what we already know. Bartlett referred to this process as **effort after meaning**.

Eyewitness testimony (EWT)

Main influences on EWT

Juries place a great deal of weight on eyewitness testimony. *The Devlin Report*, published in 1976, found that in more than 300 cases, eyewitness identification was the *only* evidence of guilt, but the conviction rate was nonetheless 74%.

Based on Bartlett's idea of memory as reconstruction, a lot of research has been carried out (notably by Loftus) that has demonstrated that the wording of a question can influence what is remembered, and that EWT can be unreliable (see Box 2.13).

| Box 2.13 | Loftus and Palmer (1974) |

Aims: To investigate the influence of wording on recall.

Procedure: One hundred and fifty participants were shown a film of a car accident in which two cars collided, and were then asked to fill in a questionnaire about what they had seen. The crucial question asked participants to estimate the speed of the cars at the point of impact. One group of participants was asked: 'How fast were the two cars going when they hit each other?' Other groups were asked the same question, but with 'bumped', 'collided', 'contacted' or 'smashed' replacing the word 'hit'. A control group was asked nothing at this stage about the speed of the car. One week later, participants were asked if they had seen any broken glass in the film of the accident; no broken glass had been shown.

Results: The average estimates of the speed at which the cars were going varied with the verb used in the question:

In the control group, 12% claimed to have seen broken glass. Of those who had heard the word 'hit', 14% said they had seen broken glass, while 32% of those who had heard the word 'smashed' remembered seeing broken glass.

Verb used	Speed given
Contacted	32 mph
Hit	34 mph
Bumped	38 mph
Collided	39 mph
Smashed	41 mph

Conclusions: The differences in the speed estimates suggest that the wording of a question about an event can distort a person's memory of the event. The use of the word 'smashed' in the question a week earlier caused participants to modify their memories of the car accident as being more serious compared with those who had heard the word 'hit', or controls who had not been asked the question. The participants' memories had been reconstructed.

However, it is not always easy to cause a memory to be reconstructed. Loftus (1979) found that 98% of people who had seen colour slides of a man stealing a red purse from a woman's bag remembered it as red, even when it was suggested that it was brown. It is more difficult to modify a memory about something that is central to an event being witnessed than something that has less importance.

However, as Loftus et al found (see Box 2.14), this focus on what is central to an event can also lead to poorer memory about other details of the event that may also be important in EWT.

Box 2.14 Loftus et al. (1987)

Aims: To investigate the effect of the presence of a weapon on witness recall.

Procedure: Participants were shown one of two versions of a video of a restaurant scene. In the 'weapon' version, a man pointed a gun at the cashier and she gave him money. In the 'non-weapon' version, he gave her a cheque and she gave him money. The eye movements of the participants were recorded and their recall for the event tested.

Results: Participants in the 'weapon' condition fixated more on the gun and less on other details of the scene than those in the 'non-weapon' condition. Their recall for other details of the scene was also poorer. They were less able to identify the man from a set of photographs than those in the 'non-weapon' condition.

Conclusions: What has been called **weapon focus** distracted participants in the 'weapon' condition from features of the situation other than the gun. The gun became the most important aspect of the situation — a phenomenon described as **detail salience** — and led to less attention being given to other potentially important aspects of the situation, such as the identity of the perpetrator.

Loftus has also investigated the effect of introducing deliberately **misleading information** into an interview with an eyewitness (see Box 2.15).

Box 2.15 Loftus (1975)

Aims: To investigate whether introducing inaccurate information after people have witnessed an event leads to a distorted reconstruction of memory.

Procedure: Participants watched a 3-minute video of a lecture being disrupted by eight demonstrators. The participants later completed a 20-item questionnaire. In one condition, this included the question: 'Was the leader of the 12 demonstrators a male?', while in the other condition the question was: 'Was the leader of the four demonstrators a male?'. A week later, all participants were asked how many demonstrators there had been.

Results: Those who had been asked the '12 demonstrators' question reported on average that there had been 8.9 demonstrators, compared with 6.4 for those who had been asked the 'four demonstrators' question.

Conclusions: Participants reconstructed their memory of the event as a result of the inaccurate information that they had been given about demonstrator numbers, though in most cases the answers given were a compromise between what they had witnessed and the misleading information.

McCloskey and Zaragoza (1985) have suggested that the influence of misleading information — the **misinformation effect** — is not so much the result of memory being modified, but has more to do with two sources of bias in the testing procedure:

■ First, they refer to **misinformation acceptance**. It is possible that participants can be misled because they have failed to take in relevant information when they witnessed the event and so accept misleading information as accurate. For example, in the 'student demonstrators' study, they may not have counted the number of demonstrators and so have been prepared to believe that there were more or fewer than there actually were.

■ Second, they argue that **demand characteristics** — aspects of the testing situation that may suggest what is being tested — may lead to participants (mis)interpreting the task. They might accept the misinformation as accurate because it was given by the researcher, and responded to it because they wanted to 'do well' on the task.

Summary

- **Bartlett** suggested that memory is a **reconstruction**, which can be both incomplete and distorted. This has important implications for the reliability of **eyewitness testimony (EWT)**.
- The **wording** used in questioning eyewitnesses can influence recall.
- Recall can also be influenced by **detail salience**, where a focus on one particular detail of what is witnessed can lead to poor memory for other potentially important information.
- **Misleading information** given during questioning can be incorporated into the memory of an event and lead to distortion. However, the influence of this kind of information — the **misinformation effect** — may be the result of testing bias rather than the distortion of memory.

Other influences on eyewitness testimony (EWT)

A further factor that may influence EWT is the **age** of the witness, particularly when the witness is a child, as found by Flin et al. (see Box 2.16).

Children may also be more easily influenced by misleading information than adults. Robinson and Briggs (1997) showed participants a filmed event and then asked them questions about it, some of which included misleading information. Children aged 8–9 years were more susceptible to misleading information than adults, and those aged 4–5 years even more so.

Comparing the amount remembered by adults of different ages, List (1986) found that older people may recall less than younger people. Similarly, Loftus et al. (1991) found that older people — especially males — were more likely to be influenced by misleading information than younger people.

Stress and the anxiety associated with it are also factors in EWT. This can be related to the Yerkes-Dodson Law (see Figure 2.6).

Box 2.16 Flin et al. (1992)

Aims: To compare the accuracy of and amount of information about a witnessed event recalled by children and by adults, both immediately and after a delay.

Procedure: There were three groups of participants: children aged 5–6 years, children aged 9–10 years and undergraduates. All watched a presentation by a nurse on foot hygiene. As the talk began, there was an accident with a slide projector and an argument between the nurse and her two assistants. The 5-minute talk followed. The whole event had in fact been staged in order to test EWT. The following day, all participants were asked to recall as much as they could about the event, including the sequence of events, the content of the talk and what people were wearing. The interview was repeated 5 months later.

Results: For immediate recall, the amount of information recalled was not related to age. However, 5 months later, the younger children remembered significantly less than the other groups. Very little information offered by participants in all groups was incorrect.

Conclusions: Children's immediate EWT is as accurate as that of an adult. However, younger children forget more information over time. This is likely to be a problem when children are witnesses of a genuine crime, as there is inevitably a delay between witnessing an event and the child being asked to give evidence in court.

Figure 2.6 *The Yerkes-Dodson Law applied to recall*

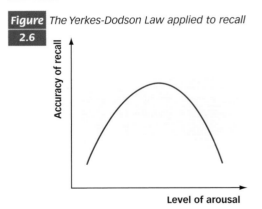

This law suggests that performance is related to arousal level. At low levels of arousal, for example when you are sleepy, performance is poor. As arousal increases, performance improves. However, as it increases still further, so that it becomes stress and is experienced as anxiety, performance falls off. In the case of EWT, it would therefore be expected that witnessing an anxiety-provoking event could reduce the accuracy of recall. This has been supported by research (see Box 2.17).

Box 2.17 Loftus and Burns (1982)

Aims: To investigate the effect of the stress associated with violence on recall of a witnessed crime.

Procedure: Participants were shown a video of a simulated armed robbery. In one condition, a boy was shot in the face while the robbers were making their getaway. The control condition was identical apart from the shooting. The amount and accuracy of recall in each condition were compared.

Results: Participants who had seen the 'violent' version of the video had less accurate and less complete recall than those who had seen the 'non-violent' version. This was true not only of the events immediately before the shooting, but also for events up to 2 minutes earlier.

Conclusions: The 'violent' version of the video heightened arousal and therefore reduced the processing of information into memory, necessary for recall.

The effect of the arousal associated with stress and anxiety on memory has also been tested in a more realistic situation (see Box 2.18).

Box 2.18   Peters (1988)

Aims: To assess the effects of stress on memory.

Procedure: People going to a surgery for an inoculation met the nurse who was to give them the injection, and another person, the researcher. They were exposed to each person for the same period of time. After they had been given the inoculation, they were asked to pick out both the nurse and the researcher from a set of photographs.

Results: Participants were significantly more successful at picking out the picture of the researcher than that of the nurse.

Conclusions: The stress of having the inoculation, associated with the nurse who gave it, led to comparatively poor memory when participants were asked to identify her. This suggests that the stress of witnessing a crime might have a negative effect on the ability of a witness to identify the criminal.

It is important to note that stress does not always have this effect (see Box 2.19).

Box 2.19   Yuille and Cutshall (1986)

Aims: To investigate the effects of stress on the accuracy of recall and susceptibility to misleading questions on witnesses of a crime.

Procedure: In Canada, 13 people who had witnessed an armed robbery gave evidence to the police. Between 4 and 5 months after they had witnessed the robbery, they were interviewed by psychologists. Two of the questions they were asked contained misleading information.

Results: Participants' recall of the events was not affected by the misleading questions. Very little of the information they gave the psychologists was inaccurate or reconstructed. There was no relationship between the degree of stress each participant had experienced at the time of the crime and the accuracy of recall.

Conclusions: In a real-life situation, recall is not necessarily inaccurate or reconstructed, or influenced by misleading questions. There is no relationship between the amount of stress experienced and accuracy of recall.

However, one problem with the Yuille and Cutshall study is that those who experienced higher levels of stress were closer to what was going on. Perhaps the effects of higher stress levels were counteracted by having better access to information about the event, thus improving their recall.

Nonetheless, this study is a good example of research with high **ecological validity**, because it relates to EWT given by people who had witnessed a genuine crime. By contrast, the ecological validity of the Loftus studies, described in Boxes 2.13, 2.14, 2.15 and 2.17, can be questioned. First, Loftus used videos, a situation that is different in many respects from witnessing a genuine event. A video does not have the immediacy of a real-life event, and participants will not have a clear view of what is going on. They are expecting to focus on what they are shown and report on it afterwards. They are also aware that they are taking part in psychological research, and so there will be no consequences as a result of the information that they provide, whereas witnesses of a crime are aware that their evidence can have serious consequences.

A similar criticism can be made of the Flin et al. study (Box 2.16). The children watching the staged event were not personally involved in what was happening and no crime was being committed. In real life (in court, for example), children are often asked to testify either for or against relatives with whom they have an emotional bond. Tye et al. (1999) carried out a study with children aged 6–10 years of age and found that almost half were prepared to lie to cover up a theft carried out by a close relative. In abuse cases, they may themselves be the victim of a crime.

Summary

- **Age** is a factor in the amount of information offered by witnesses and their susceptibility to misleading questions.
- While the information that **children** offer is generally accurate, they are more likely than adults to be influenced by **misleading questions** and **misinformation**.
- Children are also more likely to forget information over **time**. This is important, given the delay between witnessing a crime and a case coming to court.
- Studies have shown that high levels of **arousal**, associated with **stress** and **anxiety**, can reduce the efficiency with which information is processed into memory. This is likely to be a factor for witnesses of **violent crime**.
- Laboratory studies can be criticised for having **low ecological validity**, because the results cannot always be replicated in real-life situations.

The cognitive interview (CI)

The role of psychology is not only to develop an understanding of how people function, but also to apply this information in practical ways. Given the weight that juries give to EWT, the findings of studies like those of Loftus, which suggest that the way questions are worded can distort recall, have important implications for the questioning techniques used by the police and lawyers.

A teenage girl being interviewed by the police

The traditional way in which the police interview a witness typically focuses on eliciting information that is immediately useful, such as gender, height, age and dress of the criminals, rather than information that may be useful later on in the proceedings. This technique may therefore not be the best way to get the maximum amount of potentially useful information from a witness.

It is widely believed that **hypnosis** may be a useful way of improving the amount of information recalled by a witness. However, a survey of research in this area, carried out by Orne et al. (1984), suggested that testimony produced under hypnosis is not reliable and should only be accepted if there is independent corroborative evidence.

Using information from psychological research about how memory works, psychologists working with the police have developed a questioning technique called the **cognitive interview** (CI). This technique aims to get as much accurate information as possible from witnesses and is commonly used by police forces in the UK and the USA.

Geiselman et al. (1984) developed a procedure called the **basic cognitive interview**, which is based on two principles established by memory research. First, there may be a number of retrieval paths to a memory, so a memory that seems to be inaccessible may be retrieved if a different retrieval path is used. Second, a memory trace is made up of several features, and the effectiveness of a retrieval cue depends on how much of it overlaps with the memory trace.

These principles can be related to psychological theory. The **spreading activation model** of organisation in LTM, developed by Collins and Loftus (1975), suggests that concepts in LTM are linked in a complex network, each concept having many links with other concepts. There are therefore numerous pathways by which a particular concept may be reached (see Figure 2.7).

Figure 2.7 *The spreading activation model*

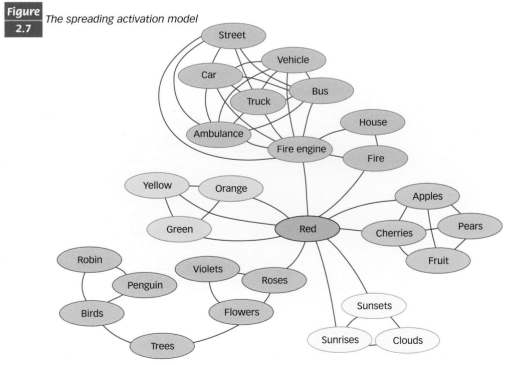

Adapted from Collins and Loftus (1975)

Cognitive psychology

The principles of the CI can also be related to **cue-dependent forgetting**, a concept developed by Tulving (1974). This theory proposes that there may be information in LTM that has apparently been forgotten but that can be retrieved using appropriate cues. It refers to two related phenomena: context-dependent forgetting and state-dependent forgetting.

In **context-dependent forgetting**, we may not be able to access a memory if we are in a different context when we are asked to recall it than we were when the information was originally taken in. If we are in the same context, that provides cues that may help to trigger the memory and so aid retrieval. For example, Godden and Baddeley (1975) asked divers to learn a list of words either on land or under water. Those who had learned the words underwater recalled them more accurately when they were tested under water than when they were tested on land, while those who had learned them on land recalled them more accurately when they were tested on land than when they were tested under water.

In **state-dependent forgetting**, we may not be able to access a memory if we are in a different physical or emotional state when we are asked to recall it than when the information was originally processed. If we are in the same state, the state provides cues that may help us to access and recall the memory.

Based on these psychological principles, the memory retrieval procedure of the basic cognitive interview was developed.

The basic cognitive interview involves:

- asking the eyewitness to reinstate mentally the environmental and personal context of the crime, reporting not only everything about the event that he or she witnessed, but also his or her own thoughts and feelings at the time
- asking the witness to recall as much as possible about the event that he or she witnessed, however trivial any details might seem
- encouraging the witness to recall the events that he or she witnessed in a variety of orders
- asking the witness to report from a variety of perspectives and points of view, for example, what another witness would have seen from a different standpoint

Cue-dependent forgetting is the reason behind asking the witness to reinstate the context of the crime. Mentally re-creating the physical environment of the event provides 'context' cues, while bringing back one's own thoughts and feelings provides 'state' cues.

The other three points of the basic cognitive interview can be linked to the spreading activation model. When a witness is asked to recall everything about the event, it is possible that recalling something apparently irrelevant could in turn trigger something important, or which later may turn out to be important. Asking a witness to recall events in different orders, for example starting with the end of the event and working backwards, and asking him or her to describe events from a different standpoint, will hopefully provide alternative pathways to crucial information.

When the CI was first used, Fisher et al. (1987) found that it produced 30% more information than a standard police interview, with no loss of accuracy. Geiselman et al. (1986) found that it also made witnesses less likely to be influenced by misleading information.

The CI has also been used with children. However, Memon and Bull (1991) suggested that not all the procedures of the cognitive interview may be useful when interviewing children. Children under the age of 7 years have difficulty understanding and following instructions to change perspectives, and the ability to organise parts of an event in the correct order is also something that is still developing during early childhood, so recalling in a different order may be something that young children find difficult. The most useful CI techniques are therefore likely to be asking children to reinstate the context, and to report everything they can remember (see Box 2.20).

Box 2.20 **Hayes and Delamothe (1997)**

Aims: To investigate the effectiveness of a modified form of the cognitive interview with children.

Procedure: Children aged 5–7 years and 9–11 years were shown a video of a story. During a narrative session, in which the story was outlined, some were given misleading information and some neutral information. The children were then interviewed, using either a standard interview technique or a CI, focusing on context reinstatement and reporting everything they could remember.

Results: Children produced more accurate information when the modified form of the CI was used. However, children in both age groups were susceptible to misleading information, whichever interview type was used.

Conclusions: The modified form of the CI was effective in increasing accurate recall in children. However, it did not affect their susceptibility to misleading information.

The basic cognitive interview has now been refined further, based on an analysis of real police interviews. The **enhanced cognitive interview** includes additional techniques, as outlined below.

The enhanced cognitive interview involves:

- minimising distractions
- asking the witness to speak slowly
- adapting the language used to suit the individual witness
- reducing anxiety
- avoiding judgemental and personal comments

Fisher et al. (1990) found that these techniques produced 45% more correct statements than the basic cognitive interview.

Geiselman (1999) points out that the CI has limitations. It has nothing to offer when a witness is asked to identify a suspect, and conflicting research findings suggest that it may have limited value with very young children. It also requires more time and effort than a standard police interview. Nonetheless, research has shown that the CI can be a useful tool for questioning witnesses.

Summary

- The **cognitive interview (CI)** was developed as a more effective questioning technique than standard police interviews.
- **Hypnosis** is not a reliable alternative.
- The CI is based on the principles of the **spreading activation model** of organisation in LTM and **cue-dependent forgetting**.
- The **basic cognitive interview** has been shown to increase the amount of accurate information that witnesses produce. A modified form has been shown to be useful when interviewing children.
- The **enhanced cognitive interview** is even more effective.
- While the CI is a useful technique, it also has **limitations**.

Strategies for memory improvement

As has been discussed earlier, there are ways in which memory can be improved. For example, use of the cognitive interview can elicit more useful information from an eyewitness than a standard police interview. The psychological principles on which the cognitive interview is based can also be used to enhance memory in everyday situations. For example, in relation to **context-dependent forgetting**, Abernathy (1940) found that people were more likely to recall information in the room in which the information had been learned than in a different room — the room provided context cues to recall.

This suggests that you might be better able to remember psychological information in the room in which you learn psychology than in the exam hall. This may not be a practical proposition, but Zechmeister and Nyberg (1982) found that imagining the environment in which you learned the information — in the same way that eye-witnesses are asked to re-create mentally the context and state in which they witnessed a crime — can be effective.

In the next sections, we will be looking in more detail at three kinds of strategy that enhance memory: the role of **meaning**, **organisation** in memory, and **imagery** as a form of organisation.

Meaning and memory

As noted earlier, one of the criticisms of the early work of Ebbinghaus on memory was his use of CVCs that have no meaning. Bartlett argued that we remember things because they are meaningful to us and so tested people using meaningful material like the story 'The war of the ghosts'. It was also mentioned that the capacity of STM can be increased by 'chunking', that is, putting several pieces of information together (for example, the letters GCSE) as a meaningful chunk. Craik and Watkins (1973) also suggested that in order to move information from STM to LTM, elaborative rehearsal is used. This kind of rehearsal is semantic, i.e. it processes the information using its meaning. All this suggests that we are more likely to remember something if it is meaningful to us.

The importance of meaning in memory is emphasised by the **levels of processing model** of memory, developed by Craik and Lockhart (1972). They suggested that memory is the result of processing information. Storage of information varies along a continuous dimension, depending on the depth to which it has been encoded. 'Depth' is defined here in terms of the meaningfulness extracted from the information. The more deeply information is processed, the better it will be stored and the more likely it is that it will be remembered. This idea has generally been tested using three levels: the **structural level**, the **phonological level** and the **semantic level** (see Figure 2.8).

Figure 2.8 *Levels in Craik and Lockhart's levels of processing model (1972)*

Structural level	What does the word look like? e.g. capitals or lower-case letters?	**Shallow**
Phonological level	What does the word sound like? e.g. does it rhyme with 'cat'?	
Semantic level	What does the word mean? e.g. is it a type of food?	**Deep**

A classic study carried out by Craik and Tulving (1975), which tested this theory used memory for words (see Box 2.21).

Box 2.21   Craik and Tulving (1975)

Aims: To investigate the role of meaning in memory.

Procedure: Participants were shown a series of words, on each of which they were asked a question. The questions required either (a) structural, (b) phonological or (c) semantic processing. For example:

(a) Is the word written in capital letters? (e.g. CAT or cat)

(b) Does the word rhyme with 'stable'? (e.g. table or chair)

(c) Does the word fit into the sentence: 'She climbed up the…'? (e.g. stairs or goat)

Participants were then given an unexpected recognition task, in which they were asked to pick out the words that they had been shown from others they had not seen.

Results: Participants were significantly better at identifying words that they had processed semantically than those they had processed structurally or phonologically.

Conclusions: The effectiveness of recall is related to the depth at which material is processed, with deep semantic processing producing better recall.

The idea of meaning being important if information is to be remembered can be applied to exam revision. If you just read and re-read your notes or the textbook, the processing that you are carrying out is relatively superficial, rather like the maintenance rehearsal that Craik and Watkins (1973) suggest is sufficient to keep information in STM, but not to move it into LTM. However, if you make summary notes of the key points as you read, you will be processing the information at a deeper semantic level and will be more likely to remember it.

Summary

- We remember information because it is **meaningful**.
- This idea underlies **levels of processing theory**. Information that is processed **semantically** is more readily remembered than information that is only processed structurally or phonologically.

Organisation in memory

Organisation of information in LTM is essential if we are to be able to retrieve it when it is needed. It is, to some extent, something that we do automatically. For example, if you were asked what the capital of France is, you would be able to access the information immediately, without having to search through all the other unrelated information that you have stored away in LTM, such as chemical symbols, the words of the British national anthem, how to do sudoku and so on. Therefore, there must be some kind of system that enables us to access information quickly and easily. One way in which this organisation takes place is by using **categories**, as explored by Bousfield (1953) (see Box 2.22).

Box 2.22   Bousfield (1953)

Aims: To investigate the effect of organisation in categories on recall.

Procedure: Participants were asked to learn 60 words, 15 in each of four categories — vegetables, animals, people's names and professions — presented in a random order. They were then asked to recall as many as possible in any order.

Results: There was a tendency to recall the items in clusters. For example, if 'carrot' was recalled, it tended to be followed by other vegetable names.

Conclusions: Material is organised in LTM in categorical clusters, i.e. meaningful groups.

The Bousfield study could be criticised for low ecological validity, as in real life we are seldom asked to remember word lists. However, Rubin and Olson (1980) found that the same kind of clustering occurred in more realistic situations: students recalled the names of Monopoly squares in the groups in which they appear on the board, and members of the university staff in groups according to the department in which they worked.

Hierarchical organisation is another way of storing information in LTM, as investigated by Bower et al. (1969) (see Box 2.23 and Figure 2.9).

Box 2.23 Bower et al. (1969)

Aims: To assess the effect on recall of the presentation of words in a hierarchy.

Procedure: Participants were asked to learn a set of words presented in a hierarchy (see Figure 2.9), with the most general term at the top and the most specific terms at the bottom. Participants in a control group were asked to learn the same words, presented in the same hierarchical structure, but with the words randomly distributed.

Results: The experimental group recalled 65% of the words accurately, while the control group remembered only 19% of the words.

Conclusions: Hierarchical organisation of information promotes recall.

Figure 2.9 *The Bower et al. hierarchy*

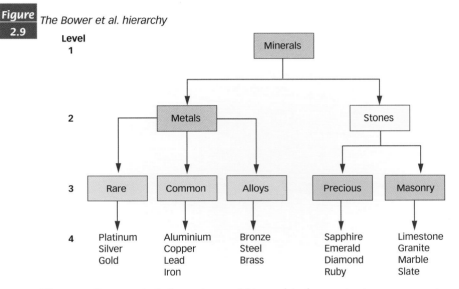

The use of categorical clustering and hierarchical organisation are ways in which we can improve memory for some kinds of material. A further kind of organisation, which may be more widely applicable, is the use of **schemas**. Schemas are cognitive structures and can be described as packets of information, based on our knowledge and experience of the world. The term can be traced back to Bartlett (1932). You will remember how he found that when people reproduced the story 'The war of the ghosts', there were omissions and distortions. This is because people changed what they had read to make it a more recognisably 'English' story, using their 'story' schemas, developed through their experience of English stories.

Schemas can relate to any number of things: types of people, social groups (such as hoodies or nurses), events (such as eating in a restaurant), and so on. They are useful in that they reduce the amount of processing necessary in new situations: we can link new experiences to the related schemas that we have already developed. Fitting new information into an existing schema makes it more likely to be remembered. However, as Bartlett demonstrated, schemas can also lead to distortions and omission of material that does not easily fit into the schema.

Summary

- Information must be **organised** in LTM to enable us to access it easily.
- Two effective forms of organisation are **categorical clustering** and **hierarchical organisation**.
- The use of **schemas** can also aid memory but may lead to distortion.

The role of imagery

Imagery can be seen as a particular form of organisation in LTM, and there is a lot of evidence that verbal material can be better remembered if it can be associated in some way with a visual image.

The use of imagery as a mnemonic technique goes back a long way. In classical times, an orator, wishing to remember the points that he intended to make in a speech, would create an image of an object relating to each point. He would then visualise a place with which he was familiar, such as a street or a building, and then mentally move around this place, placing each object in a specific location. When giving the speech, he would then visualise the location that he had chosen and mentally move around it, 'retrieving' each object in turn. This method is known as the **method of loci** ('loci' is the Latin word for 'places').

The usefulness of imagery as an aid to memory has been shown experimentally, for example by Bower (1972) (see Box 2.24).

Box 2.24   Bower (1972)

Aims: To investigate the role of visual imagery in promoting recall.

Procedure: A method called **paired associate learning** was used. In the learning phase, participants are shown a pair of unrelated words, e.g. 'dolphin' and 'tray', and are asked to remember the pairs. In the recall phase, they are shown the first word of the pair and are asked to recall the second word. In this study, participants were shown a series of 100 cards, each with a pair of words. Those in the experimental group were instructed to form a mental image that linked the words in some way, while those in the control group were just asked to try to remember the word pairs.

Results: Those in the experimental group remembered 80% of the word pairs, while for those in the control group, recall was only 45%.

Conclusions: The use of visual imagery is an effective way of improving recall.

The Bower study just presented pairs of words and asked participants themselves to form an image linking them. Other studies have built on this by presenting participants with images, to try to establish which aspects of images are most effective in increasing recall. Toyota (2002) found that bizarre images are effective for people who find it easy to create mental images. Wollen et al. (1972) found that memory is enhanced if the images are interacting in some way.

The finding that interactive images can aid recall has been applied to the practical situation of vocabulary learning for students of a foreign language. Atkinson and Raugh (1975) found the **keyword method** to be effective in vocabulary learning:

The keyword method

This has two stages:

- First, an English word (the keyword) that is similar in sound or appearance to the new foreign-language word is identified. For example, the Spanish word 'apio' is similar to the English word 'ape'.

- Then an interactive image is created, linking the keyword and the definition of the new word. For example, 'apio' means 'celery', so the learner could create an interactive image of an ape carrying a bunch of celery.

  For retrieval of the English meaning when the learner is given the foreign-language word, he or she would need to recall the keyword, in this case 'ape', to access the image of the ape holding the celery. A similar process would be carried out when the learner is presented with the English word and asked for the foreign-language equivalent.

Recent research by Wyra et al. (2007) examined this method in more detail (see Box 2.25).

Box 2.25   Wyra et al. (2007)

Aims: To investigate whether additional training in retrieval techniques improves the effectiveness of the keyword method, and whether its effectiveness is related to the individual's ability to create images.

Procedure: The participants were 71 students, aged 11–12 years, who had studied Spanish for 5 years. Six words unfamiliar to the students were used for instruction and practice, and a further 22 to test its effectiveness. The students were asked to create appropriate images containing just two elements, with the definition image larger than the keyword image. Recall was tested in both directions, i.e. participants were given the new Spanish word and asked for its English equivalent (forwards), and given the English word and asked to give the Spanish equivalent (backwards). Some students were given extra training on backwards recall, because the effectiveness of keyword training on this aspect is seldom tested. Students also completed an 'ability to make images' questionnaire, designed specifically for this study.

Results: Recall for the students who had received extra training was around 20% higher for forwards recall and 16% higher for backwards recall. The method was significantly more effective for students who rated their ability to create images as high.

Conclusions: The use of images in the keyword method is useful in learning foreign vocabulary, particularly if students are given sufficient training and practice in its use and if they are able to create interactive images easily.

Summary

- **Imagery** is an effective way of enhancing recall.
- There is some evidence that **bizarre** and **interactive** imagery may increase its effectiveness.
- The use of interactive imagery can be beneficial in the **keyword method** of learning **foreign-language vocabulary**.

Terms explained

anterograde amnesia: inability to form new memories, as the result either of brain damage, as in the cases of HM and Clive Wearing, or of shock or trauma.

ecological validity: the extent to which a piece of research represents a real-life event or experience. For example, a study of memory in which people are asked to remember a list of nonsense syllables would have low ecological validity, as it is very unlike the way we use memory in real life. Ecological validity is important if the conclusions drawn from the findings of the study are to be applied beyond the research situation.

hippocampus: part of the limbic system in the brain, which plays an important role in memory.

As in the cases of HM and Clive Wearing, damage to this area of the brain leads to an inability to form new long-term memories

reconstructive memory: Bartlett suggested that remembering is not a straightforward reproduction of an experience; instead, we store key aspects and reconstruct the details in line with the schemas we have developed from other similar experiences. This may lead to distortions in memory.

working memory model (WM): an alternative to the STM of the multi-store model. The WM model suggests that there are different sub-systems within STM, and focuses on active processing of information, together with temporary storage.

Chapter 3

Attachment

In this chapter, we will be looking at:
- the nature of attachment and its development
- explanations of attachment
- secure and insecure attachment
- cultural variations in attachment
- disruption of attachment and privation
- day care and social development
- the implications of research for childcare practices

The nature of attachment and its development

Attachment can be defined as a strong and reciprocal emotional bond with another person. This is particularly evident in the attachment of babies to their mothers or other major caregivers. Maccoby (1980) suggested that there are four key behaviours that indicate that an attachment has been formed:

Key behaviours demonstrating attachment

- Seeking to be near the attachment figure.
- Being distressed when separated from them.
- Showing pleasure when reunited with them.
- Orientation towards them, being aware of their presence and frequently making contact with them.

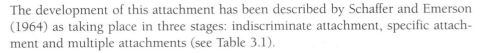

The development of this attachment has been described by Schaffer and Emerson (1964) as taking place in three stages: indiscriminate attachment, specific attachment and multiple attachments (see Table 3.1).

Table 3.1 *The development of attachment (Schaffer and Emerson, 1964)*

Stage	Approximate age range	Characteristics
Indiscriminate attachment	Up to about 6 months	It doesn't matter who is holding the baby. The baby smiles at anyone and protests when put down, whoever is holding them.
Specific attachment	From about 7 months to a year	One specific attachment emerges, usually to the mother or major caregiver. In the earlier period, the baby is distressed when separated from this person (**separation anxiety**) and is wary of strangers (**stranger anxiety**).
Multiple attachments	From about a year onwards	Attachment to another person is shown, and then to a number of other people who are important in the child's life.

However, there is quite a lot of individual variation. Schaffer and Emerson found that the second stage of specific attachment could start at any time between 6 months and a year, and the number of multiple attachments formed, and when they were formed, also varied. Only half of the 60 babies studied formed their main attachment with the mother, with a third showing a preference for the father, and others with a grandparent or with a brother or sister.

Explanations of attachment

Several theories have been put forward to explain why infants form and maintain attachments. We will now look at those based on learning theory and on the ethological perspective.

Learning theory

You will remember from Chapter 1 that behaviourists believe that all behaviour is learned, through either classical or operant conditioning. Both forms of conditioning have been used to explain the development of attachment.

Within a classical conditioning framework, food produces a sense of pleasure. The person providing the food — usually the mother — is linked to food, and so she becomes a source of pleasure (see Figure 3.1).

Figure 3.1 *Attachment as classical conditioning*

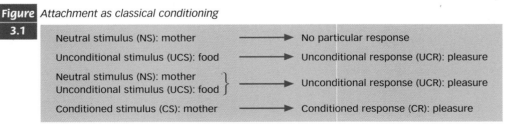

Neutral stimulus (NS): mother ⟶ No particular response

Unconditional stimulus (UCS): food ⟶ Unconditional response (UCR): pleasure

Neutral stimulus (NS): mother
Unconditional stimulus (UCS): food } ⟶ Unconditional response (UCR): pleasure

Conditioned stimulus (CS): mother ⟶ Conditioned response (CR): pleasure

This explanation has been further developed in the **secondary drive hypothesis** proposed by Dollard and Miller (1950). They proposed that we have **primary drives**, that is, motivational states arising from basic physiological needs, such as hunger. Since this basic need is repeatedly met by the mother, her presence becomes associated with the satisfaction of the need and so becomes a **secondary** (or **learned**) **drive**. The infant is therefore motivated to seek the mother's presence and to become distressed if she is not there.

Operant conditioning also suggests that attachment is learned. Feeding is reinforcing to a hungry child. As the mother is close to the child during feeding, feeding positively reinforces attachment.

However, there are problems with theories that explain attachment in terms of feeding. Schaffer and Emerson found that quite a large proportion of infants formed their primary attachment with someone who seldom, if ever, fed them, so attachment cannot adequately be explained by feeding alone. This has been further demonstrated in animal research (see Box 3.1).

Box 3.1 Harlow and Zimmerman (1959)

Aims: To investigate the basis of attachment in rhesus monkeys.

Procedure: Infant monkeys were separated from their mothers shortly after birth and raised in isolation. They had access to two surrogate mothers: wire frames that looked similar to an adult monkey. One was covered in soft terry cloth, and the other was left bare but had a teat through which the infant could obtain milk. The infant monkeys were deliberately frightened by introducing a clockwork teddy bear beating a drum, into the cage.

Results: The infant monkeys showed their extreme distress through behaviours such as screaming, rocking, crouching in a corner and thumb sucking. Most of the time, they clung to the cloth mother, even though it did not give milk. They also clung to her when frightened by the teddy bear. There was no attempt to cling to the wire monkey.

Conclusions: Mothering is not just about feeding. Young primates also need a source of psychological warmth (Harlow called it **contact comfort**), which here was provided by the cloth mother.

However, this study presents some weaknesses. Firstly, there are ethical concerns, as the infant monkeys clearly suffered as a result of this experience. Secondly, there are methodological issues, i.e. with the way that the study was carried out, given that the two surrogate mothers differed in ways other than being covered in cloth or giving milk. For example, they had somewhat different head shapes, and this kind of difference cannot be ruled out as an influence on the behaviour of the infants. Thirdly, there is the issue of **extrapolation**: though monkeys are genetically quite similar to humans, can we assume that what is true of monkeys is also true of humans? Nonetheless, the series of studies that Harlow carried out adds weight to the idea that attachment cannot be explained purely in terms of learned behaviour based on feeding.

The ethological perspective: Bowlby's theory of attachment

A different kind of explanation of attachment was put forward by **John Bowlby** (1907–90). His theory was much influenced by **ethology**, the study of animals in their natural surroundings, and in particular by **imprinting**. Imprinting is the phenomenon observed in some birds, such as geese, which follow the first moving object that they see on hatching. In most cases, this is the mother, but Lorenz, an ethologist, demonstrated that goslings would also imprint on him if he was there when they first hatched. Once this bond was formed, it was irreversible: the goslings never learned to follow the mother.

It was initially thought by ethnologists that there was a **critical period** when imprinting had to occur, a brief period of time within which it had to take place. If it did not happen then, it would not happen at all. This principle was later modified, with the suggestion that instead there is a **sensitive period**, when imprinting is more likely to take place, though it can still occur outside this restricted window of time. However, the idea of a critical period was still accepted when Bowlby developed his attachment theory.

Imprinting has obvious survival value. The mother will protect the young from predators and make sure that they are fed and cared for. She will also help them to acquire the skills they need for survival. However, Lorenz demonstrated that successful imprinting has wider implications. He found that goslings that did not successfully imprint on an appropriate carer had serious social and sexual problems as they matured, and he believed these problems to be irreversible. This was supported by Immelmann (1972), who found that zebra finches that had imprinted on Bengalese finches preferred to mate with this species rather than their own.

Konrad Lorenz walking with 'his' goslings

Bowlby extended these ideas to attachment in infants, proposing that human infants have an innate predisposition to form a strong attachment to one individual, who will most usually be the mother. The bond between mother and infant is **reciprocal**, with the mother also being predisposed to bond with her infant. In evolutionary terms, infant attachment is **adaptive**. In our evolutionary past, those infants genetically predisposed to form a strong attachment would be more likely to survive to maturity and reproduce, passing on their genes, including those coding for attachment, to their offspring. For the mother, attachment is adaptive in that it will motivate her to care for the infant and so promote its survival, and ultimately the survival of her genes when the infant reaches maturity and reproduces successfully.

Attachment in the infant is adaptive in several ways:

Attachment is adaptive because:

- It promotes **safety**: the infant wishes to be close to the mother, and both are distressed by separation.

- It promotes the development of **healthy emotional relationships**: within this first relationship, Bowlby suggests that the infant develops an **internal working model (IWM)** of the self, the mother and the relationship between the two, which acts as a template for future relationships.

- It provides a **secure base for exploration**: exploration is an important factor in mental development, but this needs to be balanced by the security offered by returning from time to time to the mother.

Bowlby proposed that there is an innate sequence in the development of attachment, with the infant moving through the phases as he or she matures (see Box 3.2).

Box 3.2 The development of attachment (Bowlby, 1969)

1 **Birth–8 weeks**: The infant is friendly towards other people, but shows little discrimination between them.

2 **8 weeks–6 months**: While still generally friendly, the infant starts to show a preference towards one primary caregiver.

3 **6 months–2 years**: The infant seeks proximity to the attachment figure and uses him or her as a secure base. The infant is distressed when separated from the attachment figure (**separation anxiety**), is less friendly towards others and is wary of strangers (**stranger anxiety**).

4 **2 years onwards**: The infant develops insight into the primary caregiver's behaviour and can consciously influence what he or she does. This marks the beginning of a relationship that is a more equal partnership between child and caregiver.

As a trigger for the attachment process, Bowlby claimed that the infant displays **social releasers**, such as smiling, crying, sucking and clinging, to which others are innately predisposed to respond.

Bowlby also suggested that there is a **critical period** for this attachment to be formed. If it had not formed by the age of around 3 years, it would be impossible for the child to form a strong attachment. There would be long-term and irreversible consequences for an infant's social and emotional well-being if an attachment was not formed by this time.

There were a number of influences on Bowlby's theory. He was a trained psychoanalyst and therefore recognised the importance of childhood experience for later development. However, the findings of ethological research were a major influence, which raises the issue of **extrapolation**, i.e. in this instance applying findings relating to non-human animals to human development. It is problematic to extrapolate from goslings to humans. Imprinting is a reflex, leading to following behaviour, whereas attachment is to do with the development of emotions, so imprinting may not be an entirely appropriate model for human attachment.

However, research evidence suggests that, like those identified in birds, there are serious long-term social and sexual problems in monkeys — genetically much closer to humans than goslings — when they are reared without a mother. Harlow and Harlow (1962) found that rhesus monkeys reared in isolation had severe social and sexual problems when they were older. When put with normally reared monkeys, they were unable to interact in a natural way. Some were extremely withdrawn, rocking back and forth repetitively; some were aggressive towards others; and some were self-harming, biting their own limbs until they bled. Males could not mate successfully, and females, if they did mate, were cruel and rejecting mothers, refusing to let their infants nurse. Of course, these monkeys had not only been separated from their mothers but also raised without any kind of social contact, so their extreme behaviour clearly cannot be accounted for solely by the lack of attachment. However, given the similarities between monkeys and humans, this suggests that an early close relationship with the mother is crucial to human social and emotional development.

Further support for Bowlby's theory comes from cross-cultural research. Kagan et al. (1978) carried out research in a range of different cultures. They found that the pattern of development of **separation anxiety** in different cultures was similar, with only relatively small variations (see Figure 3.2): it emerges in the second half of the first year and increases until approximately 15 months; it then declines steadily.

Bowlby believed that separation anxiety indicates that a bond has been formed with the mother, the fear of strangers that occurs at around the same time preventing another bond being formed. He used the term **monotropism** to describe the child's need to become attached to one particular person. This would also be adaptive, in terms of protecting the infant from possible harm, and since the Kagan et al. study suggests that it is universal, there is support for it being innate.

Further support for Bowlby's ideas, and in particular the internal working model (IWM) as a template for future relationships, comes from research looking at links between the nature of early attachment and later characteristics. This will be examined in the next section.

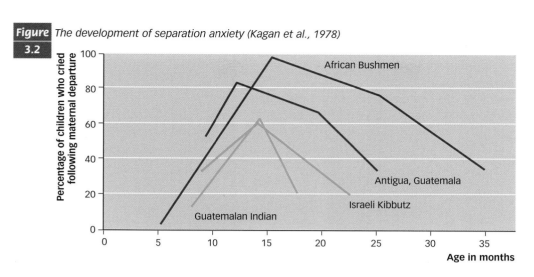

Figure 3.2 The development of separation anxiety (Kagan et al., 1978)

Percentage of children who cried following maternal departure — Age in months

African Bushmen
Antigua, Guatemala
Israeli Kibbutz
Guatemalan Indian

However, there are also some problems with Bowlby's theory. First, it rests on evolutionary ideas, and as we discussed in Chapter 1, ideas associated with this theory are speculative — it is not possible to test them directly. Second, Bowlby suggests that the early attachment with the mother acts as a template for future relationships: if a good relationship is established with the mother, then future relationships should also be sound. However, even if this were the case, there are ways in which this could be explained other than by the establishment of an IWM. For example, it could be explained in terms of the temperament of the child: a child with an easy temperament is likely to form a secure attachment with the mother, and it may be that this kind of temperament also makes it easy for him or her to form good relationships with others later in life, rather than the pattern of relationships being laid down in infancy.

Summary

- Bowlby's theory of attachment was influenced by **ethology** and in particular by **imprinting**.
- Imprinting was thought to take place within a **critical period**, later adapted as a **sensitive period**.
- Imprinting has **survival value**, and failure to imprint appropriately leads to poor social and sexual development.
- Bowlby applied these principles to the attachment between a mother and her baby. It is **reciprocal**; both are innately pre-programmed to form a bond.
- As with animals, this attachment is **adaptive**, in that it is likely to promote survival.
- For the infant, this attachment is **monotropic** and is different in kind from other attachments. It allows the infant to develop an **internal working model (IWM)** of relationships.
- Animal research supports these ideas, although **extrapolation** from non-human animals to humans is problematic.

Developmental psychology

Secure and insecure attachment

A major research tool in investigating mother–infant attachment is the laboratory-based **Strange Situation** technique. This was developed by **Ainsworth**, a student of Bowlby's, and identified the characteristics of both secure and different types of insecure attachment in infants. Children are usually tested between the ages of 12 months and 18 months, and the procedure consists of a series of eight episodes involving collaboration between the mother and the experimenter. Each episode lasts approximately 3 minutes, but is cut short if the child becomes distressed. The interactions are filmed for analysis. Figure 3.3 shows the eight stages of Ainsworth's Strange Situation technique.

Most children use their mothers as a secure base

Figure 3.3 *Ainsworth's Strange Situation technique*

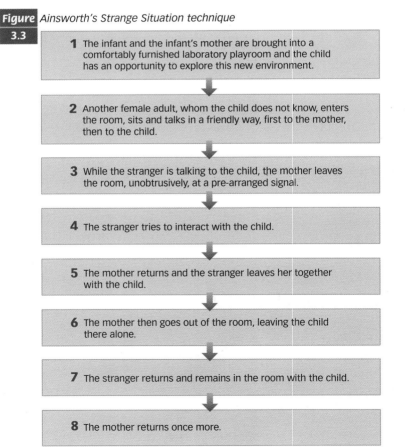

1 The infant and the infant's mother are brought into a comfortably furnished laboratory playroom and the child has an opportunity to explore this new environment.

2 Another female adult, whom the child does not know, enters the room, sits and talks in a friendly way, first to the mother, then to the child.

3 While the stranger is talking to the child, the mother leaves the room, unobtrusively, at a pre-arranged signal.

4 The stranger tries to interact with the child.

5 The mother returns and the stranger leaves her together with the child.

6 The mother then goes out of the room, leaving the child there alone.

7 The stranger returns and remains in the room with the child.

8 The mother returns once more.

Four different aspects of behaviour are assessed using this technique:

Assessment of the child's behaviour in the Strange Situation

1 The use of the mother as a **secure base**, i.e. leaving her side to explore the environment, but returning at intervals to her side.

2 The response of the child on separation from the mother when she leaves the room (**separation anxiety**).

3 The way the child responds when the stranger seeks to interact with him or her (**stranger anxiety**).

4 The child's behaviour on **reunion** with the mother.

Using this technique, Ainsworth identified three contrasting patterns of attachment:

Types of attachment

Type A (insecure: anxious-avoidant): The child does not use the mother as a secure base; is not distressed when the mother leaves the room; treats the mother and the stranger in much the same way; avoids interaction with the mother when she returns.

Type B (secure): The child uses the mother as a secure base; is distressed when the mother leaves the room; is somewhat wary of the stranger; is easily comforted when reunited with the mother.

Type C (insecure: anxious-ambivalent, sometimes referred to as anxious-resistant): The child does not use the mother as a secure base; is extremely distressed when the mother leaves the room; rejects the stranger; seeks to be with the mother when she returns, but at the same time rejects her, and is not easily soothed.

Van IJzendoorn and Kroonenberg (1988) used this assessment of attachment type in a number of different countries and found that typically, approximately 65% of children are Type B, 20% Type A and 15% Type C. However, there was considerable variation both between and within countries, and we will be returning to this issue in the next section.

Main and Solomon (1986) later added **Type D**, an additional form of insecure attachment, which they described as 'insecure: disorganised'. Children falling into this category seem dazed, confused and apprehensive, and seem to have no coherent system for dealing with separation and reunion. This pattern, fortunately rare, is most commonly found in children where there is child abuse, the child is at high social risk, or one or both of the parents have serious mental health problems.

Attachment theory suggests that each attachment type is linked to a different IWM of 'self', 'the other' and the relationship between the two. **Type B** children feel worthy of their parents' affection and love, and are confident that the mother will return when they are separated, so separation, whilst distressing, does not lead to panic. They have an expectation of closeness and warmth between people, so are able to accept some contact with the stranger. **Type A** children seem to feel unworthy of affection and expect the relationship with the mother to be difficult, so tend not to get too close to her, even when they are reunited after a separation. For **Type C** children, the mother's presence is important, but children seem to lack a firm belief that their mothers will return or will be able to provide effective comfort.

These attachment types have been linked to the way in which the mother interacts with the child, as established by Vondra et al. (1995) (see Box 3.3).

Box 3.3	**Vondra et al. (1995)**

Aims: To establish links between Strange Situation categories and maternal behaviour during interaction with the child.

Procedure: The interaction between mothers and their 1-year-old infants was filmed. To start with, the mother started to answer a questionnaire, with the child in a highchair at the other end of the room. The mother then continued with the questionnaire, with the child free to move around the room. Finally, the mother carried out various tasks with the child, such as putting wooden blocks in a box and stacking plastic rings. On the basis of their behaviour during these tasks, the mothers were classified into one of three groups: **controlling**, **unresponsive** or **sensitive**. A Strange Situation assessment was also carried out to define the child's attachment type.

Results: Sensitive mothers tended to have securely attached infants (Type B), controlling mothers were more likely to have Type A infants, and unresponsive mothers to have Type C infants.

Conclusions: The mothers' classifications were good predictors of the infant's attachment type. The kind of mothering that the child receives shapes the child's IWM.

The experiment shown in Box 3.3 was brief, but still seems to indicate that attachment type can be linked to the way the mother interacts with the child.

The expression of **emotion** and emotional responses has also been shown to have links with Strange Situation classifications. In an analysis of 30 video recordings of Strange Situations, Goldberg et al. (1994) found that Type B children frequently experienced emotional events, both positive and negative, and the mother responded to these events. This would give the child opportunities to learn that in a relationship all emotions are valid. Type A children had few emotional experiences, especially negative ones, to which the mother rarely responded. The child would learn from this that negative feelings should be suppressed. Type C children had many emotional experiences, especially negative ones, and although the mother rarely showed any kind of response, it was to negative experiences that she was more likely to respond, giving the child the message that negative emotions attract attention.

Links have also been made between infant attachment type and **characteristics later in childhood**, supporting the idea of an IWM, established in infancy and shaping later relationships. Main and Cassidy (1988) investigated possible links between infant attachment type and the behaviour and self-image of children aged 3–6 years. They found quite wide variations. Some children see themselves as lovable and value close relationships with others, linked to the Type B classification. Type A children see themselves as unlovable and act in ways that may lead others to reject them. They seem more interested in activities than people. Type C children at this age are still distressed by separation from the parent and show whiny, clinging behaviour.

In a related study, Main and Goldwyn (1984) used the **Adult Attachment Interview (AAI)** to investigate whether these early patterns of attachment could influence adult relationships, and in particular the quality of attachment of the adult with his or her own child. Each adult was classified into one of four groups, and the quality of attachment of his or her child(ren) assessed (see Table 3.2).

Table 3.2 *Adult behaviour and own child's attachment (Main and Goldwyn, 1984)*

Adult classification	Characteristics	Infant attachment type
Dismissing-detached	Childhood experiences are not seen as important; neither are personal relationships	Type A
Autonomous-secure	Relationships, both past and current, are important; both positive and negative experiences are recalled, with insight into their influence on the self	Type B
Preoccupied-entangled	The emotional significance of past experience is recognised, but past issues are unresolved	Type C
Unresolved-disorganised	These adults had suffered traumatic separation from the attachment figure, with which they had not come to terms; they had often been abused	Type D

This idea has been extended by Hazan and Shaver (1987), to look at possible links with the nature of adult romantic relationships (see Box 3.4).

Box 3.4 Hazan and Shaver (1987)

Aims: To investigate a possible link between the kind of mothering experienced as an infant and the experience of adult romantic love.

Procedure: Hazan and Shaver used Ainsworth's three basic infant attachment types to compare descriptions of three corresponding types of adult attachment (see Table 3.3). Their Love Quiz was then published in a newspaper and readers were asked to pick which description of adult romantic relationships best applied to them. They were also asked to complete an adjective check list to describe the kind of parenting they had received as children. The first 620 replies were analysed.

Results: There was a significant correlation between attachment classification, based on the check list, and the choice of the participants' description of their adult relationships.

Conclusions: There is a link between early attachment experience and the nature of relationships formed as an adult.

There are some problems with Hazan and Shaver's study. The sample was self-selecting, in that people chose whether to respond to the newspaper quiz or not, and it is possible that a particular kind of person might choose to do so, not necessarily representative of people in general. In addition, part of the study asked people to respond to adjectives describing the kind of parenting that they had received, so asking them to recall experiences that had happened many years previously; it is possible that their memories were not entirely reliable. Finally, given that the respondents were giving information about themselves, it is also possible that they were not completely truthful.

Table 3.3 *Hazan and Shaver (1987): attachment type, parenting and adult relationships*

Attachment style	Type of parenting	Adult relationships: self-description
Securely attached	Readily available, responsive	I find it relatively easy to get close to others and am comfortable depending on them and having them depend on me. I don't often worry about being abandoned or about someone getting too close to me.
Anxious-avoidant	Unresponsive, rejecting, inattentive	I am somewhat uncomfortable being close to others; I find it difficult to trust them completely, and difficult to allow myself to depend on them. I am nervous when anyone gets too close and, often, love partners want me to be more intimate than I feel comfortable being.
Anxious-ambivalent	Anxious, fussy, out of step with child's needs; only available/responsive some of the time	I find that others are reluctant to get as close as I would like. I often worry that my partner doesn't really love me or won't want to stay with me. I want to merge completely with another person, and this desire sometimes scares people away.

There is also evidence that the quality of relationships cannot be explained fully by the quality of early attachment, as shown by Zimmermann (2000) (see Box 3.5).

Box 3.5 **The Bielefeld longitudinal study (Zimmermann, 2000)**

Aims: To investigate links between infant attachment type and adult attachment type at adolescence.

Procedure: A longitudinal study was carried out with 44 children, whose attachment was assessed as infants and whose adult attachment type was assessed when they were 16. There was also a systematic collection of data on various life events, such as divorce, death or illness of parents during the intervening years.

Results: The Strange Situation classification was not a good predictor of adult attachment. Life events, and in particular divorce or serious parental illness occurring in childhood, was a much greater influence.

Conclusions: Attachment classification in infancy alone is not a good predictor of adult attachment type. Life events also have an influence.

However, in a similar study, Hamilton (1994) found a strong correspondence between Strange Situation classification and adult attachment type, though this was strongest for those whose family circumstances had remained stable throughout the period between the two measures. Where there was change in the classification, children were more likely to have experienced major changes in family circumstances.

These studies suggest that while there is some link between infant and adult attachment, **life events** also have a part to play. Bowlby's notion of the IWM is perhaps rather too limited in its explanation of the causes of the nature of attachment in later relationships. As for the Strange Situation technique, although it has been used widely in research and the classification into three main types of attachment is useful in demonstrating differences in behaviour, the categorisation of attachment types is an over-simplification. For example, infants who have been placed in the same category are nonetheless likely to be quite different from each other. In addition, in several studies, researchers have been unable to classify some infants: in a study by Nakagawa et al. (1992), for example, 4% of the infants observed were unclassified because their behaviour did not fit into any of the categories. As Takahashi (1990) points out, other factors, such as individual temperament, need to be taken into account when an assessment of the quality of attachment is made.

A child at nursery waves good-bye to her mother, knowing that she will return

Another problem with the Strange Situation technique is that it is an artificial situation. Mothers are aware of being observed, so it is possible that they interact differently with their child under these conditions than they would in their normal surroundings at home. Moreover, it does not take into account the child's previous experience of separation. For example, a child who regularly goes to nursery may be used to the mother leaving and has learned that she will return. The child might therefore appear unworried when the mother leaves the room and, though securely attached, could be categorised as Type A (anxious-avoidant).

Finally, the technique was developed in the USA, so it may be culturally biased. It may be that a particular behaviour has different implications in different cultures. This will be examined in the next section.

Summary

- The **Strange Situation** technique has been widely used in attachment research. It classifies attachment into three main types. A fourth type was added later.
- Attachment type is linked to the child's **internal working model (IWM)** of self, the mother and the nature of relationships.
- Attachment type has been associated with the **ways in which the mother responds to the child** and with the **child's experience of emotional events**.
- A modified form of the technique has demonstrated links to **later relationships**, both in childhood and as adults. However, **life events** may also be important in changes in attachment over time.
- While the technique is widely used in attachment research, there are several grounds on which it can be criticised.

Developmental psychology

Cultural variations in attachment

Cultures vary in terms of beliefs, attitudes, norms and values. One broad distinction can be drawn between individualist and collectivist cultures, though countries that fall into the same general category nevertheless vary among themselves.

In **individualist** cultures, typically Western cultures (such as the UK and the USA), the focus is on the rights and responsibilities of the individual, with an emphasis on individual achievement and personal choice. People feel that it is their right to choose how they wish to organise their lives in areas such as marriage and career. At the same time, they must take personal responsibility for the results of their decisions.

In **collectivist** cultures, typically Eastern cultures (such as mainland China and Korea), the emphasis is on the needs and goals of the social group. While the preferences of the individual are taken into account, decisions such as choosing a marriage partner are made by the social group, and the responsibility for the outcomes of these decisions is also shared by the group.

These kinds of differences are likely to impact on child rearing across the world. Cultural values and beliefs seem to influence child-rearing styles, and thus the ways in which mothers and infants interact. **Cross-cultural research** has been carried out to explore this issue, for example by Jin (2005) (see Box 3.6).

Box 3.6 **Jin (2005)**

Aims: To compare the pattern of attachment classifications in Eastern and Western cultures by assessing mother–infant pairs in Korea and the USA.

Procedure: Eighty-seven Korean mother–infant pairs and 113 American mother–infant pairs, with the infants aged between 12 and 18 months, were observed using the Strange Situation technique. The behaviour of both infants and mothers was observed.

Results: In the two samples, there was a similar percentage of securely and insecurely attached infants. However, fewer babies in the Korean sample were classified as Type A (insecure: anxious-avoidant) than in the American sample. In the Strange Situation, the Korean infants and their mothers showed different behaviours from American babies and mothers. The Korean infants showed less proximity and contact-maintaining behaviours than the American infants. At reunion, the Korean mothers immediately approached their babies and stayed on the floor with them unlike the American mothers. The Korean infants were less likely to approach the mother on reunion.

Conclusions: There are cultural differences in the way mothers and infants interact.

Hautamäki (2007) gives a further example of how culture could influence attachment classification. In Finland, the Strange Situation technique identifies a larger than expected proportion of Type A children. Hautamäki points out that Finland has a culture of self-reliance and hard work, and that the strategies the Finns have developed to protect themselves from the risks of the long, cold winters, along with a difficult geopolitical position, may create a culture in which emotions are inhibited, and this is mirrored in the response of children in the Strange Situation.

Research has also directly explored cultural differences in beliefs about attachment, and what are seen as desirable outcomes as the child develops (see Box 3.7).

Box 3.7   Rothbaum et al. (2007)

Aims: To explore cultural similarities and differences in the understanding of attachment, and how secure or insecure attachment is linked to behaviour.

Procedure: Thirty-nine American mothers and 32 Japanese mothers were interviewed to explore their beliefs about attachment, and how secure and insecure attachment is shown in behaviour.

Results: Both groups of mothers considered maternal responsiveness to be an important factor in the development of a secure attachment, and saw secure attachment as being shown in desirable child characteristics. However, whereas American mothers believed that secure children show more exploratory behaviour and insecure ones show more anger and aggression, Japanese mothers linked security to obedient behaviour. In mildly stressful situations, Japanese mothers were more likely to interpret children's poor behaviour as a need for security and dependence on the mother, while American mothers interpreted this kind of behaviour as self-assertiveness.

Conclusions: While different cultures share some beliefs about the nature of attachment and see a secure attachment as desirable, there are variations in how they interpret behaviour in relation to attachment.

In the previous section it was noted that research using the Strange Situation technique carried out by Van IJzendoorn and Kroonenberg (1988) found that in general, 65% of children can be classified as Type B, 20% as Type A and 15% as Type C. It is also relevant to this section because it was a major study into cultural variations in attachment. Its procedure, results and conclusions are described in Box 3.8 and the figures are provided in Table 3.4.

Box 3.8   Van IJzendoorn and Kroonenberg (1988)

Aims: To investigate possible cultural variations in patterns of attachment by way of a meta-analysis of studies using the Strange Situation technique.

Procedure: A meta-analysis combines data from existing studies and re-analyses them. Thirty-two studies using the Strange Situation were examined. Research was used from eight cultures: the USA, the UK, Germany, the Netherlands, Sweden, Israel, Japan and China, and the percentages of children in each culture falling into each category were compared.

Results: In all cultures, with the exception of China, Type B was the most common attachment category. However, there was a lot of variation in the percentages of insecure attachment types. Israel and Japan had high levels of Type C attachment, with low levels of Type A, while Germany had high levels of Type A attachment. There was nearly 1.5 times as much variation within cultures as there was between cultures.

Conclusions: Overall, there is wide inter-cultural variation in the percentages of different attachment types, with Type A classifications relatively more common in Western European countries and Type C classifications more common in Israel and Japan. However, the variation within cultures suggests that it is misleading to think of averages as describing attachment patterns within a culture, as in most countries there are several sub-cultures. Differences between sub-cultures are lost when a country is treated as being equivalent to a culture.

| Table 3.4 | Van IJzendoorn and Kroonenberg (1988): infant behaviour in the Strange Situation, from studies in different cultures |

Country	Number of studies	Percentage of each attachment type (to the nearest whole number)		
		Secure	Avoidant	Resistant
West Germany	3	57	35	8
UK	1	75	22	3
Netherlands	4	67	26	7
Sweden	1	74	22	4
Israel	2	64	7	29
Japan	2	68	5	27
China	1	50	25	25
USA	18	65	21	14
Overall average		**65**	**20**	**15**

It is highly improbable that the wide variation shown in this study in the percentages of infants being classified as secure means that babies in cultures such as China are less likely to form a secure attachment with the mother. It seems much more likely that different patterns of mother–child relationships lead to different patterns of response in the Strange Situation. For example, Takahashi (1990) reports that infants in Japan are rarely left alone at this age, which could account for their distress in the Strange Situation: to them, it would be a situation unlike any they had ever experienced. This is supported by Nakagawa et al. (1989), who compared the initial reaction of Japanese and American infants to the Strange Situation. While American infants seemed to find the situation ambiguous, the Japanese infants were fearful, leading to the conclusion that lack of previous experience made the Strange Situation more stressful for Japanese infants. This could lead to a Type C classification for infants who in their normal environment were securely attached.

Similarly, Grossmann et al. (1985) claim that German parents encourage independence in infants. The pattern of response in German infants in the Strange Situation, leading to a Type A classification, might therefore be the result of cultural beliefs and practices, rather than indicating an insecure attachment.

This kind of explanation could also be applied to the findings of True's study in 1995, which used the Strange Situation technique in an African community for the first time (see Box 3.9).

| **Box 3.9** | **True (1995)** |

Aims: To carry out a cross-cultural investigation of the possible effect of differences in communication patterns in different cultures on classification in the Strange Situation.

Procedure: Twenty-six mothers and their 1-year-old infants from the Dogon ethnic group of Mali were filmed, once in the Strange Situation, and twice when the babies were being weighed. During the weigh-ins, the communication patterns of mothers and infants were assessed, including aspects such as direct and cooperative communication, typical of Western samples, and behaviours such as infant avoidance and maternal withdrawal.

Results: In the Strange Situation, 69% of infants were classified as securely attached (Type B), 0% as anxious-avoidant (Type A), 8% as insecure-resistant (Type C) and 23% as insecure-disorganised (Type D). There was a significant negative correlation between secure attachment and behaviours such as infant avoidance and maternal withdrawal, i.e. the mother–infant pairs that showed this communication pattern were less likely to be classified as securely attached.

Conclusions: There is a link between the kinds of culturally accepted communication patterns between mother and infant and classification in the Strange Situation. The behaviour of the infant in the Strange Situation needs to be seen in the context of cultural practices.

These studies show that we need to be aware there may be a **cultural bias** in using the Strange Situation to assess attachment, and be careful in the conclusions that we draw from this kind of research. There might well be common factors across cultures in the mother–child relationship that lead to a secure attachment. However, different cultures place different values on particular behaviours and characteristics, so there are likely to be wide cultural differences in the way that these patterns are expressed.

Summary

- Cultures vary in their beliefs and attitudes. One distinction is between **individualist** and **collectivist** cultures. **Cultural variation** is likely to influence patterns of child rearing.
- To avoid misclassifying children as insecurely attached, researchers using the **Strange Situation** technique need to view their findings in relation to the culture within which it is carried out.

Disruption of attachment and privation

On the basis of his attachment theory, Bowlby went on to develop the **maternal deprivation hypothesis**. He was asked by the World Health Organization to investigate the effects on children made homeless in the Second World War of being without their mothers. His report was later published as a book: *Child Care and the Growth of Love* (1953). In it he claimed:

What is believed to be essential for mental health is that an infant and young child should experience a warm, intimate and continuous relationship with his mother (or permanent mother-substitute — one person who steadily mothers him) in which both find satisfaction and enjoyment.

(Bowlby, 1953)

It is worth noting here that Bowlby does not claim the relationship needs to be formed with the biological mother, but in the following discussion, the term 'mother' will be used to refer to the major caregiver.

3

Young children can be wary of strangers (stranger anxiety) which, according to Bowlby, demonstrates that a bond has been formed with the mother

In his work with children, Bowlby had observed that at around the age of 9 months, children protest and show extreme distress if separated from the mother (**separation anxiety**) and cannot easily be comforted by someone else. They are also at this stage wary of strangers (**stranger anxiety**). Bowlby believed that this demonstrated that a bond had been formed with the mother, with the fear of strangers preventing another bond being formed. He used the term **monotropism** to describe the child's need to become attached to one particular person, and believed that this was crucial for the development of good mental health. If there was any separation from the mother in these early years, he believed there would be irreversible social, cognitive and emotional consequences. He suggested that long-term separation could lead to **affectionless psychopathy**, where children do not seem to care for anyone and are incapable of guilt or remorse, **anaclitic depression**, where children are apathetic and lose interest in what is going on around them, and even physical effects, such as **deprivation dwarfism**, where growth is stunted.

Bowlby's own research influenced and supported these ideas of the serious consequences of separation from the mother (see Box 3.10).

Box 3.10   **Bowlby (1944)**

Aims: To investigate the long-term effects of early separation from the mother.

Procedure: Bowlby compared 44 juvenile thieves who attended a child guidance unit with a control group of another 44 juveniles who had emotional problems but had not committed any criminal offence. He was interested in how many in each group had experienced separation from their mothers in their early years.

Results: Seventeen of the 'thieves' group but only two of the control group had been separated from their mothers for a period of at least a week in the first 5 years of their lives. In some of the children, he diagnosed affectionless psychopathy.

Conclusions: Early separation from the mother is likely to cause delinquency.

The results of this study do seem to suggest that a close and continuous relationship with the mother is necessary for good later development. However, there are also some problems with the study. Bowlby himself carried it out, so it could be that there was an element of **experimenter bias** in his analysis of the results. It is also a **correlational study**: it suggests that there is a link between separation from the mother and later problems, but it does not show a cause-and-effect relationship. It could be that there were other factors that influenced the outcome, for example, the *reasons* why the children were separated from their mothers. Moreover, it is a **retrospective study** (participants were asked about events that had taken place in the past), so the accuracy of the information given is open to question. Perhaps most importantly, the use as a control group of young people who had emotional problems seems odd, given that Bowlby proposed that the development of emotional problems would be the outcome of separation from the mother. A control group of individuals with no emotional problems would have provided a better comparison.

However, Bowlby's views were extremely influential. His ideas were readily accepted in the political climate of the day. During the Second World War, while the men were away fighting, women were needed in the workforce and were still at work when the war ended. Large numbers of servicemen were now returning to the UK and needed jobs, so Bowlby's recommendation that children should not be separated from their mothers in the early years was a powerful argument against women working, thereby freeing up jobs for the men. Bowlby's ideas were therefore widely publicised, both to provide jobs and to save the expense of providing care for children who could be looked after at home. Since these ideas meshed with public concerns, people were in general receptive to what Bowlby had to say.

There has been a good deal of research into the effects on children of being separated from the mother. One area of research addresses Bowlby's claim of monotropism: that infants form one attachment that is different in kind from other attachments, and that any substitute care in the early years, for however brief a period of time, damages children.

There is little support for the claim that **short-term separation** causes the damage that Bowlby suggests. For example, Stacy et al. (1970) carried out a study of 4-year-old children in Wales who went into hospital to have their tonsils removed. They stayed in hospital for four days, and at that time parents were not allowed to stay with them overnight. Most of the children coped well with this separation, and it emerged that many had previously experienced separation, having stayed overnight with grandparents or a friend. This supports the findings of Schaffer and Emerson (see page 58), who concluded that children are capable of forming more than one attachment and that other attachments mean they do not find temporary separation as distressing as Bowlby claimed. However, **longer-term separation** may indeed be — though not necessarily always — as serious for the child as Bowlby suggested.

Rutter (1972) queried the use of the term '*de*privation' in the maternal deprivation hypothesis. Deprivation implies the loss of maternal care, whereas a child may never have formed an attachment in the first place. Rutter suggested that this distinction could be made using the terms '**disruption**' and '**privation**'. Privation refers to circumstances in which no attachment has been formed. Disruption refers to circumstances where an attachment has been formed but is later broken, for example by the death of the caregiver, when a child is taken into care by the local authority, or when the parents separate or divorce. Bowlby stressed the relationship between a broken home and later delinquency, and he believed that the origin of later delinquency was to be found in inadequate maternal care. However, there are other problems associated with family break-up, and in particular the tension and discord in the home leading up to the break-up, which are likely to continue afterwards. Rutter therefore made a further distinction between the disruption brought about by bereavement and the **distortion** of relationships associated with divorce.

Going back to Bowlby's notion of delinquency being the result of deprivation, Rutter (1972) compared the effects of disruption and distortion. He found that the delinquency rates for boys who had lost a parent (disruption) were very similar to those for boys in intact families. However, the rate for boys whose parents had divorced (distortion) was significantly higher. There was also a high rate for boys living in intact but unhappy families (distortion), compared with those whose parents had divorced but where relationships remained good (disruption). He concluded that disruption was less of a problem than distortion.

The effects of divorce have also been examined (see Box 3.11).

Box 3.11 | Hetherington et al. (1979 and 1982)

Aims: To study the effects, over time, on children whose parents had divorced and who were living with the mother.

Procedure: This longitudinal study assessed the characteristics of children (aged around 4 at the start of the study) immediately after divorce, 2 years later and a further 2 years after that. Comparisons were made with a control group of children living in intact families.

Results: At the first assessment, the children of divorced parents were less mature in their play and tended to be negative, attention-seeking, dependent and aggressive, compared with controls. After 2 years, there was no difference between girls with divorced parents and those in intact families. Boys continued to have problems, though they had become less extreme. After 4 years, the differences between boys and girls persisted. Boys were more aggressive and lacking in social skills compared with controls.

Conclusions: Disruption and distortion brought about by divorce affect children, though the gender of the child also plays a role: girls seem to adjust better than boys.

There is mixed evidence, then, as to the effects on a child when a bond is disrupted, i.e. has been formed but is then broken. In general, it seems that more problems arise where relationships are distorted, which can occur in an intact but dysfunctional family, than in families where a bond has been broken.

Summary

- **Bowlby's maternal deprivation hypothesis** states that any separation from the mother has irreversible social, emotional and cognitive consequences. His ideas were extremely influential at the time.
- There is little evidence that **short-term separation** necessarily has a negative effect.
- Rutter distinguished between privation, disruption and distortion. There is evidence that **disruption** is less likely to have a negative effect on children's development than **privation** or **distortion**.
- Other factors such as **gender** influence the outcomes of disruption and distortion.

Institutionalisation

In research into the **effects of privation**, there have been a number of studies that focused on the ways children are affected by being brought up in an institution, where it may not be possible for them to make an attachment. There is some evidence that privation in this context can have the effects that Bowlby described. Johnson et al. (2006) reported a survey showing that a large number of children in institutional care are at risk of harm in terms of attachment disorder and delay in social, behavioural and cognitive development, along with delays in physical growth, neural atrophy and abnormal brain development. The survey suggests that children are at risk if they are not moved to family-based care by the age of 6 months.

An early study on the effects of **institutionalisation** reached the same conclusion, and it influenced the development of Bowlby's maternal deprivation hypothesis. Goldfarb's study (1943) was one that took advantage of naturally occurring events rather than manipulating variables (see Box 3.12).

Box 3.12	Goldfarb (1943)

Aims: To investigate the effects of institutionalisation in early childhood on children's cognitive, emotional and social development.

Procedure: Two groups of 15 children were compared, matched for mother's occupation and level of education. The children in the 'institution' group were raised in a children's home until they were three and a half, and then went to foster homes. The children in the 'fostered' group went straight to foster homers after birth. Comparisons were made at the age of 3 years, and again when the children were aged between 10 and 14 years of age.

Results: At 3 years old, in comparison with the 'fostered' group, the 'institution' children were behind in language development, had difficulty in forming relationships, craved affection and demonstrated a lack of guilt. At the later assessment, their average IQ was 72, compared with 95 for the fostered group. 'Institution' group children had difficulty concentrating and were unpopular with other children.

Conclusions: The lack of opportunity for the 'institution' group to form an attachment during the early years led to emotional problems and to social and intellectual retardation.

There are, however, some problems with accepting the conclusion that the difficulties experienced by children in the 'institution' group arose from the lack of an early attachment. At the time when this study was carried out, institutions were generally unstimulating, and this lack of stimulation could well have contributed to the poor development of the children who spent their early years there. In the institution that Goldfarb studied, babies under 9 months were kept in isolation from each other for fear of the spread of infection and had little contact with adults except for routine changing and feeding. There was a high turnover of carers, and for this reason carers were discouraged from forming bonds with the infants.

Moreover, although there was some attempt to match the children in the two groups so that individual differences did not affect the outcome, the matching was far from complete. For example, the infants in the two groups may well have differed in terms of general health or temperament. Temperamental characteristics and factors such as how alert or intelligent a child seemed may have been factors in whether they found foster homes immediately or spent their early years in the institution.

Later studies (such as that carried out by Hodges and Tizard, 1989), when institutions were far more stimulating places than the one in which Goldberg carried out his study, have also looked at the effects of institutionalisation on children's development, with somewhat different findings (see Box 3.13).

Box 3.13   Hodges and Tizard (1989)

Aims: To carry out a longitudinal study into the effects of institutionalisation.

Procedure: A comparison was made between 65 children who had entered an institution before the age of 4 months, and a control group brought up at home. By the age of 2 years, each of the children in the institutionalised group had been looked after by an average of 24 carers, which had risen to 50 by the age of four and a half. At the age of 4 years, 24 children had been adopted, 15 returned to their birth parents and the remainder stayed in the institution. Comparisons were made when the children were 4, 8 and 16 years old.

Results: At the age of 4 years, the institution children had not formed attachments. At 8 and 16 years of age, most of the adopted children had formed close attachments, as strong as those in the control group, with their adoptive parents. The children who had returned to their natural homes had formed poorer attachments than the adopted group. However, both the adopted children and those who had been restored to their natural homes had difficulties at school; they were attention-seeking and had problems forming relationships with other children. More than two-thirds of the children who had remained in the institution were described at four and a half years old as 'not to care deeply about anyone', and many were attention-seeking. At 8 years old, they had serious problems at school.

Conclusions: The attachments that the adopted children formed with their adoptive parents suggest that, contrary to Bowlby's claim, the effects of privation can be reversed to some extent. However, the problems that the adopted children experienced at school suggest that some of the effects of privation are indeed long lasting. The characteristics of the children who stayed in the institution and the problems experienced by the other two groups suggest that the lack of an early close relationship with one particular person could contribute to later social and emotional problems.

One of the strengths of this study is that it followed the children's progress over a number of years and thus could demonstrate the possible long-term effects of privation. However, longitudinal studies suffer from drop-out, where some participants no longer wish to be part of the study, and those who remain could be a biased sample. Adopted children who continued to participate in the study had been those who had shown better adjustment at the age of 4 years, while those who had returned to their natural homes had shown poorer adjustment at 4 years of age, which may have distorted the differences between the groups. This would have biased the samples, so it is difficult to generalise from the results.

There are also further factors to take into consideration, for example the reasons why the children who went back to their natural homes had entered the institution in the first place: it is likely that there were problems in their families at that time.

It may be that these problems continued when they returned home, so they were offered little support and affection, which could have contributed to their poor outcomes. In contrast, those children who were adopted are likely to have gone to homes where they were much wanted and offered a lot of love and affection. This could also help to explain why the adopted children who had few problems at home nonetheless continued to have some outside the home, away from the support that their adoptive parents offered.

A more recent longitudinal study, by Rutter et al. (2001), is still ongoing, and has also explored the effects on children of institutional care (see Box 3.14).

Box 3.14 **Rutter et al. (2001)**

Aims: To investigate the patterns of behaviour of children suffering privation as a result of being reared in institutions, and to identify those areas most affected.

Procedure: A group of 165 children adopted from Romania into UK families before the age of three and a half years was compared at the ages of 4 years and 6 years with 52 UK children adopted by the age of 6 months. Level of functioning was assessed in both groups in seven areas (see box below).

Results: Attachment problems, inattention/overactivity, quasi-autistic features and cognitive impairment were much more common in the Romanian children than in the UK controls, but emotional difficulties, poor peer relationships and conduct problems were not. Some children in both groups showed dysfunction in only one area, but more often there were problems in several areas. Dysfunction tended to be more extreme in those children who had left Romania when they were older. Nevertheless, more than one-fifth of children who were older than 2 years when they were adopted, and had therefore spent the longest time in institutions, showed normal functioning.

Conclusions: Some aspects of functioning are impaired in children who have experienced privation in institutions, while other areas are relatively unaffected. There is considerable individual variation in the effects of being reared in an institution. It is still possible for children who have experienced profound institutional privation from infancy to the age of 3 years to have normal psychological functioning, provided that the child has experienced several years in a good adoptive family.

The areas of functioning assessed in the study by Rutter et al. (2001)

1 **Attachment difficulties**: the child makes no distinction between adults, will readily go off with a stranger and does not check back with the parent when anxious. Assessed by interviews with the parents.

2 **Inattention/overactivity**: the child is restless, has a short attention span, is easily distracted, is attention seeking. Assessed by questionnaires completed by parents and teachers.

3 **Emotional difficulties**: the child is often fearful and miserable, and complains of aches and pains. Assessed by questionnaires completed by parents and teachers.

4 Quasi-autistic features: the child is assessed by a test for signs of autism, such as obsessive behaviour and responding inappropriately during interaction with others.

5 Cognitive impairment: the child's general cognitive ability is assessed using an IQ test.

6 Peer difficulties: the child does not get on with other children and is not liked by them, teases or is teased by others, and bullies or is bullied by others. Assessed by questionnaires completed by parents and teachers.

7 Conduct problems: the child often gets into fights, is disobedient, tells lies and is quarrelsome. Assessed by questionnaires completed by parents and teachers.

The research of Rutter et al. suggests that the effects of privation are not as global as Bowlby had suggested. However, this study only followed the children up to the age of 6 years, so it is possible that problems could emerge later. Rutter planned to carry out further assessments when the children were 11 years old, and in adolescence. As he points out, one limitation of the research is that the children could not be studied while they were still in the Romanian institution, so it is not possible to identify which aspects of the privation they experienced had the most influence, and this should be an area for future research.

Extreme privation

As well as studies into the effects of institutionalisation on children, there have been studies of individual cases of extreme privation. Koluchova (1976) carried out a case study in Czechoslovakia of identical twins. They were kept locked in isolation in a cellar for the first 7 years of their lives and had been mistreated and often beaten. They communicated mainly in gestures, having very little speech. After they were discovered, they were fostered by two sisters who gave them a loving home. By the age of 14 years, they had recovered to the extent that they were basically normal, and at the age of 20 years had above-average intelligence and good relationships with others.

In contrast is a case study by Curtiss (1977), with a much less happy outcome (see Box 3.15).

Box 3.15 | Curtiss (1977)

Genie spent the first years of her life alone. She was tied to a potty chair and fed baby food. She had lived her life in silence, not being spoken to and punished if she made any sound. When she was found at the age of thirteen and a half, she was severely undernourished, could not stand properly, did not understand language and could not speak.

She was given intensive help in developing skills, and in some areas she improved very quickly. However, her language did not develop properly, and she never got beyond communicating using telegraphic speech, for example, 'Go store applesauce' for 'We need to go to the store to buy some applesauce'.

She developed attachments to her foster carers, but as she grew older she was moved to a succession of short-term foster homes, in some of which she was mistreated. Her mother regained custody of her and refused to allow anyone access to her. It is not known what happened to her in later life.

The differences in these cases are marked, with the Czech twins apparently making a full recovery and Genie showing limited development, particularly in language skills. One possible reason is the age at which the children were found. As Genie was so much older, it is possible that she had passed the age when language can be learned, while the twins were still young enough for this to be possible. The Czech twins were together, so although their language was extremely limited, they could communicate with each other using gestures, while Genie had no one with whom to communicate. The Czech twins went to a loving home, whereas Genie was soon moved from the foster carer to whom she had become attached and went to homes that did not offer the love and support that the twins received.

However, it is possible of course that Genie was not normal at birth and that her lack of development was not entirely the result of the privation she experienced. A major drawback with case studies such as these is that personal characteristics of the individuals being studied may have a major effect on their development, so it is unwise to draw broad general conclusions from them.

Summary

- Research into the effects of **institutionalisation** is one method of investigating **privation**.
- Early studies supported the claim that lack of an attachment figure would have extreme negative effects, but the children were also in an **unstimulating environment**, so the role of lack of attachment cannot be established.
- In contradiction to Bowlby's claim, later studies suggest that some effects of privation can be **reversed** and that some areas of psychological functioning are more likely to be affected than others.
- Case studies of **extreme privation** have produced mixed findings and do not allow **generalisations** to be made.

The effects of day care on children's social development

Bowlby believed that any separation from the mother would have a negative effect on a child's development and in particular would weaken the attachment bond with the mother. In his 1951 report to the World Health Organization, he claimed that the use of day care would lead to 'permanent damage to the emotional health of a future generation' (WHO, 1951, quoted in Tizard, 1991).

Bowlby's beliefs continued to be influential, with Penelope Leach, a popularly accepted authority for new mothers, writing in 1979: 'My ideal society has no day nurseries…Babies and very small children each need a "special" and continuous person or people and they need to have their daily lives based on somewhere they know as "home".'

There has been considerable research into the effects of day care, particularly in whether day care is necessarily damaging to young children, whether it has little —

if any — effect, or whether it might also carry some benefits. Research has tried to establish what factors influence the outcome for children who are cared for in this way. This is an important issue, as more mothers now want or need to work. For example, in 1994, the US Bureau of the Census found that 60% of mothers with a child under the age of 2 years were employed and their children were therefore experiencing day care.

There are different kinds of day care, with some children looked after by family members, some by childminders, and some in day nurseries. We will focus here on childminding and day nurseries.

Childminding

Mayall and Petrie (1983) found that the effects on the child being cared for by a childminder appear to depend heavily on the **quality of care** that he or she receives, with some caregivers providing excellent care, but others offering a somewhat unstimulating environment, with a negative effect on the child's development. Mayall and Petrie argue that childminding is unreliable, as there is no guarantee that the childminder will have acceptable experience and premises, and no guarantee of continuity of care. They point out that childminding is poorly paid, which influences who is likely to become a childminder, and that attempts to raise standards by imposing more stringent conditions on registered childminders would be counterproductive and likely to lead to an increase in the use of unregistered childminders.

Some child-minders provide excellent care

Bryant et al. (1980) take a similar view, suggesting that some child minders do not wish to form emotional bonds with the children that they care for, and do not provide them with a stimulating environment. Instead, they reward them for being quiet, leading to children becoming passive and apathetic.

Melhuish et al. (1990) compared the experiences of 18-month-olds interacting with others in different kinds of day-care settings: at home, cared for by a relative, cared for by a childminder, and in a nursery. Although there was a lot of variation within each kind of setting, overall, children cared for at home, by a relative or by a childminder, had more stimulating interactional experiences with their carer than children in a nursery.

Shinman (1981) also takes a positive view. In her research, she found that most childminders cared for the children that they minded as competently as they cared for their own children. Problems were only likely to arise when children had particular problems that were outside the minder's experience, an issue that could be addressed by making more support available to carers.

Day nurseries

Most studies have concluded that day care need not have adverse consequences for young children, and in particular does not threaten the attachment bond with the mother. However, a study by Belsky (1988) challenged this view (see Box 3.16 and Table 3.5).

Box 3.16 | **Belsky (1988)**

Aims: To assess the quality of attachment in children who spent time in day care, and the effect on attachment of the amount of time spent in day care.

Procedure: The quality of attachment of children who spent time in day care was compared with that of children staying at home with their mothers, using the Strange Situation technique. The quality of attachment was also analysed in terms of the age at which children started day care and the length of time they spent there each week. There were 464 children in the sample.

Results: Children were more likely to have an insecure attachment to the mother if they had started day care before their first birthday, or if they spent more than 20 hours a week there. A large number of children in day care had a secure attachment, but children in day care were more likely to have an insecure attachment than those who were not.

Conclusions: Day care can lead to insecure attachment, particularly if it starts when the child is very young or a lot of time is spent there.

Table 3.5 *Security of attachment and extent of non-maternal care (Belsky, 1988)*

	Extent of non-maternal care	
	More than 20 hours/week	**Less than 20 hours/week**
Secure attachment	59%	74%
Insecure attachment	41%	26%

At first glance these findings are worrying, because they imply that children in day care are likely to form insecure attachments, which may put their future development at risk. However, as was noted earlier, the Strange Situation technique does not take the child's previous experience into account. It could be argued that children in day care have learned that separation is only temporary and that the mother will return. They are therefore not overly distressed when the mother leaves, nor particularly demonstrative when she returns, and could therefore be classified as Type A (insecure: anxious-avoidant), even though they are in fact securely attached.

In addition, Belsky's study does not take into account factors other than being in day care that could lead to children showing insecure attachment. For example, there could be differences between mothers who use day care and those who do not.

Other studies demonstrate that day care can in some respects be beneficial for a child. For example, McCartney et al. (1985) carried out a study in Bermuda, where 85% of children enter day care before they are 2 years old. They found that good-quality day care, where the environment was stimulating, predicted good cognitive, language and social skills in the pre-school years, with the children showing none of the cognitive and social damage that Bowlby predicted would be the result of separation from the mother (and therefore of a weakening of the attachment bond).

More recently, research has moved away from considering whether day care may be harmful because of preventing or disrupting the formation of a strong attachment, and has focused instead on its possible effect on **aggression**. As children in day care experience group care, it has been suggested that these children may be more aggressive than those cared for at home, because there is more opportunity for physical aggression. On the other hand, they could be less aggressive, as in day care they have the opportunity of learning to resolve disputes with others without resorting to fighting. There is particular interest in this area, because aggressive behaviour reaches a peak in the pre-school years and because research has shown that early aggression is a major risk factor for later antisocial behaviour (Tremblay, 2000).

Findings in this area have been inconsistent. For example, Honig and Park (1993) found that there was a link between higher levels of aggression and children having spent longer in day care, while Schindler et al. (1987) found that time spent in day care was positively correlated with social play, suggesting lower levels of aggression. Hegland and Rix (1990) found no significant difference in observer ratings of aggression when comparing children who had been attending day care with children who had been cared for at home.

A large-scale study carried out by Borge et al. (2004) in Canada has taken a rather more detailed approach to investigating a possible link between day care and aggression, looking also at the potential influence of **family background** (see Box 3.17).

Borge et al. suggest that day care may help to protect children in high-risk families because it dilutes the child's exposure to family risks. This has been supported by Papero (2005), who suggested that high-quality day care may be an appropriate intervention for children with mothers suffering from depression. Day care may also provide positive opportunities, not readily available in the home, to learn ways of managing disputes.

However, it is also possible that there are factors that have not been taken into account in this study and might therefore limit the conclusions to be drawn. For example, it is possible that some children were looked after at home by their mothers rather than sent to day care *because* they had shown early signs of disruptive behaviour, so the higher levels of aggression could be related to the characteristics of the child rather than the type of care that they experienced. Nonetheless, with such a large sample, this seems unlikely to have had an effect.

The influence of factors such as **child temperament** and **gender** on a possible link between the kind of care experienced and the development of social skills has also been investigated, for example by DiLalla (1998) (see Box 3.18).

DiLalla points out that aggressive behaviour should not necessarily be seen negatively. It may well be adaptive, leading to the more socially positive characteristic of assertiveness when the child gets older. In support of this, she reports findings that children classed as aggressive in pre-school interactions with peers were later rated by teachers as more likeable and as having fewer behaviour problems.

Box 3.17 **Borge et al. (2004)**

Aims: To compare rates of physical aggression shown by children in day care and those looked after at home by their mothers, and to look at the possible effects on aggressive behaviour of factors relating to family background.

Procedure: The mothers of 3431 Canadian 2–3-year-olds completed a questionnaire. Three questions were included, which asked how often, from a choice of 'never', 'sometimes' or 'often', their child:
- kicks, bites and hits other children
- reacts with anger and fighting when another child accidentally hurts him or her
- gets into many fights

A measure of family risk factors was also developed. High-risk factors included low socio-economic status, mother's low educational standard, a greater number of siblings and poor family functioning. This aimed to assess whether social factors led to an increased risk for physical aggression.

Results: Aggression was significantly more common in children looked after by their own mothers than in those attending day care. Physical aggression was significantly more common in children from high-risk families looked after by their own parents than those in day care. There was no difference in levels of aggression between children in low-risk families (84%) in day care and those looked after at home.

Conclusion: Day care does not lead to aggression in children and may even be a protective factor for those in high-risk homes.

Box 3.18 **DiLalla (1998)**

Aims: To investigate the relationship between day-care experience, temperament and social behaviour.

Procedure: In a laboratory playroom, 62 pairs of same-sex 5-year-olds who had not met before played together for 20 minutes. They were rated for pro-social behaviour (talking politely, inviting the other child to play, smiling at the other child in acknowledgement or praise and helping) and aggression (teasing, hitting, grabbing, yelling and throwing toys). Parents completed questionnaires on day-care experience, temperament and behaviour problems.

Results: Children who experienced little or no day care were more likely to behave pro-socially, and those with a difficult temperament showed less pro-social behaviour. However, day care and temperament did not overall seem to be important factors in aggressive behaviour, though boys who had experienced day care when they were toddlers tended to be more aggressive than those who had experienced day care from infancy or not at all. Gender was a significant predictor of both aggressive and pro-social behaviours, with boys being both more aggressive and more pro-social.

Conclusions: Day care may have a negative effect on the development of pro-social behaviour, but does not affect aggressive behaviour. Other factors, such as gender and temperament, need to be taken into account when assessing the effects of day care on social development.

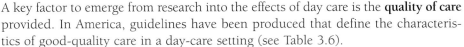

A key factor to emerge from research into the effects of day care is the **quality of care** provided. In America, guidelines have been produced that define the characteristics of good-quality care in a day-care setting (see Table 3.6).

Table 3.6 *Appropriate infant and toddler day care (National Association for the Education of Young Children, 1991)*

Characteristic	Signs of quality
Physical setting	Clean, well-lit, well-ventilated and uncrowded environment; fenced outdoor play space available
Child-to-carer ratio	Ratio of no more than 3:1 for infants and 6:1 for toddlers; consistent staffing so that relationships with particular carers can be formed
Daily activities	Schedule includes active play, quiet play, naps and meals; flexibility to meet children's individual needs
Adult–child interaction	Prompt carer response to distress; carers hold, talk to and read to children, and are responsive to the needs of the individual child
Carer qualifications	Training in child development, first aid and safety
Relationships with parents	Parents are welcome at any time; carers discuss children's behaviour and development with them
Toys and equipment	Appropriate play materials, both for indoor and outdoor play, are available and within reach of the children

The importance of some of these factors, in particular the **quality of care**, has been supported by research. The quality of care in 64 Dutch childcare centres was assessed by De Schipper et al. (2007) through extensive observation of 237 carers during interaction with the children, aged from birth to 4 years of age, in their care. They found that lower-quality care was given by carers who were younger and with higher workloads. However, they found that the differences in quality of care were more to do with differences between the care centres than between individual carers.

The importance of quality of care can be demonstrated by comparing studies of the effects of good-quality and poor-quality day care. In Sweden, Andersson (1992) carried out a longitudinal study, assessing children's cognitive and social skills when they were coming up to their fourth birthday, and again when they were 8 and 13 years old. School performance was highest for those who had entered day school earlier, before their first birthday, and was lowest for those who did not have any day care, suggesting that day care can have a beneficial effect on children's development. However, Andersson stresses that childcare in Sweden is of very high quality, with a low child : staff ratio, highly trained carers and good financial support from the government. Moreover, Sweden has a system whereby one or both parents spend most of the first year with the child, so Swedish infants have the opportunity to form strong attachments during this time.

In contrast, Howes (1990) assessed children entering poor-quality day care before their first birthday and who remained there until they started school. When they went to school, teachers rated these children as being easily distracted and less considerate of others than children who had not experienced day care. This suggests that poor-quality day care may lead to a lack of the skills necessary for good cognitive and social development.

Summary

- **Bowlby** suggested that any kind of day care could damage a child's development.
- Research into the effects of **childminding** has produced conflicting results.
- Earlier research focused on the possible disruption of **attachment** as the result of day care, but there is little evidence that day care has this effect.
- Later research has focused on **social development**. There are conflicting findings in this area too.
- Day care may be particularly beneficial for children from **high-risk families**, or where the mother suffers from **depression**.
- Research into the effects of day care on social development needs to take into account factors such as **temperament** and **gender**.
- The **quality** of day care is a central issue in determining its effects.

The implications of research for childcare practices

Bowlby's theory of attachment and maternal deprivation hypothesis have been influential in shaping childcare practices. For example, his belief that separation from the mother would damage a child has led to reform in hospital practice. Indeed, when Bowlby was first developing his ideas, a mother was not allowed to stay with a child who had to go to hospital. Robertson and Bowlby (1952) made a study of children's response to this separation. Typically a child would go through three stages:

The protest-despair detachment (PDD) model

Protest: the child cries a lot of the time and seems panic-stricken.

Despair: the child seems to lose hope, and is apathetic and lethargic.

Detachment: the child is less distressed, but shows little interest when the mother returns.

The detachment stage was thought to show that the child had adapted well to hospital, and for this reason mothers were discouraged from visiting as it was believed that this would only upset the child unnecessarily. However, as Robertson and Bowlby found, the lack of interest in the mother on her return suggested that this apparent adaptation masked very different feelings. Thankfully, it is now standard practice for mothers to stay with their children in hospital, or close by, so that they can spend time together.

Stevie Grand/SPL

Nowadays, it is usual for a mother to stay with her child in hospital

However, some of Bowlby's claims have been challenged. The idea that children form a special kind of bond with the main caregiver — monotropism — and that substitute care is not acceptable, seems to be an overstatement. Children do seem to have a special attachment for one person, but adapt well to different caregivers, provided that they are familiar to them and there are not too many of them. For example, there is little evidence for the claim that day care weakens the emotional bond with the mother.

Bowlby's proposal that the lack of a secure attachment would have long-lasting and irreversible effects on children's cognitive, social and emotional development has also been challenged. Later research has shown that in most cases, even when deprivation in the early years is severe, it is possible to reverse the effects, at least in part.

Similarly, although the research findings are far from clear, the claim that day care necessarily inhibits development seems to be an exaggeration. There is evidence that it may be beneficial to cognitive and social development, particularly where there are family problems and when it is of good quality.

Terms explained

control group: in an experiment, a group of participants whose data provide a baseline with which the effect of the manipulation of the independent variable (IV) on the data of the experimental group(s) can be compared. The control group should be similar in every way to the experimental group(s), apart from receiving the IV.

cross-cultural studies: research into behaviour, beliefs and so on in different cultures. One aim is to compare the results from different cultures to establish whether there are cultural universals, which would suggest that a characteristic is innate. These studies also investigate the effects of cultural influences.

ethology: the study of animals in the wild. Ethologists are interested in describing patterns of animals behaviour, observing changes in behaviour across the lifespan, and explaining the functions of behaviour. They are interested in animal behaviour for its own sake, and so differ from comparative

psychologists, who investigate animal behaviour to establish whether general laws can be established which may also apply to human behaviour.

longitudinal study: a study in which the same group of people is studied over a period of time, often years, with data being collected at intervals to assess change and development, for example an association between early attachment pattern and the nature of later relationships. However, because of the time involved, this method is expensive, and some participants are likely to drop out. This leaves a smaller sample, which may also be biased if a particular kind of participant is more likely to drop out.

temperament: consistencies in the ways in which children respond to their world, for example how active or emotional they are, which are relatively stable across time and different situations. Temperamental differences are assumed to be strongly genetic, and link to adult personality.

Chapter 4

Research methods

In this chapter, we will be looking at:
- methods and techniques in psychology
- the design of research studies
- ethical issues
- data analysis and presentation

Methods and techniques in psychology

You will remember from Chapter 1 that one of the ways in which psychology differs from common sense is that it aims to explore ideas in a systematic way, rather than rely on casual observation. The latter can provide ideas, but in psychology ideas are followed up using organised methods; the simple observation turning into research.

Research aims to provide data that can support or challenge ideas. If specfic ideas are supported by the research findings, these may then suggest ways in which the ideas could be followed up to provide more detailed information. If they are not supported, researchers can pursue alternative ideas, which might better explain the phenomenon in which they are interested.

Not all areas of psychology give priority to research. For example, humanistic psychologists focus on the experience of the individual and how this can contribute to bringing about positive changes in their lives. Although Rogers did carry out some research into clients' experiences of person-centred therapy, research is much less a priority for humanistic psychologists than for cognitive psychologists or behaviourists. However, most areas of psychology are research-based, using a wide range of methods. A broadly experimental approach has traditionally been the main method of research, but there are a number of alternative approaches. Which method is used will depend on what is being investigated, the kinds of questions being asked and the orientation of the researcher.

The experimental method

Variables

For a piece of research to be an experiment, two criteria need to be met:

- An independent variable must be manipulated between conditions.
- There must be an element of random allocation of participants to conditions.

However, some methods that are broadly experimental do not necessarily meet these conditions fully. We will look more closely at what the two criteria mean and what is involved in an experiment, in relation to the basic Bobo doll study carried out by Bandura (1963), which was discussed in Chapter 1 (page 16) in the section on social learning theory. We will then look at different kinds of broadly experimental methods.

A variable is anything that can vary. In an experiment, the **independent variable (IV)** is what is different between conditions. Creating this difference is what is meant by 'manipulating the independent variable'. In Bandura's study, the independent variable was whether or not the children had observed the adult attacking the Bobo doll.

The **dependent variable (DV)** is the outcome of the study, i.e. what is being measured. In the Bobo doll study, it was the number of aggressive behaviours produced by each group — those who had observed the adult and those who had not — which were similar to those demonstrated by the adult model.

In an experiment, the aim is to show cause-and-effect relationships between the IV and the DV, i.e. to demonstrate that manipulating (or varying) the IV has caused a change in the DV. All differences between the groups other than the IV — the variable in which the researcher is interested — should therefore be eliminated as far as possible. If there are any other differences between the groups, then they, rather than the IV, could account for any differences in the outcome, i.e. in the DV, between the groups being compared, and so would be **confounding variables**.

Confounding variables can take two forms: subject variables, i.e. differences between the participants in the groups to be compared, or situation variables. For example, if the children in one of the groups in the Bobo doll study were aged 4–5 years, and those in the other group were aged 9–10 years, this would be a **subject variable**. Any difference in the DV between the groups could have been the result of the children's ages, rather than whether or not they had observed an adult attacking the doll. If the children in one group were all girls, and those in the other all boys, any differences could be explained by gender, rather than the observation of the adult model.

Similarly, if all the children in one group were greeted by a friendly lady and made to feel welcome, while those in the other group were treated brusquely, this would be a **situation variable**, as this difference could have affected the children's behaviour and therefore the results of the study. The same reasoning would apply if one group was tested early in the morning and the other at 6 p.m.: differences in behaviour could be the result of the time of testing.

In an experiment, participants are **randomly allocated** to conditions (groups). There should be no kind of system for putting a particular participant in a condition; rather, every participant should have an equal chance of being allocated to each condition. If large samples are to be tested, potential participants could each be given a number, and a computer programme that generates random numbers could decide the condition into which each participant is to be placed. This would ensure that there was no bias in the allocation, for example participants being allocated in a way that was likely to support the hypothesis being tested.

Sometimes random allocation is not possible. For example, if Bandura had been interested in whether boys or girls were more likely to imitate the adult's behaviour towards the Bobo doll, participants could not have been randomly allocated to the 'boy' condition or the 'girl' condition. In the same way, if he had been interested in whether older or younger children were more affected, they could not be allocated randomly to the 'older' or 'younger' condition. Studies of this kind are **quasi-experiments**, i.e. they are broadly experimental but they do not quite meet the criteria for a true experiment.

Laboratory and field experiments

Laboratory experiments are carried out in controlled conditions, which makes it easier for the experimenter to eliminate possible confounding variables and to isolate the IV. If this is done successfully, the experimenter can claim that the manipulation of the IV is responsible for differences in the DV, i.e. a cause-and-effect relationship between the two has been established. The control that the experimenter has in a laboratory experiment also makes **replication** possible: other researchers can carry out the study in exactly the same way to see if they get the same or similar results. A laboratory experiment also makes it possible to use complex technical equipment, for example exposing a participant to a visual stimulus for a precisely measured fraction of a second.

The major drawback to laboratory experiments is that they may often have low **ecological validity**, i.e. the procedures followed and the situation in which the study takes place may not relate closely to real-life experience. For example, many memory experiments require participants to learn and recall lists of words, yet there are very few occasions in our everyday lives when we would need to do this. Ebbinghaus's use of nonsense syllables is an even more extreme example.

A related problem is that of **demand characteristics**. In a laboratory experiment, people are usually aware that they are taking part in a study, and so may try to guess what is being tested and what the expected outcome is. They may pick up on cues from what the researcher says or does, or the layout of the laboratory, or any materials with which they are presented. Whether their guesses are correct or not, they may alter a participant's behaviour, either to try to respond in the way they think the experimenter expects, or deliberately to go against what they see as the aims of the study, which Masling (1966) has referred to as the **'screw you' effect**. In either case, if participants are responding to demand characteristics, the ecological validity of the experiment is compromised.

An experiment carried out by Berkowitz and LePage (1967), which tested Berkowitz's **aggressive cue theory**, is a good example of the possible effects of demand characteristics. They were interested in whether people were more likely to behave in an aggressive way in the presence of items associated with aggression, in this case guns. A confederate of the experimenters gave participants a series of seven mild electric shocks, supposedly as a way of assessing the effects of stress (induced by the shocks) on problem-solving behaviour, but in reality to make them angry. Participants were then asked to evaluate the confederate's performance on a problem-solving task by way of giving him, in turn, small electric shocks. Participants gave more shocks, and were therefore considered to be more aggressive, when there was a shotgun and a revolver in the room than when there were no weapons present.

This study was criticised on the grounds that the participants might have found the presence of weapons in a laboratory distinctly odd and guessed that they were intended to increase aggression. The experimenters did provide a cover story — that the weapons were needed for an experiment later on — but this was somewhat unconvincing. In a later replication of the study by Page and Scheidt (1971), participants were interviewed after the experiment. Eighty-one per cent claimed to have guessed that the study was about revenge, and many of these had guessed that the weapons were there to increase the aggression that they might show in the shocks given to the confederate. The conclusions of the Berkowitz and LePage study could therefore have been the result of the participants guessing (correctly, in this instance) what the aim of the study was, and cooperating with the experimenters, thus distorting the findings.

A related consideration is **evaluation apprehension**, where participants are concerned that they will be judged by the experimenter and so act in a way they believe will put them across in a good light. This can lead to **social desirability effects**, where behaviour is changed to achieve a good impression, thereby lowering the ecological validity of the study.

A further problem with experiments is **experimenter effects**, where the characteristics or behaviour of the experimenter might affect the behaviour of the participants. These characteristics include the age, sex, race or physical attractiveness of the experimenter, or the treatment of participants in an overly friendly, brusque or patronising way.

Experimenter bias can also cause problems. Experimenters have a clear idea of what they expect or hope will be the results of their study, so there may be a bias, however unintentional, when they are recording the data. One way of overcoming this

is to use a **double-blind technique**. In most experiments, participants do not know what the aims of the study are or what the results are expected to be (though, of course, demand characteristics may make this less true). Withholding this information from participants is known as a **single-blind technique**. For a double-blind technique, someone other than the experimenter collects the data, so that neither the participants nor the person running the study is aware of the expected outcomes.

It is worth noting that not all studies carried out in laboratory conditions are experiments. For example, the Strange Situation technique, used to classify infants' attachment types and described in Chapter 3, is carried out in laboratory conditions. However, there is neither manipulation of an independent variable, nor random allocation of participants to conditions. Rather, this is an **observational study** looking at naturally occurring behaviour.

Not all experiments are carried out in laboratory conditions. **Field experiments** are studies that meet the criteria for an experiment but they take place in natural conditions. For example, an experiment by Piliavin et al. (1975) explored the effect of appearance on willingness to help. They found that people were less likely to offer help to someone who had apparently collapsed in the subway if he had an ugly facial birthmark than if he had no birthmark. Here the IV, manipulated by the experimenters, is the presence or absence of a birthmark, and the passers-by were not systematically assigned to one or other of the conditions. Another example is the study of nurses' obedience to orders given by a doctor, carried out by Hofling et al. (1966), which you will read about in the section on obedience in Chapter 6.

The main advantage of field experiments over laboratory experiments is that they have high ecological validity, because they are looking at naturally occurring behaviour in a real-life situation, and so reduce the possibility of demand characteristics affecting the outcome; in most cases, people are not aware that they are participants in a psychology experiment. However, **control** is more of a problem. Experimenters can make sure as far as possible that they have controlled for confounding variables, but there are likely to be circumstances beyond their control — such as changes in the weather, or the number of people around when the experiment is taking place — which could affect the results.

Since field experiments have high ecological validity, the conclusions drawn from the results may be more easily **generalised** than those drawn from the results of laboratory experiments, that is, they may be assumed to apply to similar situations. However, it may also be more difficult to apply the conclusions to situations that differ in some respect from the situation in which the study was carried out. For example, it may not be possible to use findings about the nature of children's play derived from a study of a particular playgroup and generalise them to other playgroups with different playgroup leaders, numbers of children in the group, facilities and so on.

Field experiments also have **ethical problems**: participants will not have given their consent to their behaviour being observed if they are unaware that they are taking part in a psychological study. These problems will be examined later in this chapter.

This kind of experiment can also take longer to carry out than a laboratory experiment because the researchers may have to wait for behaviour to occur. Also, they do not allow complex technical equipment to be used.

Table 4.1 shows a comparison between laboratory and field experiments, using a selection of criteria such as control and ecological validity.

Table 4.1	Laboratory and field experiments compared	
Criteria	**Laboratory experiments**	**Field experiments**
Control	High	Lower
Ecological validity	Sometimes low	High
Replication	Easy	Difficult
Demand characteristics	Quite likely	Rare
Generalisability	Sometimes low	Variable
Ethical problems	Variable	Variable

Natural experiments

A final kind of experiment is the **natural experiment**. Strictly speaking, this is not an experiment at all because it does not meet the necessary criteria, i.e. the manipulation of the IV by the experimenter and an element of random allocation. Natural experiments take advantage of naturally occurring events, over which the researcher has little, if any, control. For example, Charlton et al. (2000) took advantage of the introduction of television into the remote island of St Helena. In a longitudinal study, they compared children's behaviour before and after television programmes started to be broadcast, to investigate whether exposure to television affected their levels of pro- and antisocial behaviour. The IV here was 'before' vs 'after' the introduction of television, not controlled by the researchers. As a matter of interest, the researchers found no rise in levels of aggressive behaviour after television was introduced.

Summary

- In an experiment, the researcher manipulates the **independent variable (IV)**, and there is an element of **random allocation**.
- The researcher assesses the effect of the IV on the **dependent variable (DV)**, controlling for **confounding variables**, to establish a **cause-and-effect relationship** between the two.
- **Quasi-experiments** do not fully meet the criteria for a study to be called an experiment.
- **Laboratory experiments** take place in controlled conditions, while **field experiments** take place in the natural environment. Both kinds have advantages and drawbacks.
- **Natural experiments** are not true experiments. They take advantage of naturally occurring events.

Correlational analysis

Correlational analysis is a widely used statistical technique for measuring the relationship between two variables. For example, Kanner et al. (1981) carried out a study to investigate the relationship between the experience of daily hassles

(relatively minor everyday events that have a negative effect, such as losing things) and uplifts (everyday events that have a positive effect, such as feeling healthy), and the psychological symptoms of stress (this study is discussed in more detail in Chapter 5).

A **positive correlation** occurs when, as the values of one variable increase, the values of the other variable also tend to do so. For example, the Kanner et al. study found a positive correlation between the number of hassles experienced and measures of stress symptoms: people who experienced more hassles tended also to experience higher levels of stress. A **negative correlation** occurs when, as the values of one variable increase, the values of the other variable tend to decrease. The Kanner et al. study found a negative correlation between the number of uplifts experienced and measures of stress symptoms: people who experienced more uplifts tended to experience lower levels of stress.

Statistical tests measuring correlation produce a **correlation coefficient** of between +1 for a perfect positive correlation and −1 for a perfect negative correlation. A coefficient of 0 indicates no relationship between the variables being measured. In practice, positive correlations rarely have a coefficient of +1 but fall somewhere between 0 and +1. A coefficient of +0.7 would indicate a fairly strong positive relationship between the variables being measured. For example, this might express the strength of the relationship between height and shoe size, as taller people on the whole have larger feet, but some tall people have smallish feet and some short people have quite large feet. Similarly, for negative correlations, a coefficient of −1 is seldom found in practice. There is likely to be a negative correlation between the amount of alcohol drunk and scores on a test requiring hand–eye coordination, with people who have consumed less alcohol tending to perform better, but the coefficient would be reduced by people who do well on the test despite alcohol consumption, and by people whose coordination is poor even when entirely sober. A coefficient in the region of −0.5 might therefore be expected.

Correlational analysis has the advantage of being able to indicate the **direction**, i.e. positive or negative, of the relationship between two variables, and the **strength** of this relationship, expressed in the size of the correlation coefficient. The method is often useful at the start of a research project to establish if there is a phenomenon worth investigating, which could then be explored more rigorously using an experimental method. As we will see later, it is also used to establish the **reliability** and **validity** of tests.

The main drawback of correlational analysis is that — unlike the experimental method — it cannot establish cause-and-effect relationships. For example, there is likely to be a strong positive correlation between the number of puddles observed on a particular day and the number of people seen carrying umbrellas. However, a variation in the number of puddles does not cause variation in the number of umbrellas, nor does the variation in the number of umbrellas cause variation in the number of puddles. The increase in both comes about through the influence of a third variable: rain.

The other limitation of correlational analysis is that it cannot show **non-linear relationships**. For example, the relationship between arousal and performance is initially a positive one: people are likely to carry out a task better when they are awake and alert rather than when they are half asleep. However, when arousal becomes too great, so that it can be described as stress, performance drops off (this is discussed in more detail in Chapter 5). This kind of relationship is called a **curvilinear relationship**. If a correlation coefficient were to be calculated for the relationship between arousal and stress, it would be likely to be close to 0, with the positive relationship shown during lower levels of arousal being cancelled out by the negative relationship when arousal becomes extreme, thus masking the real relationship between the two variables.

Table 4.2	Strengths and limitations of correlational analysis	
Strengths	It can show the **direction** of the relationship between variables	
	It can show the **strength** of the relationship between variables	
Limitations	It cannot show **cause-and-effect** relationships	
	It cannot show **non-linear** relationships	

Summary

- The statistical technique of correlational analysis describes the **relationship** between variables.
- It is a **useful** technique, but it has some **limitations**.

Observational techniques

Observational studies make no attempt to manipulate variables. They simply record behaviour as it occurs. This can happen within a laboratory setting, as in the Strange Situation technique, where the security of an infant's attachment is assessed, but more often it is **naturalistic observation**, carried out in a natural setting. Therefore, it has high ecological validity, and if people are unaware of being observed it eliminates demand characteristics. It can take the form of **non-participant** or **participant observation**.

In non-participant observation, as, for example, in the method used in the Strange Situation technique, the researcher remains apart from the people being studied.

In participant observation, the researcher becomes part of the group of people being studied. For example, Marsh (1978) was interested in the behaviour of groups of football fans, and in particular the rules underlying aggression towards fans of other teams. In order to explore this, he attended football matches with a group of fans, travelling with them to away matches, talked to them and observed their behaviour. The advantage of this method is that people may be more likely to be open and honest with someone whom they perceive as a member of the group to which they belong, rather than seeing themselves as the object of study by an outsider. However, participants are often unaware that they are being observed, and this — as noted earlier in relation to field experiments — can raise ethical problems, to be discussed later in this chapter. Nonetheless, if carried out carefully, participant observation allows naturally occurring behaviour to be studied and analysed.

Because of the researcher's lack of control when observational methods are being used, careful planning before the study starts is necessary, in terms of what is to be observed and how observations are to be recorded. It is often possible to film behaviour, which has the advantage of allowing repeated viewing. This enables the researcher to pick up on details that might have been missed during an earlier viewing, and so allows a fuller analysis to be made of the behaviour observed. For example, in an observation of children at play, there would be so much movement and so many different things going on at the same time that it would be impossible to record all the relevant details while they were happening. If filming is not possible, the observation can be made more manageable through either time sampling or event sampling.

In **time sampling**, observations are made for only short periods of time within the observation period. For example, if children's play was being observed, it would not be possible both to observe and make detailed notes on all the behaviours occurring in their play. The researchers might therefore divide the observation period into 10-minute slots, and within each slot observe the behaviour for 3 minutes and use the remaining 7 minutes to make notes on their observations while they were still fresh in their minds.

In **event sampling**, a specific event is noted each time it occurs. For example, in an observation of children's play, a researcher might have a check list of expected behaviours, based on previous observation during the planning stage of the study. If he or she were interested in comparing the frequency of aggressive behaviours shown by girls and by boys during play, the check list could include items such as 'hits another child' or 'name calling'. The researcher would then put a tick next to each behaviour on the list each time it occurred.

Naturalistic observation is a useful technique when the researcher is interested in something that it would be hard, if not impossible, to re-create realistically under laboratory conditions, for example, driver behaviour or children's spontaneous interaction. It can also play a part in exploratory studies to identify phenomena that could subsequently be investigated under the more controlled conditions of a laboratory setting.

One practical problem of observational studies is the **observer effect**, where observing a phenomenon may in itself affect what is being observed. The classic example of this is the **Hawthorne effect**, which takes its name from the Hawthorne works of the Bell Telephone Company. It refers to observation of workers at the factory and the finding that productivity increased, not because of suggestions as to how changes in working practices might improve productivity, but merely because the workers were aware of being observed. When people know that they are being observed, issues of evaluation apprehension and social desirability (mentioned earlier) also arise.

As with experimenter bias, **observer bias** is also possible. Observers may interpret what they see in line with the expectations and beliefs that they bring to the study. For instance, to return to the example of observing aggressive behaviour in children at play, if the researcher expects boys to behave more aggressively than girls, he or she may well interpret a boy pushing another child as aggressive behaviour, but would not do so if this behaviour were observed in a girl. One way to try to overcome this problem is to have two people making observations of the same event(s), each collecting data independently. If their observations are similar, the data are said to have **inter-observer reliability**. We will be returning to the issue of reliability in the next section.

Replication is also an issue in observational studies. It is highly unlikely that a precise replication could be carried out, as some aspects of the observation would inevitably be different if the study were to be repeated. For this reason, **generalisation**, i.e. applying the conclusions drawn from the outcome of the study more widely, is also difficult. For example, it would be unwise to apply general conclusions drawn from one study of the nature of children's play in a playground to all children's play, as there are likely to be differences in replication that cannot be controlled by the researcher, such as the number of children playing, the balance in numbers between boys and girls, the size of the play area and so on.

Summary

- Observational techniques record behaviour as it occurs. They can take the form of **participant** or **non-participant observation**.
- Ideally, behaviour is filmed to allow a full analysis of what is being observed. If this is not possible, **time sampling** or **event sampling** may be used.
- Observational techniques are useful when studying phenomena that cannot easily be created in a laboratory setting.
- **The observer effect** and **observer bias** can create problems. **Replication**, and therefore **generalisation**, are also difficult.

Self-report techniques: questionnaires and interviews

There are several variations of these techniques, but they all involve asking people to provide information about themselves.

Questionnaires

Questionnaires are widely used in psychology as they have the great advantage of allowing the researcher to collect a lot of data relatively easily, and they do not require him or her to be present when they are completed. Both closed-ended and open-ended questions can be used.

Closed-ended questions provide the respondents with a choice of answers from which they are asked to select the one that they feel is most appropriate. For example, the **Eysenck Personality Inventory (EPI)** asks questions such as: 'Do you find it hard to take no for an answer?', and the respondent must choose between 'yes' and 'no'. This format has the advantage of being easy to score and to analyse. Indeed, scoring of this kind of questionnaire is often carried out by computers.

However, it is possible that none of the answers provided corresponds exactly with the answer that the respondent would ideally like to give.

Open-ended questions address this issue, in that respondents are free to answer the questions in any way they like, so that what they have to say is likely to be more detailed and accurate, and a better reflection of their thoughts and feelings, than just choosing one from a limited number of options. However, this kind of questionnaire is more difficult to score.

One of the problems with questionnaires in general is that respondents might not be prepared to be honest in the information they give: there is the possibility of evaluation apprehension and social desirability affecting their responses. However, this kind of issue is less likely to arise when people are completing questionnaires than when questions are asked in interviews, face to face. It can also be minimised by allowing people to complete questionnaires anonymously, only giving information that is relevant to the aims of the study, for example age and/or sex.

Postal questionnaires allow data to be collected from a large number of people without making too many demands on the researcher. However, the return rate of questionnaires that collect information in this way is relatively low. Perhaps even more importantly, the people who choose to complete and return questionnaires are a **self-selected sample** and so may not be representative of the group of people in which the researcher is interested (sampling will be examined in more detail in the next section).

Interviews

Interviews can also take several forms. At its most structured, an interview can be identical to a questionnaire, except that it is carried out face to face, with a standard set of questions and a limited number of answers from which the respondent is asked to choose. At the other end of the scale, interviews can be open-ended and unstructured. The researcher has a set number of topic areas that he or she wishes to investigate, but the respondents are encouraged to talk about the topics in any way they think appropriate, with the interviewer being free to follow up any points raised that he or she feels are interesting. This method has the advantage of producing rich and detailed data and of being quite flexible, often giving access to information that could not be gained easily in any other way. On the other hand, analysis of the data is open to **researcher bias**, and because of the potentially large variation in the information given by respondents, is **time-consuming** to analyse.

In practice, a **semi-structured interview** technique is often used, to draw on the advantages of both structured and unstructured approaches. The **clinical interview** is an example of a semi-structured interview, used to assess a person who has a mental disorder. Specific questions are asked that require simple answers, but this information is also followed up in more detail where this is felt to be useful. This technique is used as part of the process of making a diagnosis about the particular disorder from which the individual is suffering, and therefore helps to determine what kinds of treatment might be appropriate. The data collected can also be used for the purposes of research. This method is used by mental-health professionals to collect information about the psychiatric, personal, medical and family history of the patient, together with his or her social circumstances and personality characteristics. In addition to the clinical interview, a more structured approach is used to assess cognitive functioning, for example memory and IQ, to test the functioning of the central nervous system. A physical examination is also made.

One of the drawbacks of both unstructured and semi-structured interviews is that the data they provide depend very much on the ease with which the individuals can express themselves. This in turn may also be affected by the skill of the interviewer. It is important that respondents should neither feel pressured into giving information, nor that judgements are being made of them on the basis of the answers they give.

Summary

- **Questionnaires** are widely used because they allow a lot of data to be collected relatively easily.
- Those using **closed-ended questions** are easy to analyse but may not provide an accurate picture, while those using **open-ended questions** provide richer data but make analysis more difficult.
- There are problems in terms of the **honesty** of respondents and the **return rate** of **postal questionnaires**.
- **Interviews** can be open-ended or tightly structured. **Semi-structured interviews** are often carried out as they provide rich data and their analysis is not as complex and time-consuming as with a completely unstructured approach.

Case studies

Case studies are **in-depth studies** of an individual or a small group of people who share a characteristic in which the researcher is interested. Case studies can use a range of methods to tap into different kinds of information, including interviews, detailed observation, information from others about the person being studied, and so on. While some of the data collected may be **quantitative**, providing precise measurements such as test scores, at least some, if not most, of the data are usually **qualitative**, i.e. largely descriptive. Perhaps the best known example of the case-study method is the work of Freud. He developed his theories from talking to patients who went to him for therapy, and he wrote up detailed accounts of the individuals that he studied in this way. Unlike research that takes a **nomothetic** approach, which is interested in understanding the general laws of behaviour that apply to everyone, case studies are **idiographic**, studying one individual or a very few people in depth.

Case studies are useful for developing an understanding of a particular individual, and also for investigating the characteristics of someone who is unusual in some way. For example, in Chapter 3 we discussed the case studies of Genie and the Czech twins, who had spent the early years of their lives shut away from interaction with other people. Similarly, in memory research, Luria (1968) studied a journalist whom he referred to as 'S', who had a phenomenal memory. Not only was 'S' able to remember vast amounts of information over long periods of time, but he was even able to do this with material that had no meaning for him, such as poems in a foreign language or chemical formulae. He did this to a large extent by using visual images, but also because he experienced **synesthesia**, the ability to link information across different modalities. For example, he said to one psychologist: 'What a crumbly yellow voice you have'.

One of the advantages of the case-study method in a clinical context is that it is a way of carrying out research for which a more experimental approach would be unethical. It is also useful in the initial stages of researching a topic, as it can identify particular areas that could then be followed up using other methods. As it is an in-depth approach, it also provides a lot of rich data. Finally, as the numbers involved are so small, it lends itself to longitudinal research, where people are followed over a long period of time to assess any changes that may have occurred. Koluchova's study of the Czech twins, discussed in Chapter 3, is a good example.

However, the case-study method also has drawbacks. A major problem is **generalisability**, the extent to which what is true of the person or small group of people who have been studied can be assumed to apply more widely. One of the criticisms often made of Freud's theories is that they were developed largely through case studies of middle-class, middle-aged Viennese women, and yet Freud believed that the basic principles (outlined in Chapter 1) were universally applicable.

Researcher bias is also a problem. Again, Freud's case studies have been criticised on the grounds that the conclusions he drew from the material that he collected involved a high degree of interpretation. For example, in his case study of Little Hans, who had a phobia of horses, Freud explained the child's problem in terms of horses being symbolic of Hans's father and expressing his feelings towards him, whereas the phobia could equally well be explained in less complex and speculative ways.

Finally, if a case study involves in-depth interviews, it relies heavily on the willingness and ability of the individual to provide accurate information. For example, if an adult is asked to recount childhood experiences, he or she may not be able to remember accurately information about events that took place many years ago, or may not wish to do so, or may reconstruct memories, as discussed in Chapter 2.

Summary

- **Case studies** are **in-depth studies** of an individual or a small group of people.
- They provide rich and **detailed data**, but there are problems of **generalisability**, **researcher bias** and **accuracy**.

The design of research studies

A great deal of planning and preparation is necessary if a research study is to provide appropriate and informative data. In this section, we will look at the areas that need to be considered when a piece of research is being developed, starting with the design of experiments and studies using correlational analysis.

Aims, hypotheses and operationalisation

Before starting a study, the first thing to do is to decide, in general terms, what the aims of the study are. For example, they may be to carry out a replication of previous research, to test the implications arising from an existing theory, or to investigate the effects of a particular factor on behaviour in a situation where this factor has not previously been considered. Once the general aims have been established, a much more precise hypothesis can be developed.

You will remember that in an experiment, the IV is systematically manipulated by the experimenter, with confounding variables being controlled, in order to assess the effects of this manipulation on the DV. From this, a cause-and-effect relationship between the IV and the DV can be shown. The hypothesis for an experiment refers to the IV and the DV, and is a precise prediction of what the result of the manipulation of the IV will be. In a correlational study, the hypothesis predicts the expected relationship between the two variables that are to be measured. In order to develop a hypothesis, the researcher needs to use a precise definition of the variables in terms of how they are to be used in a particular study. This is called **operationalisation**.

As an example of an experiment, let us take the Bower et al. study on semantic hierarchies examined in Chapter 2 (see Box 2.23, page 53). Its general aims were to assess whether memory for material is improved when the material is organised in such a way as to highlight semantic links. In order to develop these aims into a hypothesis, the IV was defined as whether a set of words is presented in the form of a semantic hierarchy or in random order, and the DV as the number of words remembered. As an example of a correlational study, we can take that carried out by Kanner et al. (page 94), where one aim was to investigate whether there is a relationship between experiencing hassles and experiencing stress. The hassles could be measured using a questionnaire, asking people to assess how frequently each of a number of listed hassles was experienced, and symptoms of stress could be measured with a similar questionnaire. The hypothesis could then operationalise hassles and stress in terms of questionnaire scores.

There are two kinds of hypotheses: the **alternative** (or **experimental**) **hypothesis** and the **null hypothesis**. The term 'alternative hypothesis' can be used with any study, but the term 'experimental hypothesis' only when the study is an experiment. All experimental hypotheses are alternative hypotheses, but not all alternative hypotheses are experimental hypotheses.

Alternative hypotheses can be **one-tailed** (**directional**) or **two-tailed** (**non-directional**). In an experiment, a **non-directional hypothesis** predicts that there will be a difference in the DV as a result of the manipulation of the IV. In the Bower et al. study, a non-directional hypothesis would be: 'There will be a difference in the number of words remembered when they are presented in a semantic hierarchy and when they are presented in random order.' In a correlational study, a non-directional hypothesis predicts that there will be a relationship between the variables being measured, so in a study such as that carried out by Kanner et al., the hypothesis would be:

'There will be a relationship between scores on a hassles questionnaire and scores on a questionnaire measuring stress.'

Non-directional hypotheses suggest that there will be a difference between conditions, or a relationship between variables, but give no indication as to the nature of the difference or relationship. By contrast, in a **directional hypothesis**, the *direction* of the difference or relationship is predicted. For the Bower et al. study, a directional hypothesis would be: 'Participants presented with words in a semantic hierarchy will remember *more words* than those who are presented with the words in random order.' For the Kanner et al. correlational study, it would be: 'There will be a *positive relationship* between scores on a hassles questionnaire and scores on a stress questionnaire.'

Directional hypotheses are used when there is some evidence — either on the basis of a theory or from the results of previous related research — as to the direction that the difference or relationship is expected to take. A non-directional hypothesis is used when there is no evidence to support a particular direction, or when there is conflicting evidence, for example when one theory (or research study) suggests one direction, but a different theory or study suggests the other direction.

A **null hypothesis** predicts that there will be no difference between conditions in an experiment, or no relationship between variables in a correlational study. To return to the previous examples, the null hypothesis for the memory experiment would be: 'There will be no difference in the number of words remembered when the words are presented in a semantic hierarchy and when they are presented in random order.' For the hassles/stress study it would be: 'There will be no relationship between scores on a hassles questionnaire and scores on a questionnaire measuring stress.' In a study, it is actually the null hypothesis that is being tested, hence the term 'alternative hypothesis', because it is the alternative to the null hypothesis.

Statistical tests carried out on the data from experiments and correlational studies tell us how likely or unlikely it is that any difference between conditions, or relationship between variables, has come about by chance. If it is unlikely, then the alternative hypothesis is accepted and the null hypothesis is rejected. If, on the other hand, it is probable that any difference or relationship has come about by chance, then the alternative hypothesis is rejected and the null hypothesis retained.

Summary

- The **aims** of a study give a general indication of why a study is being carried out, while **hypotheses** make precise predictions about what the results of a study are expected to be.
- To write hypotheses, variables must be **operationalised**.
- **Alternative hypotheses** can be **directional** or **non-directional**, depending on whether or not they predict the nature of the difference between conditions in an experiment, or the direction of a relationship in a correlational study.
- The **null hypothesis** predicts that there will be no difference between conditions, or no relationship between variables.

Experimental design

Before carrying out an experiment, a decision needs to be made about which kind of design would be most appropriate. We will now examine three possible designs.

Independent groups design

One possibility is an **independent groups design**, sometimes also referred to as an **independent measures design** or a **between-groups design**. In this design, different participants take part in each condition, and participants should be randomly allocated to conditions. For example, in the Bower et al. study, one group of participants would be asked to learn the words presented in a meaningful hierarchy, and a different group to learn them in a random presentation.

In an experiment using this design, there could be two (or more) **experimental conditions** receiving variations in experimental treatment. For example, the effectiveness of two different strategies on memory for a word list could be compared by asking participants in one condition to try to remember the words using visual imagery, and those in the second condition to use rehearsal, saying the words over and over to themselves in their heads.

It is also possible to have one or more experimental condition, together with a **control condition**, where participants are given no particular treatment. In the memory strategies example, participants in the control condition would just be asked to try to remember the words, with no strategy suggested. A control condition provides a baseline measure against which the results from the other conditions can be compared. With the inclusion of a control condition, it would be possible to assess not only whether the use of visual imagery is more effective than rehearsal, but also whether suggesting either strategy would enhance recall.

Since participants are only exposed to one condition, this design eliminates possible **order effects** (when carrying out a task in one condition may affect performance in the other condition(s)). However, there is a problem with **individual differences**, because the participants in one condition may be different in some important respect from those in the other condition(s), which would bias the results.

Repeated measures design

A second possible experimental design is a **repeated measures design**, sometimes also referred to as a **related design** or **within-groups design**. In this design, each participant provides data in both (or all) conditions, and his or her performance in each condition is compared. An important advantage of this design over an independent groups design is that any effects of individual differences are eliminated, because the performance of each participant in one condition is compared with that same person's performance in the other condition(s).

However, the main problem with this design is possible **order effects**. These effects include practice, boredom and fatigue. For example, participants may have settled into the task by the time they take part in the second condition, and so do better for this reason and not because of the experimental manipulation of the IV. Alternatively, they may do worse in the second condition because they are starting to find it tedious or have difficulty in continuing to concentrate.

It is often possible to minimise these effects by **counterbalancing**, that is, by varying the order in which participants do the tasks. If some participants start by carrying out the task in condition A, followed by condition B, while others start with B, followed by A, then any order effects should affect both conditions equally. However, this is not always a solution. In the example of comparing the memory techniques of using visual imagery or rehearsal, it could be that those participants who carried out the 'visual imagery' condition first found it so effective that they also used it in the condition in which rehearsal was the strategy to be used. Sometimes counterbalancing may not even be possible. For example, if the effectiveness of two teaching methods for learning were to be compared, participants could only take part in one condition. An independent groups design would need to be used here.

Another drawback is that more **materials** may need to be prepared when a repeated measures design is used than when the design uses independent groups. For example, in the word list study, two different lists would need to be prepared, as the experiment would be compromised if participants were to be asked to learn the same list again in the second condition: they would probably remember more of the words simply because they have already seen them once, rather than because of the experimental manipulation of the IV. The lists would also need to be matched on word length and usage (how common they are in the language), which could be a time-consuming process. A word list in one condition with words such as 'tree', 'dog' and 'chair' could not be matched with a list containing words such as 'harbinger', 'recidivist' and 'fandango' without introducing an unwanted bias!

You will remember that one of the criteria for a study to be an experiment is that there should be an element of **random allocation**, to avoid the possibility of bias in the way in which the experiment is carried out. In an independent groups design, participants would be randomly allocated to a condition, i.e. all participants would have an equal chance of being placed in either condition, or any condition if there are more than two. However, in a repeated measures design, random allocation to conditions is not possible, as participants take part in both or all the conditions. However, the order in which they carry out each condition should be randomised, within the constraints of counterbalancing.

Matched pairs design

A final possible experimental design is a **matched pairs design**. This design aims to exploit the advantages of both independent groups design and repeated measures design, while avoiding some of the drawbacks of both. In this design, each participant is matched with another participant on characteristics that are thought to be relevant to the experiment, such as age, sex, personality characteristics and/or intelligence. One participant from each pair is then randomly allocated to each condition and takes part only in that condition. For example, in the semantic hierarchy study of Bower et al., participants could be pre-tested on their memory ability and matched on this basis, with one of each pair being randomly allocated to each condition. It is assumed that the matching process produces pairs who are so similar that they can be treated as if they were the same person. Indeed, the statistical tests used to analyse the data from an experiment using a matched pairs design are the same tests that would be used for a repeated measures design. The main drawback of a matched pairs design is that the process of matching participants is time-consuming, and the pair may also not be matched on a characteristic that turns out to be important. Furthermore, if one of the pair withdraws from the study, the other one must also be withdrawn.

Summary of the three experimental designs

These three designs vary in how susceptible they are to **demand characteristics**. In a repeated measures design, participants get an overview of the whole study, because they take part in all conditions. They may consequently work out — correctly or not — the aims of the experiment and adjust their behaviour. In independent groups and matched pairs designs, demand characteristics are less of a problem, because each participant will only have experienced one condition and so has less of a basis on which to work out the aims.

In summary, there are positive aspects and drawbacks to all three designs, as shown in Table 4.3.

Table 4.3 *Three experimental designs: strengths and drawbacks*

Design	Strengths	Drawbacks
Repeated measures	Eliminates the effects of individual differences Requires fewer participants	Possible order effects, though sometimes counterbalancing is possible More susceptible to demand characteristics May require more materials
Independent groups	No order effects Less susceptible to demand characteristics Only one set of materials required across conditions	Possible effect of individual differences Requires more participants
Matched pairs	Reduces the effect of individual differences No order effects Less susceptible to demand characteristics Only one set of materials required across conditions	Requires more participants Matching is time-consuming and may be incomplete If one participant withdraws, the 'pair' must also be withdrawn

Summary

- Experimental designs include **independent groups**, **repeated measures** and **matched pairs**.
- Each design has both **strengths** and **drawbacks**.

Design of naturalistic observations

Naturalistic observation can be defined as a systematic description of events and behaviours in a particular social setting. It aims to try to understand 'real' people in everyday situations. We have already looked briefly at this method, and in

particular at the distinction between participant and non-participant observation, and at the methods of time sampling and event sampling. In this section, we will examine in a little more detail some of the elements that need to be considered when planning a study of this kind.

The methods used show considerable variation. For example, they can be highly structured and detailed, or relatively unstructured and more impressionistic. Data collection can be simple note taking or involve making video or audio recordings. It may also include the use of behavioural check lists, or timing events using stop-watches. The data could be verbal or non-verbal behaviour, or even evidence (from which conclusions may be drawn) from what people have produced, rather than the people themselves. For example, Webb et al. (1981) analysed carpet wear and 'nose prints' on glass protecting exhibits at an art exhibition to assess the relative popularity of what was on display. People may be made aware that their behaviour is being observed, or not (something that, again, raises ethical issues, but we will discuss this later in the chapter).

Data collection can be **quantitative**, i.e. in the form of measurements that may be analysed using statistical techniques. There are some set techniques that can be used for this. For example, Bales (1950) developed techniques for analysing group interactions, in which specific instances of verbal behaviour were classified in terms of whether the contribution was positive or negative, whether it was asking for, or giving, information, and so on.

Researchers may also develop their own way of measuring the behaviour they observe. For example, if researchers were interested in children's playground behaviour, they could develop a check list of possible behaviours and count how frequently each occurred. They could also use rating scales, where the children observed are rated for particular characteristics by observers.

As stated earlier, research needs to start with aims — why is the study to be carried out? This can then be developed to create a more precise hypothesis, as with an experiment, but is sometimes refined instead into a research question, i.e. a statement of precisely what is to be observed and with what purpose, rather than a prediction of what is expected to happen. Again, as with an experiment, research should arise from theory or previous related research. The researcher needs to decide who are to be observed and in what setting. At this point, ethical concerns will need to be considered, particularly the issue of whether or not people will be aware they are being observed, and if not, whether this is ethically acceptable. Decisions then need to be made in terms of what exactly is to be observed and how these observations are going to be recorded.

The data collected can also be **qualitative**, where no measurements are made. These observations will be reported in a more descriptive way, using examples from what has been observed to support the description, and the researcher's interpretations of the meaning of participants' behaviour. If this approach is taken, it is particularly important that the observer should recognise his or her own part in the observation and the subjectivity of his or her interpretation of it. What is observed and how

it is interpreted may well be influenced by the observer's beliefs and expectations, so reports of this kind of research usually include a **reflexive analysis**, where these issues are considered. It is not unusual for both quantitative and qualitative methods to be used together.

Summary

- **Naturalistic observation** focuses on the behaviour of people in particular social settings. There is wide **variation** in how it is carried out.
- Data can be **quantitative** or **qualitative** or both.

Design of questionnaires and interviews

As with any other research method, the researcher needs to establish the aims of research where questionnaires are to be used, and from these to decide exactly what information it is hoped that the completed questionnaires will offer. If too much ground is covered, the questionnaire might need to be unreasonably long in order to provide enough information on all aspects of the topic to be covered, whereas if the scope is too limited, very little useful information will be collected.

The researcher will then need to decide what form the questions will take, i.e. whether to use closed-ended or open-ended questions, or a mixture of both. As discussed earlier, both have strengths and limitations, and the format chosen will depend on the priorities of the researcher. For example, if it is considered important to collect data from a lot of people, closed-ended questions will be more practical in terms of time constraints on analysis. However, if the focus is to be on the collection of more detailed data and individual variation, open-ended questions will be more useful.

In questionnaires with closed-ended questions, there are different ways in which items can be presented. They can be in the form of questions with a choice of answers, perhaps just 'yes' or 'no', but perhaps also including a greater spread of possible responses, such as 'to some extent' or 'don't know'. For example, the **Eysenck Personality Inventory (EPI)** uses the 'yes or no' method, and in a **Likert Scale**, items are presented in the form of statements, with possible answers on a five-point scale, the different points being given numerical values for ease of scoring. Box 4.1 shows items from these two questionnaires.

The next step will be generating possible items to be included in the questionnaire that are relevant to the topic being explored, later discarding those that are perhaps less relevant. It is also necessary to avoid questions that might be ambiguous and therefore unlikely to provide accurate information, or that are biased. For example: 'As watching television has been shown to cause aggressive behaviour in children, should the amount of television that children are allowed to watch be limited?' is a biased question: the first part reflects the opinion of the researcher on the effects on children of watching television. Questions that are long or complex should also be avoided, as they can easily be misunderstood.

Box 4.1 Sample items from two questionnaires

Sample items from the Eysenck Personality Inventory (EPI)

Do your moods go up and down? ☐ YES ☐ NO

Are you usually carefree? ☐ YES ☐ NO

Sample items using a Likert Scale to measure beliefs about the effect on children of watching television

Watching TV is often a useful educational experience for children.

☐ strongly agree | ☐ agree somewhat | ☐ undecided | ☐ disagree somewhat | ☐ strongly disagree

Most children watch too much TV.

☐ strongly agree | ☐ agree somewhat | ☐ undecided | ☐ disagree somewhat | ☐ strongly disagree

In order for a questionnaire to be good, there must be a balance in the way that the questions are asked, or between positive and negative statements, with the different kinds of questions or statements being presented in random order. This should be done so as to avoid a **response set**. For example, in the EPI and Likert Scale examples above (see Box 4.1), a person might be expected to respond differently to the two items in each case because the questions posed are varied and unexpected. However, if all the statements in a questionnaire were positive or similar, people might soon start to respond to all of them in the same way, without reading the questions carefully.

The scores given to each answer will need to reflect the variation in the order of the way in which questions are asked, or between positive and negative statements. For instance, the EPI, which in the example above is assessing neuroticism, would score positively for 'yes' on the first item and for 'no' on the second item. Similarly, if the Likert Scale for the first item scored 5 for 'strongly agree', 'strongly disagree' would score 5 on the second item.

There are similar considerations when planning research using **face-to-face interviews**, which are usually more open-ended than questionnaires. A good deal of thought needs to be given to the wording of questions, to avoid bias and ambiguity and to encourage respondents to expand on what they have to say rather than offer limited and uninformative answers. The analysis of the material also needs to be considered carefully, particularly when the data do not lend themselves to quantitative analysis using statistical tests. We will return to the analysis of qualitative data later in the chapter.

Since interviews are face to face, ethical issues are extremely important. Participants should feel comfortable talking to the interviewer. They should be assured that the information they give will be confidential, and that in any report of the study it will not be possible for them to be personally identified. We will return to this in more detail in the section on ethics.

4

Summary

- As with any research, questionnaires and interviews need careful **planning**.
- Decisions must be made in terms of the **form** that the questionnaire or interview will take, depending on the aims of the research.
- **Ethical issues** are of particular importance in interviews.

Pilot studies

A **pilot study** is a small-scale study, carried out with a restricted number of participants who will not take part in the study itself, before the process of collecting data begins. The aim is to make sure that the materials the researcher is planning to use are suitable and to identify any potential problems with the procedure. Pilot studies are carried out whichever method of research is used, and the feedback provided by those taking part in the pilot study can be useful in adapting the study where necessary.

In an **experiment**, a pilot study is useful in ensuring that any instructions given to participants are clear. It is also helpful in determining how long participants should be exposed to stimulus materials. For example, in a memory study, if the participant is exposed to the materials for too long, there is likely to be a **ceiling effect**, where most of the participants remember virtually everything and the procedure fails to discriminate between participants. If the time is too short, there is likely to be a **floor effect**, where little is remembered by anyone and so again there is a lack of discrimination. A pilot study can also indicate how much material it is reasonable to ask a person to remember — neither too much nor too little.

In **naturalistic observation**, the control of the researcher over the phenomena to be observed is usually minimal. A pilot study will therefore help to establish the possibilities and potential problems of the planned observation. This could identify items for a check list of behaviours, or define the particular points on a rating scale. It could also clarify issues such as whether note taking will be sufficient to cover all the relevant aspects of the interaction, or establish the most appropriate positioning of a camera, if the interaction is to be filmed.

For **questionnaires** and **interviews**, a pilot study can help to identify questions that are ambiguous or do not produce relevant material. Participants may also suggest whether the length of the questionnaire or interview seems too long, too short or about right.

Summary

- A **pilot study** should be carried out before starting the main study, in order to refine the precise ways in which the study will be carried out and data collected.

Reliability and validity

In psychological research, the term **reliability** refers to **consistency**. Researchers need to be sure that the measures they use are reliable, i.e. provide consistent results.

For instance, you know that a 1-litre bottle of milk will always contain the same amount of milk. A good example of a reliable test is the EPI: the results are relatively consistent if a person takes it more than once. The term 'reliability' can be used in different contexts, in relation to psychological tests and in relation to observations in observational studies.

In relation to the reliability of psychological tests, **test-retest reliability** assesses *external* reliability, i.e. the consistency of the test over time. Participants are given the test on two different occasions, and if the test is reliable, the results should be very similar. Clearly, the timing here is important. If participants retake a test soon after they took it the first time, it is possible that can remember how they responded before, and give very similar if not identical answers. On the other hand, if there is too big a gap between the two tests, it is possible that the results are different, not because the test is not reliable, but because the person has changed in some significant way.

Split-half reliability assesses the *internal* consistency of a test, i.e. the extent to which all parts of the test contribute to what the test is measuring. This is done by comparing the results from one half of the test with the results from the other half. The test could be split in several ways, for example the first half and the second half, odd-numbered and even-numbered questions, or even at random. If the test is reliable, the results of the two halves should be very similar.

To test the reliability of observational studies, **inter-rater** (or **inter-observer**) **reliability** is tested, in other words the extent to which two or more people rating the same event agree on the ratings that they give. For example, if a rating scale were to be used to assess levels of aggression shown by children playing in a playground, two or more raters would independently rate each child and their ratings would be compared. A rating scale would need to be worked out and the points on the scale described before the start of data collection for the study.

In all these cases, the comparison would be made using **correlational analysis**. If a measure is reliable, there will be a high positive correlation between the two measures.

Validity refers to whether a test is actually testing what it sets out to test, or a study provides genuine information about what it is aiming to investigate. A distinction can be made between **internal validity** (that is, in an experiment, that the effects observed are genuine and brought about through the manipulation of an IV) and **external (ecological) validity** (that the results of a study can be generalised to situations and samples outside the study). A criticism frequently made of laboratory studies is that they lack ecological validity. For example, the research of Ebbinghaus using nonsense syllables was a highly artificial way of testing memory, so the extent to which the findings may be generalised is open to question.

In relation to psychological tests, it is possible for a test to be reliable but not valid. For example, the Eysenck Personality Questionnaire (EPQ) is a reliable personality test but not a valid test of, say, intelligence. Therefore, in order to be useful, a test needs to be both reliable and valid.

Face validity is a straightforward way of assessing the validity of a test. This is the extent to which it seems to be testing what it aims to test. The sample items from the EPI (see Box 4.1) appear to be related to personality, so the test has face validity. **Construct validity** refers to the extent to which test items link to the theory on which the tests are based. In the case of the EPI, the items clearly relate to the theoretical constructs of Eysenck's theory of personality on which the test is based. These two types of validity relate to the **content** of the test.

Predictive validity is slightly different. It is a kind of criterion-related validity that refers to the validity of a test in terms of how well it relates to other measures. It is the ability of a test to predict performance on another related criterion. The old 11+ test is a good example of a test assumed to have predictive validity. All children used to take this test to determine whether they went to a grammar school, offering an academic education, or a secondary modern school that was less academically orientated. It was assumed that results from the 11+ could predict how well pupils were likely to do later on in their academic life, for example, in exams taken at age 16.

Summary

- **Reliablity** refers to **consistency**. **Test-retest** and **split-half** reliability assess the reliability of psychological tests. **Inter-rater** reliability assesses the reliability of ratings in observational studies. This is done using **correlational analysis**.
- **Validity** refers to how genuinely a test or study achieves what it sets out to do.
- A distinction is made between **internal** and **external** (**ecological**) **validity**.
- There are several methods to assess the validity of tests.

Sampling techniques

When carrying out a study, a sample of people to be tested must be selected. They are drawn from the **population** in which the researcher is interested — for example, primary school children or A-level psychology students. As the whole population is too large for everyone to be tested, a sample is drawn that should ideally be representative of the population as a whole, that is, all the characteristics of the parent population should be represented. If a representative sample is tested, any conclusions drawn from the study can then be generalised to the population as a whole.

The larger the sample, the more likely it is to be representative. If it is not representative, it is said to be **biased**, in that some of the characteristics of the population are either over- or under-represented, and generalisation is more open to question. In selecting a sample size, there are practical considerations. If the sample is small, it is unlikely to be representative. If it is too big, testing will be time-consuming. Whatever the sample size, there is likely to be **sampling error**, i.e. inaccuracies in terms of the sample's representativeness of the parent population. The larger the sample, the more this is likely to be reduced, but not necessarily eliminated.

There are several ways in which a sample may be selected. We will look here at random, opportunity and volunteer sampling.

Random sampling

In a **random sample**, every member of the parent population has an equal chance of being selected to form part of the sample, with no bias as to who is selected and who is not. If the population is small, for example students studying art at a further education college, a random sample could be achieved by writing the name of each art student on a piece of paper, putting all the names in a hat and then drawing out names until the sample is the planned size. Alternatively, if the parent population is too large for this to be practicable, every member of the parent population could be given a number. A computer program that generates random numbers could then be used to select the sample, matching up the numbers with the numbers assigned to members of the population.

The advantage of this sampling method is that there is no bias in the selection of the sample. However, a random sample may not be representative of the parent population. For instance, in the art student example, it could be that by chance, only male students were selected, so female students would not be represented, though this kind of bias would become less likely as the sample size increased. To overcome this problem, a **quasi-random sample** could be selected, where a system is used to avoid this kind of bias. In this example, all the girls' names could be put in one hat and all the boys' names in another, with half the sample being drawn from each hat.

Opportunity sampling

An **opportunity sample** is a sample that is selected on the basis that anyone who is available at the time and willing to participate becomes part of it. This is often used, for example in student projects, as it is easy and convenient. The main problem with this method is that it is easily biased. For example, a student may only approach people he or she knows, or a researcher carrying out a questionnaire survey in the street might only approach people who look friendly. Therefore, the people asked to take part might not be representative of the parent population. Whether this is a serious problem depends on what is to be tested. For example, in a study measuring physiological responses to stress, an opportunity sample would be unlikely to differ radically from samples selected in other ways.

Volunteer sampling

In a **volunteer sample**, people offer — either directly or indirectly — to be part of the sample. This method was used by Milgram (1963). He placed an advertisement in the newspaper, asking for volunteers for a scientific study at Yale University, and tested those who responded. This method is often used in universities, where advertisements on notice boards ask for students willing to take part in psychological research in return for a small fee. The problem is that those who volunteer may not be typical of the target population, so here again the sample would be biased (a problem also mentioned earlier in relation to the return rate of postal questionnaires).

People may also volunteer indirectly. For example, if researchers were interested in whether men or women were more superstitious, they might set up a ladder and note how many males and how many females walked under the ladder or avoided it. The people whose behaviour was being observed would be unaware that they were taking part in a study, but would indirectly be volunteering to participate by walking along the street where the ladder was set up. Volunteer sampling was used in a study carried out by Mann (1977), which investigated queuing behaviour by noting the circumstances under which people queued or failed to do so when at a bus stop. However, observing people without their consent potentially raises ethical problems, which we will look at in the next section.

Summary

- **Samples** tested in psychological research should ideally be **representative**.
- There are several methods of selecting a sample, including **random**, **opportunity** and **volunteer** sampling, but none of them is unproblematic.

Ethical issues

Ethical issues in psychology are not straightforward as there are many grey areas in establishing what is morally right. The ethics of a study often involves a **cost–benefit analysis**; a weighing-up of the positive aspects expected to come out of a study against possible ethical dilemmas that it might raise. The most problematic point is that this is always going to be a **subjective** judgement.

Because research in psychology is done with people (and sometimes animals), there are special concerns about the way in which research studies are carried out. Ethical issues arise more in psychology than in other scientific disciplines because the subject matter is people, who can experience pain, fear and stress. In a research setting, they are capable of feeling embarrassed, humiliated or inadequate, so when planning a study, researchers need to think carefully about how the experience of taking part in their research might affect the participants.

Until fairly recently, participants in psychological research were referred to as 'subjects', a term that you may come across in older textbooks. The term 'participants' is now widely used, and recommended by the **British Psychological Society (BPS)**, to acknowledge the fact that people give of their time to help with research and should be treated with respect, and with concern for their well-being.

Milgram's study of obedience, discussed in detail in Chapter 6 (see page 174), was carried out in 1963 and is perhaps the study that most psychologists first think of in the context of ethics.

Summary

In Milgram's study, participants were led (incorrectly) to believe that they were giving painful and perhaps lethal electric shocks to someone they believed to be a fellow participant, when he failed to remember word pairs. The man receiving the fake shocks was actually a confederate of the experimenter.

The study has been widely criticised on ethical grounds, and in particular for deceiving the participants about the nature of what was being researched and for causing them stress. Even so, there is a certain amount of disagreement about the ethics of the study, with some seeing it as extremely unethical, while others see it as work of a highly moral quality. It is worth mentioning that an ethical investigation of Milgram's studies, carried out by the **American Psychological Association (APA)** shortly after they were published, came to the conclusion that the research was morally acceptable, and in 1965 the American Association for the Advancement of Science awarded Milgram a prize for his outstanding contribution to psychological research.

One of the results of Milgram's studies was to highlight the need for careful consideration of the ethics of psychological research. To assist researchers with these issues, professional bodies such as the BPS and the APA produce ethical guidelines that are regularly updated. Both these sets of guidelines stress that the aims of psychological research should be a better understanding of people and the promotion of human welfare, which require an atmosphere of free enquiry. At the same time, research needs to be carried out responsibly and professionally, and with due regard for the welfare of participants.

In this section we will be looking at the *Ethical Principles for Conducting Research with Human Participants (1993)*, produced by the BPS. The BPS has a register of chartered psychologists who work professionally in research or in a number of applied fields. Psychologists can be struck off the register if they do not maintain professional standards, including, most importantly, the ethics of the work that they carry out as psychologists. It is hoped that this system will create an accredited body of professional psychologists in whom the general public can have confidence. The term 'unethical' in this context refers to procedures that are not only morally wrong but are also professionally unacceptable.

Over recent years, ethical concerns have come very much to the fore. For example, psychologists in universities who are planning a research study have to put a proposal for it to an ethics committee. The committee will consider the ethics of what is proposed and decide whether the study should be allowed to proceed. It may also suggest ways in which ethical concerns relating to the study should be eliminated or minimised. In the next part of this section, we will examine some of the issues covered in these guidelines (summarised in Box 4.2).

Box 4.2	Summary of BPS *Ethical Principles for Conducting Research with Human Participants (1993)*

1 Introduction
In good psychological research, there should be mutual confidence and respect between participants and researchers. Guidelines are necessary to help to establish whether research is acceptable.

2 General

Researchers have a duty to consider the ethical implications of their research before it is carried out. They should eliminate possible threats to the physical and psychological well-being of participants. When researchers do not have sufficient knowledge of possible implications of their research for people varying in age, gender or social background, they should consult people with relevant characteristics.

3 Consent

Whenever possible, participants should be given full information about an investigation so that they can make an informed decision about whether or not to take part. Special care should be taken with research involving children or others who may be unable to give full informed consent. Participants should not be pressurised into taking part in research when the researcher is in a position of influence or authority over them, or by financial reward.

4 Deception

Deception should be avoided wherever possible, and particularly if participants are likely to feel troubled when debriefed.

5 Debriefing

When participants are aware of having taken part in a study, at the end of their participation the researcher should offer full information. He/she should discuss any aspects of the research that may have had negative consequences for the participants.

6 Withdrawal from the investigation

Participants should be told at the outset that they have the right to withdraw from the study at any time and have their data destroyed, even when the study has been completed and whether or not they have been paid to take part.

7 Confidentiality

Information gathered about participants during research should be kept confidential, and if published, participants should not be identifiable.

8 Protection of participants

Participants should be protected from any physical or psychological harm greater than that experienced in everyday life. Where personal information is collected, participants should be protected from stress and assured that personal questions need not be answered.

9 Observational research

Unless consent is given for behaviour to be observed, observation only of behaviour that could normally be observed by strangers is acceptable. Researchers should be sensitive to cultural values and to intruding on the privacy of people being observed, even if they are in a public place.

10 Giving advice

If the researcher becomes aware of physical or psychological problems of which the participant is apparently unaware, these problems should be raised with the participant. An appropriate source of professional advice should be recommended.

11 Colleagues

A researcher who is aware of a colleague carrying out research not following these principles should encourage the colleague to consider ethical issues arising from the research.

Consent

In order to consent to take part in a study, potential participants should be provided with full information about the aims and procedures of the study before they decide whether or not they are willing to take part. Ideally, participants should give **fully informed consent**, but there is some evidence that this information is not always routinely provided. For example, Epstein and Lasagna (1969) found that only about a third of research participants had any real understanding at the outset of what was involved in studies in which they had taken part. Menges (1973) discovered that participants were given incomplete information about the study in 80% of a sample of studies. They were given full information about the DV in only 25% of the studies, and about the IV in only 3%. Although withholding information is sometimes necessary if the aims of the study are not to be compromised, this appears to be an extremely low level of information provided. However, these surveys were carried out some time ago, and with the current emphasis on ethics in research, psychologists should be more aware of this issue.

In some circumstances, it can be difficult to obtain fully informed consent based on understanding the full implications of taking part in a study. The study of children is a case in point, because young children are unlikely to be able to understand fully the information provided, or even what a study involves. If children are too young to understand, or are below the legal age of consent, consent must be obtained from the parents or guardians. Researchers should also gain children's **assent**, as well as such consent as they are competent to give. The principle of assent requires that researchers pay particular attention to the non-verbal behaviour of children who are being studied. If the child seems to be becoming uncomfortable, for example is becoming very quiet, or sighs, or appears anxious, then withdrawal of assent is implied and the procedure should be modified or stopped. Informed consent can also be an issue with some adults, for example those with a mental disorder or learning difficulties.

A further problem arises when there is an existing relationship between the researcher and potential participants. This is particularly problematic when the researcher is in a position of authority over participants. For example, many research studies are carried out by psychology lecturers in universities, with their students as participants. In this case, steps must be taken to ensure that consent is freely given. There should be no inducements to take part, such as participation being counted towards course grades, and it should be made clear that deciding not to take part will have no negative consequences.

In the USA, students must participate in research as part of their course. Participation counts towards their course grades and they are paid for participation. **Enforced participation** explains why so many American studies are carried out with psychology students as participants. The choice for students is not whether or not to take part, but only which research to participate in. However, students know before they sign up for the course that this is a course requirement, and it could be argued that their participation in research is a good preparation for carrying out research themselves and increases their sensitivity towards participants when they do so.

4

If informed consent is not possible, one way to tackle the problem is to discuss the study with people from the population from which the sample is drawn but who are not themselves going to participate. This is known as **presumptive consent** and may be particularly useful when the participants are drawn from a population of whom the researcher has little knowledge, for example from different ethnic or national groups.

Deception

Deception can be linked to informed consent: if participants are deceived about the nature of the study, they are unable to give fully informed consent. Deception may also have wider repercussions. Participants who have been deceived may well be angry and disillusioned about psychology as a discipline, with the danger of psychology being brought into disrepute. For these reasons, the use of deception needs to be considered extremely carefully.

Of course, there are degrees of deception. For example, Brewer and Treyins (1981) carried out a study of schemas in memory (see Chapter 2 for a discussion of schemas). Participants were asked to wait in an office, supposedly while the experimenter went to check the laboratory to see if the previous participant had finished. After 35 seconds, he returned, took the participants into the laboratory and asked them to write down everything that they had seen in the office. The researchers found that people 'remembered' items that are usually found in an office, such as books, but that hadn't actually *been* in the office, and failed to remember items that were in the office but would not normally be expected to be found there, such as a skull. It is unlikely that participants were upset by this minor deception. However, deception such as that in the Milgram experiment, where people believed they were delivering painful electric shocks, could potentially have been more serious.

The guidelines do not state that participants should *never* be deceived. In some studies, deception is unavoidable, and therefore acceptable, because providing participants with full information would invalidate the (otherwise ethical) studies. For example, if the participants in Milgram's experiment had been told that the study was about people's readiness to obey an order, that no electric shocks would be given and that the person they thought was a fellow participant was in fact a confederate of the experimenter, the research could not have produced valid results. It is difficult to see how any study of a topic such as obedience could realistically be carried out if participants were given full information about the study before taking part.

Kelman (1967) suggested that the issue of deception could be addressed by asking people to role-play. However, the validity of the findings would be in question. There would inevitably be some doubt as to whether role-play produces behaviour that accurately represents people's normal behaviour.

Debriefing

Debriefing involves giving participants full information about the study, if this has not been done before they have agreed to take part, and answering any questions they may have. It is particularly important if information has had to be withheld for the study to be viable, or if deception has been involved. Participants should also be reassured about their own performance and that it was in no way unusual or shameful. It can be linked to the guideline stating that participants should be **protected from harm**, as it helps to ensure that they leave the study in as positive a frame of mind as when they arrived.

In many cases, debriefing is not problematic. However, participants who have no prior experience of taking part in psychological research — ideal participants since, unlike psychology students, the way they respond to research is unlikely to be influenced by previous knowledge of psychology — may have concerns about being judged by researchers, and in particular be worried that opinions could be formed about their intellectual ability or mental health. Careful and thorough debriefing is therefore essential.

It is perhaps also worth noting that debriefing can offer benefits to researchers, as participants can report on their experiences of taking part in the study. This may provide additional information to the researcher that is useful in helping them to understand the phenomenon being studied. For the participant, the understanding gained during debriefing can be an educational experience shared with the researcher.

Right to withdraw

This guideline links to that of informed consent. Consent is given before the study takes place, but participants need to know at the outset that they are free to withdraw at any time and to have their data destroyed, even after they have completed their part in the research. They should also know that this right still applies even when they have accepted payment for participation. In some cases, the right to withdraw with no negative consequences needs to be given particular consideration — for example, if lecturers are using their students as participants.

Confidentiality

The BPS guidelines highlight the importance of **confidentiality**. If participants have agreed in advance to waive this right, the researcher needs to make sure that participants fully understand the implications of doing so. Moreover, confidentiality is a legal right under the Data Protection Act. From a practical point of view, Coolican (1990) also points out that if confidentiality were not assured, it could become extremely difficult to find people who were prepared to take part in psychological research.

Anonymity is part of confidentiality. The standard practice to maintain anonymity in reporting the findings of psychological research is to assign each participant a number. If that particular person's results are referred to individually in the report, they are then only identified by that number. Of course, it is also essential that no other details are provided that could lead to their identification. In a case study, the participant is often referred to by initials, as in the case of HM in Chapter 2.

However, there are exceptions to the rule of confidentiality when psychologists feel that they have a wider ethical duty. For example, if a researcher were investigating gang behaviour and in the process found out that a criminal act was being planned, he might consider his ethical responsibility to society as a whole outweighed his ethical responsibility to the participants and therefore feel that he should report the planned crime. Similarly, if a psychologist became aware that one of her participants was contemplating suicide, she might not feel bound to respect the participant's confidentiality and should make sure that help was offered. In borderline cases, serious consideration needs to be given to whether confidentiality should be breached, and perhaps the position should be discussed with colleagues before doing so.

Protection from harm

There is rarely any risk of physical harm in psychological research. Occasionally, studies have made use of mild electric shocks, or have induced nausea in participants, but in these cases participants are informed beforehand so that they can decide whether or not to take part in the research.

In relation to psychological harm, Aronson (1988) proposed that participants should leave the research study in a frame of mind that is at least as sound as when they entered it. In almost all cases this is not problematic, providing that participants are given full information before they agree to take part in the study, are fully debriefed when it is over and are reassured that their performance was in no way out of the ordinary.

It is a well-accepted principle of psychological research that if researchers are in any way unsure about the procedures in a study and their possible effects on participants, they should ask a colleague for advice. Ideally, this should be someone who has carried out similar research, and who will not be affected by the outcome of the research, so can offer an unbiased opinion. Milgram carried out this consultation process fully, seeking advice from several psychiatrists. The general consensus was that fewer than one person in 100 would continue to obey up to the point of giving 450 V shocks. As is well known, their predictions were wildly inaccurate in this case. Nevertheless, the basic principle of consulting colleagues when in doubt can help to ensure that any possible harm to participants, if not eliminated, is at least minimised.

Protection from harm is a contentious issue in some circumstances. For example, in Milgram's study, it is highly likely that, in spite of the thorough debriefing Milgram provided, at least some participants did not leave the study in the same frame of mind as that in which they arrived. They left with the realisation that they were willing to harm an innocent person when instructed to do so, which may well have had a negative effect on their self-image and self-esteem. However, it can be argued that it is not a psychologist's responsibility to protect people against self-knowledge, even when this knowledge is unwelcome.

Observational studies

In many observational studies, participants are not aware that their behaviour is being observed. They have not consented to take part and are not debriefed afterwards. Deception may also be involved. For example, in a study by West et al.

(1975), a female confederate or a male confederate stood by the side of the road with the bonnet of a car raised, apparently having broken down, to observe helping behaviour in relation to gender. This kind of study calls for what is termed **involuntary participation** and may involve **invasion of privacy**.

It could be argued that if a behaviour occurs in a public place, consent is implicitly being given for it to be observed. Certainly, if the observation is concerned with something as uncontroversial as looking at factors that influence people to hold doors open for others, ethical problems are relatively minimal. However, this is not so clear cut if the observation relates to how parents interact with their children, or public courtship behaviour. A study carried out by Humphreys (1970) illustrates this in rather an extreme form. He investigated the behaviour of consenting gay men, himself acting as 'lookout' at a public convenience. The men had no idea that they were being studied, nor that Humphreys was noting down their car registration numbers so he could obtain more background information later on. It seems highly unlikely that the men would have given consent had they known what was going on.

Psychology and the ethical imperative

Brehm (1956) claimed that 'We must not overlook the other side of the ethical issue: the ethical imperative to gain more understanding of important areas of human behaviour'. The BPS guidelines suggest that increasing our understanding of human behaviour improves people's lives and 'enhances human dignity'. In other words, if psychology is to contribute to our understanding of human behaviour and improve the quality of people's lives, research must be carried out. But it must be done with an awareness of the rights of, and respect for, participants.

Summary

- The **British Psychological Society (BPS)** has produced **guidelines** for carrying out ethical research in psychology in the UK.
- Ideally, participants should give **fully informed consent** to taking part in a study and can **withdraw** their consent at any time, leaving the study and having their data destroyed.
- **Deception** should be avoided wherever possible, unless full information would invalidate an otherwise ethical study.
- **Debriefing** is essential, particularly when full information about the study has not been given at the outset.
- **Confidentiality** should be observed except in the rare cases when the researcher feels that he or she has a wider social responsibility to breach it.
- Participants should be **protected from harm**. If in doubt about this aspect of his or her study, the researcher should **consult colleagues** before carrying it out.
- **Observational studies** raise the issue of **invasion of privacy**, where people are unaware that they are being observed.
- Although research raises ethical concerns, there is an **ethical imperative** for studies to be carried out.

Data analysis and presentation

Quantitative data are analysed using statistical tests, which are known as **inferential statistics**. These tests give information about the likelihood of a result, for example a difference between conditions in the DV of an experiment, having come about by chance. If the probability of a chance difference is very small — conventionally in psychology, equal to or less than 5% — then the difference is considered to be significant. The results are then interpreted in terms of the manipulation of the IV having caused the difference in the DV. Similarly, in correlational analysis, statistical tests tell us the probability of a relationship between the two variables being measured coming about by chance. Again, if this is equal to or less than 5%, it is accepted that there is a genuine relationship, either positive or negative, between the variables.

Descriptive statistics refers to ways in which quantitative data can be summarised or presented so that they are easily accessible. One way in which this can be done is to use **measures of central tendency** and **measures of dispersion**, which are ways of summarising the data provided by all the participants. Charts and graphs can also be used to present a clear overview of the findings of a study. We will look at each of these in turn.

Measures of central tendency

Quite often, research tests a great many participants, in some cases thousands. A measure of central tendency is a way of reducing a set of numerical data to one value, to give an average of the findings. Three different measures are used: the mean, the median and the mode. Which is used will depend on the nature of the data collected, as each has strengths and drawbacks.

For the **mean**, the scores of every participant are added together and the total is divided by the number of participants. This measure is used when the data collected are precise, such as the time in seconds that it takes to complete a task. To calculate a mean, all the scores are taken into the calculation. Their values are important: if one value is changed, then the mean will be changed too. Therefore, this measure has the advantages of using all the data in its calculation, making it a **sensitive measure**. However, it is not always appropriate. For example, the average number of children in a British family is 2.4, but there are no families who actually have 2.4 children! This measure can also be misleading. Let us take a set of scores on a memory test: 4 23 25 26 27 27 29. The mean here would be 161 ÷ 7 = 23, even though five of the seven scores are higher than 23; the extreme score of 4 has reduced the mean, giving a distorted view of the test results.

The **median** is a less precise measure. It is used when the scores themselves are less precise, such as ratings on a rating scale. The median would be the measure used to find the average rating of a behaviour, given by a group of observers. If a set of scores is put in numerical order, the central score is the median. If there is an even number of scores, the two central scores are added together and divided by 2. Like the mean, this measure takes all the scores into account. It has the advantage over the mean of not being distorted by an extreme score. However, it does not use all the information provided by the scores. Using the same set of scores as we did for the mean, the median would be 26, but it would still be 26 even if the lowest score were 7, or 12, instead of 4. It is therefore not as sensitive a measure as the mean. Sometimes it is not even an actual score. For example, for this set of scores: 23 25 26 27 27 29, as there are an even number of scores, the median would be 26 + 27 ÷ 2 = 26.5.

The **mode** is the most frequently occurring score. This is the measure used when behaviour is put into categories rather than measured: it describes which category is most heavily populated. Sometimes there may be two equally frequent scores, in which case there are two modes, known as **bimodal values**, or even more, giving **multimodal values**. This measure has the advantage of always being an actual score, and like the median it is not distorted by an extreme value. However, it does not use the values of all the scores in its calculation, nor all the scores themselves, so it is the least sensitive measure of central tendency. Table 4.4 summarises the advantages and disadvantages of all three measures of central tendency.

Table 4.4 Mean, median and mode: advantages and disadvantages

Measure of central tendency	Advantage	Disadvantage
Mean	Uses all the scores	Is not always an actual score
	Uses the values of all the scores	Is distorted by an extreme value
Median	Uses all the scores	Is not always an actual score
	Is not distorted by an extreme value	Does not use the values of all the scores
Mode	Is always an actual score	Does not use all the scores
	Is not distorted by an extreme value	Does not use the values of all the scores

Measures of dispersion

Measures of dispersion are another way of summarising data. These give an indication of how spread out the scores are, i.e. the extent to which they deviate from the measure of central tendency. If we take two sets of scores: 8 9 10 11 12 and 4 6 10 14 16, the mean in each case would be the same, i.e. 10. However, the second set of scores is more widely spread than the first set, so a measure of dispersion adds to the information provided by a measure of central tendency.

A simple way of expressing the spread of scores is to use the **range**. It is normally used when the data are rather imprecise, such as ratings, where the median would be used as the measure of central tendency. The range is simply the smallest score subtracted from the largest score. In the previous example, the range in each case would be 12 − 8 = 4, and 16 − 4 = 12. For technical reasons, if there is an even number of scores, 1 is usually added to this figure, so in this set of scores: 4 6 7 7 9 10, the range would be 10 − 4 + 1 = 7. If the values are calculated to one decimal place, for example the extreme scores are 4.2 and 10.3, 0.1 is added, so the range here would be 6.2. Similarly, if the calculation is to two decimal places, for example 4.24 and 10.75, 0.01 is added, so the range here would be 6.52.

When using the range, the smaller the figure, the more closely clustered the scores are around the median.

This measure has the advantage of being simple to work out. However, like the mean, it is distorted by an extreme score, out of line with the other scores. For example, in this set of scores: 2 17 19 19 23 24 26 27, the range is $27 - 2 + 1 = 26$. This is misleading since the set of scores minus the smallest member has a range of $27 - 17 = 10$. To overcome this drawback, the **interquartile range** is used. The range is calculated using the middle 50% of score. In this case, the interquartile range would be $24 - 19 + 1 = 6$. This avoids the distortion produced by an extreme score. Again, the smaller this figure is, the more tightly clustered the set of scores is.

The **standard deviation** is a more precise and sophisticated measure of dispersion. It is used with precise data, where the mean would be used as the measure of central tendency. This measure calculates the average difference from the mean of all the scores, and is more sensitive than the range because it uses the values of all the scores to make the calculation, rather than just the extreme scores.

Summary

- **Inferential statistics** refers to statistical tests that provide information about the likelihood of a result coming about by chance.
- **Descriptive statistics** are ways of summarising large amounts of data. They include **measures of central tendency** and **measures of dispersion**, together with charts and graphs.
- The **mean**, **median** and **mode** are all measures of central tendency, i.e. ways of describing average scores.
- The **mean** is the **most sensitive**, and the **mode** the **least sensitive**.
- All these measures of central tendency have **strengths** and **drawbacks**.
- The **range**, the **interquartile range** and the **standard deviation** are **measures of dispersion**.
- The standard deviation is calculated when the data are precise, while the range and interquartile range are used for less precise data.

Graphical presentation of data

Various kinds of graphs, appropriately titled and labelled, are used in presenting quantitative data, providing a *visual* summary of facts and figures. The simplest graphical presentation of information is a **bar chart** (or **bar graph**). Bar charts are often used to show the means or medians for the different conditions of an experiment, or the percentages of participants who fall into different categories. They therefore allow visual comparisons to be made easily.

The first chart in Figure 4.1 shows the means for a memory experiment, such as that of Bower (described in Chapter 2), comparing recall for words presented in a semantic hierarchy with that for words presented randomly. The second chart in Figure 4.1 compares the pro-social behaviour of males and females in terms of helping someone to pick up dropped groceries.

Figure 4.1 Examples of bar charts

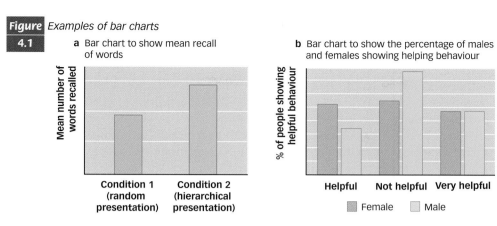

a Bar chart to show mean recall of words

b Bar chart to show the percentage of males and females showing helping behaviour

Data from correlational studies are presented using a **scattergraph**. Each of the two variables being correlated is represented on one of the axes. For example, in the Kanner et al. (1981) study investigating the relationship between the experience of daily hassles and psychological symptoms of stress, one axis would be labelled 'Experience of hassles' and the other 'Symptoms of stress'. The point where the two scores of each individual intersect is marked (see Figure 4.2).

Figure 4.2 Examples of scattergraphs

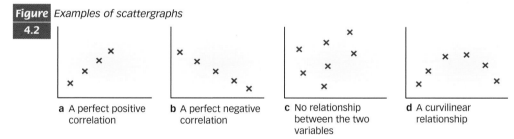

a A perfect positive correlation

b A perfect negative correlation

c No relationship between the two variables

d A curvilinear relationship

In practice there is rarely a perfect positive or a perfect negative correlation, so it is helpful to draw on **a line of best fit**, i.e. a line that is as close as possible to all the points that have been marked. This will indicate the direction of any relationship. The closeness to this line of the points marked suggests how strong that relationship is: the closer the points, the stronger the relationship. Any **outliers**, i.e. points well away from the line, will indicate a reduction in the size of the relationship (see Figure 4.3).

Figure 4.3 Scattergraph with line of best fit marked and outliers identified

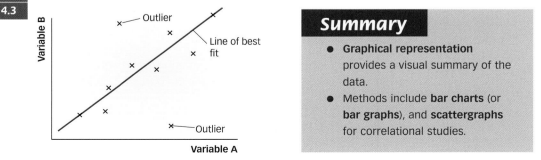

Summary

- **Graphical representation** provides a visual summary of the data.
- Methods include **bar charts** (or **bar graphs**), and **scattergraphs** for correlational studies.

Presentation of qualitative data

Qualitative data are essentially **descriptive**, rather than focusing on measurement. However, although the main emphasis is on detailed description of behaviour, the data may quite often be put into **categories**, and percentages in each category given. An example is the Strange Situation (see Chapter 3). In Ainsworth's original use of this technique, the percentages of children falling into each of the three categories that she identified were reported. Graphical techniques such as bar charts can be used to display this kind of information. The use of categorisation is widespread in qualitative research, but does not necessarily involve quantitative analysis.

Although the presentation of qualitative data is descriptive, many of the same principles apply as with quantitative data. Information needs to be presented in such a way as to give a clear picture of what are felt to be important aspects of the findings, in a structured way and with evidence to support the analysis of the data.

Along with categorisation, one way in which the presentation of data can be structured is the use of **thematic analysis**, where themes that emerge from the material are identified and discussed. For example, a researcher might interview participants about their beliefs relating to what is important in caring for children. Here, themes that arose in the interviews, such as the role of fathers or the flexibility of childcare arrangements, could be identified and explored,

A study by Stevenson et al. (2007) is an example of thematic analysis. In the context of growing concern about obesity, the researchers were interested in what stops young people eating healthily. They asked groups of teenagers to discuss healthy eating and analysed their discussions. The analysis identified four themes to emerge: how eating behaviour is reinforced, both physically and psychologically; perceptions of food and eating behaviour; perceptions of contradictory food-related social pressures; and perceptions of the concept of healthy eating itself. The general conclusion to emerge from the researchers' analysis of these themes was that healthy eating did not appear to be a goal in its own right and that young people face competing pressures to eat unhealthily and to lose weight.

With quantitative research, the results of statistical tests provide objective evidence that allows conclusions to be drawn, in terms of the research hypothesis that is being tested. In qualitative research, there is no such objective evidence on which conclusions can be based. Interpretation of the findings is necessarily **subjective**, so it is important that interpretation be supported by evidence drawn from the behaviour that is being analysed. Instead of using statistics such as measures of central tendency and measures of dispersion, specific examples of behaviour can be used to illustrate the main points to emerge. If a verbal interaction is being analysed, for example, quotations can be used to highlight important points.

As mentioned earlier, in observational studies, researchers using qualitative methods also include a **reflexive analysis** with their interpretation of the data. This acknowledges the essentially subjective nature of the analysis and discusses how researchers' own experiences, beliefs and expectations might influence their analysis and interpretation of the data. This analysis may also discuss issues arising from the interpretations that the researchers have made, and suggest other ways that the data might by analysed and interpreted. This is in sharp contrast to studies using quantitative data, where the role of the researchers and the possible influence of their subjectivity on the studies, are not explicitly addressed.

Summary

- Qualitative analysis is **descriptive**, with the meanings of data being **interpreted** by the researcher, supported by evidence arising from the study.
- There is often an element of quantitative analysis in predominantly qualitative studies.
- **Thematic analysis** is one way in which the data can be structured.
- Qualitative research acknowledges the role of the researcher in the study through a **reflexive analysis**.

Content analysis

Content analysis is a method that does not analyse people directly, but instead examines what they produce, for example films, television programmes, books, newspaper and magazine articles, advertisements, nursery rhymes, pop music lyrics, children's drawings and even psychology journals, such as a study carried out by Carter and Forsyth (2007) into the treatment of race and culture in seven forensic psychology journals.

For example, Robinson et al. (2007) were interested in the possible influence of films on the views — often negative — that young children hold of older people. Their research looked at how older people are represented in Disney animated films. They found that while most older characters were portrayed positively, there were quite a few who were portrayed in a negative way.

Although content analysis is generally largely qualitative, there is often also an element of quantitative analysis. For example, Chermak and Chapman (2007) carried out a qualitative analysis of the presentation of crime stories in the media in American cities of different sizes and with very different crime rates. However, as well as content analysis, they also used statistical techniques to explore the factors that influenced the prominence given to crime stories in the media, such as how serious the crime was and the occupation of the defendant. They emphasised the usefulness of using both quantitative and qualitative techniques in this kind of study.

In carrying out a content analysis, once the topic to be explored has been decided, the first step is **sampling**, i.e. deciding what material will make up the sample to be analysed. For example, if magazine articles are to be examined, which magazines will be used? Are they representative of the topic in which the researcher is interested?

The next step is to develop **coding units**, i.e. categories into which the material is to be divided. For example, in the Disney films study, the categories used were gender, race, appearance, role, personality and physical characteristics. The researcher will not only record instances where these are relevant in the material being analysed, but also where they are missing, for example the lack of older female characters in particular kinds of film. Coding can take the form of simply recording instances of a particular category, or could be more complex, such as **ranking** items in terms of the coverage that they are given, or using **rating scales** (e.g. rating the amount of detail in children's drawings). These kinds of data allow statistical analysis to be carried out, together with a more qualitative analysis of the data.

As with other kinds of research, a form of **pilot study** is likely to be done, with coders practising use of the coding system, and employing materials similar to those that will be used in the real study before it is carried out. This helps to establish whether the coding system is adequate and appropriate. Studies may also attempt to reduce researcher bias, by using coders who are unaware of the aims of the study.

Summary

- **Content analysis** analyses people **indirectly** through what they produce.
- It often combines **quantitative** with **qualitative** analysis.
- The process involves **sampling** material and using **coding units**.

Terms explained

generalisation: applying the findings and conclusions of a study beyond the participants and specific situation of the study.

hypothesis: a precise prediction made at the outset of a study, stating what the outcome is expected to be.

replication: repeating a study as precisely as possible with different participants on a different occasion, to see whether there are broadly similar findings. This is important in allowing the findings to be generalised. It will establish whether the findings of the original study have come about by chance, and can lend support to a psychological theory.

AQA (A)
AS Psychology

Unit 2:

Biological psychology, social psychology and individual differences

Chapter 5

Stress

The nature of stress

Most people claim to have experienced stress at some point, but how stress is defined and what it involves is rather more complex within psychology than in everyday usage. We tend to think of stress as something unpleasant, but broadly speaking it can be seen as a response to any kind of stimulation. The absence of stress would therefore mean the lack of any kind of stimulation, so using this definition, a certain amount of stress can be seen as beneficial. Indeed, Selye (1974) distinguishes between **distress**, where stress is perceived negatively, and **eustress**, the pleasant stress that we experience, for example, when we take part in moderate exercise. However, in this chapter, we will be concentrating on the more negative side of stress.

Stress can be related to the **Yerkes-Dodson Law**, which states that performance is linked to arousal (see Figure 5.1). If we are to perform effectively, we need a certain amount of arousal. For example, it is difficult to carry out a task like making notes on a psychology topic if you are half asleep. However, there is an optimal level of arousal, and if arousal increases beyond this point (see the shaded part in Figure 5.1), performance deteriorates and we experience stress. The more complex the task that we are attempting to carry out, the lower the optimal level of arousal (see Figure 5.2).

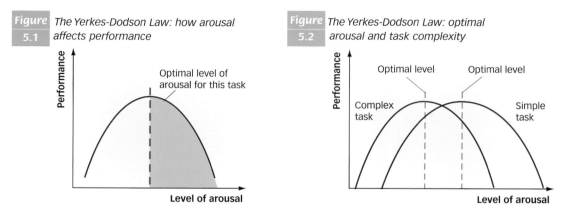

Figure 5.1 *The Yerkes-Dodson Law: how arousal affects performance*

Figure 5.2 *The Yerkes-Dodson Law: optimal arousal and task complexity*

Cox (1975) has suggested that there are three models of stress, each of which places a different emphasis on internal and external factors. The first is the **engineering model**. A metal structure like a bridge, if heavily used, will become weakened and eventually suffer from metal fatigue. In the same way, people become stressed as the result of their experiences. This model therefore looks at **external causes** of stress. Some of these causes, such as life events, will be examined later in the chapter.

The second, **physiological model**, focuses on **internal factors**. It is concerned with how our bodies respond to a **stressor**, which is anything that causes stress. Selye (1956) defines stress as 'the non-specific response of the body to any demands made on it'. We will be looking at the physiological stress response in the next section.

The third stress model is the **transactional model** (see Figure 5.3), which sees stress in terms of an interaction between people and their environment, and thus focuses on the **relationship between external and internal factors**. It is concerned with the relationship between external stressors, the physiological stress response and ways of coping with stress. In this model, stress may be defined as an imbalance between a person's perception of the demands that a situation makes on the individual, and that person's estimation of his or her ability to cope with these demands. Note that this definition is not concerned with an objective appraisal of the actual demands that a situation makes on a person, but the person's *perception* of these demands. If two people are faced with similar situations, one might feel that it is more than they can cope with, while another might find it perfectly manageable. There are individual differences in what is felt to be stressful and the precise physiological response to a stressful situation.

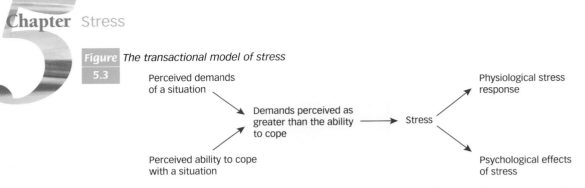

Figure 5.3 *The transactional model of stress*

The effects of stress are both physical and psychological. As well as the immediate physiological response, stress has been linked to physical illness, such as heart disease, ulcers and headaches. The psychological effects can be emotional (such as poor self-esteem), cognitive (such as difficulty in concentrating) and behavioural (such as restlessness and excessive drinking).

Along with the causes, processes and effects of stress, psychologists are also interested in strategies that can be used to cope with it. There are individual differences here, too, in terms of how stress and its effects may best be combated. A variety of methods for dealing with stress, both physical and psychological, have been put forward, and some of these will be looked at later in the chapter.

Summary

- Models of stress look at **external** factors leading to stress, the **internal** physiological response to stress, or the **interaction** of the two.
- There are **individual differences** in the experience of stress.
- Stress has **physical** and **psychological effects**.
- Psychologists are also interested in **coping strategies** for dealing with stress and in **stress management** techniques.

The physiological response to stress

We need to start with a brief outline of those aspects of physiology that relate to stress. The stress response basically involves the **autonomic nervous system (ANS)**. The ANS regulates many aspects of our functioning over which we do not need to have conscious control, such as breathing and digestion. This system controls certain internal organs, such as the heart and the gut, and a number of glands, such as the salivary and adrenal glands. It achieves its effects via the **endocrine system**, which is made up of glands that secrete hormones into the bloodstream, which in turn control ANS activity.

The ANS has two sub-systems, the **sympathetic nervous system (SNS)** and the **parasympathetic nervous system (PNS)**. These sub-systems are generally in balance, but when the SNS is dominant, there is a pattern of arousal, associated with physical activity, whereas when the PNS is dominant, there is a pattern of relaxation. It is the sympathetic nervous system that is active in the stress response.

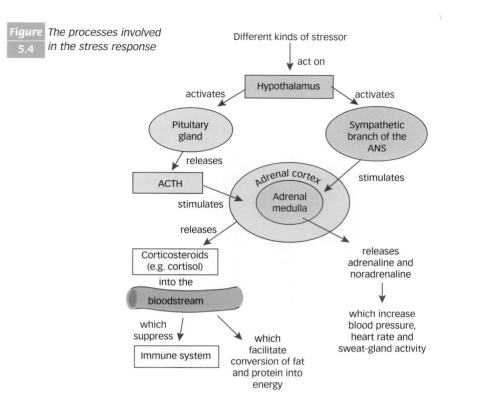

Figure 5.4 *The processes involved in the stress response*

The **hypothalamic–pituitary–adrenal axis** is highly sensitive to environmental change and is the main system involved in the stress response. The elements that make up this system are the hypothalamus, the pituitary gland and the adrenal glands.

The **hypothalamus** is a small structure in the forebrain, just above the pituitary gland, to which it is connected by a structure called the infundibulum. Through this connection, the hypothalamus controls the secretion of all the hormones released by the pituitary gland. The hypothalamus controls ANS centres in the brain stem, which in turn control the ANS. It is particularly involved in states of arousal and is therefore important in the stress response.

We have two **adrenal glands**, situated above the kidneys, each made up of the **adrenal medulla** and the **adrenal cortex**. The **pituitary gland**, at the base of the brain, controls the adrenal cortex. When the adrenal cortex is stimulated by the pituitary hormone **adrenocorticotrophic hormone (ACTH)**, it secretes **corticosteroids** into the bloodstream. Even very mild stimuli, particularly if they are unexpected, can trigger the release of ACTH and set this process in motion. There are many different corticosteroids, but those relevant to stress are the **glucocorticoids**, for example, **cortisol**. High levels of this hormone are found in the urine of someone who is experiencing stress. Glucocorticoids facilitate the conversion of stored fat and protein into energy. They also suppress the body's **immune system**.

The ANS controls the adrenal medulla. When stimulated, the adrenal medulla releases two hormones into the bloodstream, **adrenaline** and **noradrenaline**. These increase heart rate, blood pressure and sweat-gland activity. They also mobilise fat reserves, in preparation for energy expenditure, so they prolong the effects of SNS arousal. There are thus two pathways involved in our physiological response to stress.

The General Adaptation Syndrome

On the basis of experiments with rats, which he exposed to a wide range of stressors — including extreme cold, electric shocks, surgical trauma, large doses of drugs and fatigue — Selye (1956) proposed that the physiological response to stress is always the same, irrespective of the nature of the stressor. He called this the **General Adaptation Syndrome (GAS)** and described three stages of the stress response: the **alarm reaction**, the **resistance stage** and **exhaustion**. You may also find the GAS referred to as the **pituitary-adrenal stress syndrome** because, as we have seen, the pituitary and adrenal glands play a major part in the stress response.

The alarm reaction is concerned with the physiological changes associated with arousal. There are two parts, the first of which is the **shock phase**, an immediate reaction to a stressor. This first phase depends mainly on the sympathetic adrenal medullary system and prepares the body for what Cannon (1929) has called '**fight or flight**', i.e. a behavioural response to a stressful situation. The person experiences tachycardia (an abnormally rapid heartbeat) and a lowering of both temperature and blood pressure. This is followed by the **counter-shock phase**, as the body tries to defend itself against the effects of the stressor and minimise damage. This involves the hypothalamic–pituitary–adrenocortical axis. The high levels of cortisol released in this phase are useful in coping with stress as they maintain a steady supply of fuel. However, the suppression of the immune system by glucocorticoids means that the person is more open to infection and illness, a consequence of stress that will be examined later in the chapter.

Preparation of the body for 'fight or flight' can be understood in evolutionary terms. Long ago in our evolutionary history, when a person was under extreme stress, such as being faced with a predator or having a stranger encroaching on his or her territory, there would be two ways of dealing with the situation: fighting off the attack or running away, both of which require physical action. There are a number of different aspects to the shock phase of the alarm reaction that would facilitate either course of action (see Table 5.1).

In our evolutionary past, the fight-or-flight response was adaptive in facilitating physical ways of dealing with stress, and it continues to be triggered as our bodies' response to stress. However, many of the stressful events and situations that we now experience cannot be dealt with by taking physical action, so this response has become maladaptive. There is no outlet for the physical responses demanded by the alarm reaction, with the result that these responses can harm our health.

The pattern of activity in the fight-or-flight response of the alarm stage cannot be maintained for long. The body then moves into the resistance stage, where it starts to recover and adapts to the stressor. The symptoms shown in the alarm stage become much less intense or disappear altogether. There is a decrease in SNS

Table 5.1 *Physiological responses in the shock phase and their functions*

Activity in the shock phase of the alarm response	Function of the response
Pupil dilation	Increases awareness of external stimuli and thus the ability to respond to them
Bronchial tubes dilate to accelerate airflow	More oxygen is taken into the lungs; muscles require oxygen to work effectively
Heartbeat increases	Speeds up blood circulation and so carries oxygen more quickly to the muscles
Sugar metabolism is speeded up	Provides an instant supply of energy
Spleen releases red blood cells	Allows the blood to carry more oxygen
Additional blood platelets are produced	Assist clotting and so prepare the body to repair potential physical damage
Sweating	Cools down the body
Neurotransmitters called endorphins are produced	Block immediate feelings of pain

activity, with less adrenaline and noradrenaline being released. If the stressor is removed, the body will revert to normal functioning. Although it may be some time before raised hormone levels return to normal, there is little chance of any permanent damage.

If the stressor persists, the parasympathetic nervous system (PNS) branch of the ANS acts to return the functioning of internal organs, such as the heart, to normal. However, the body is only partially successful in defending itself against the effects of stressors. Cell repair is inhibited and the immune system may be damaged, making the body more vulnerable to infection and disease. If the stressor is severe and experienced over a long period of time, the final exhaustion stage follows. If there is a second stressor, resistance is lower and the exhaustion stage is reached more quickly (Figure 5.5).

Figure 5.5 *The effects of a second stressor*

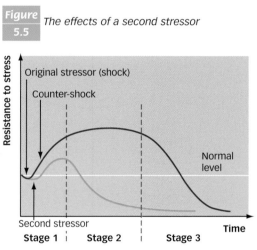

In the exhaustion stage, heart rate and blood pressure return to apparently normal levels, but the excessive levels of adrenaline and noradrenaline in the bloodstream cause the adrenal glands to stop functioning properly. Symptoms shown in the alarm stage reappear, body tissues and internal organs are likely to be adversely affected, and even mild sources of additional stress cause an immediate and strong reaction. At this stage, resistance to illness is lowered, due to suppression of the immune system. It is at this stage that what Selye refers to as **illnesses of adaptation**, such as ulcers and coronary heart disease, can occur. If stress continues, the individual suffers from **burnout**, when he or she is no longer able to function adequately and may even die.

The GAS model (Figure 5.6) provides a useful guide to the physiological responses to stress. However, it was based on research using non-human animals, so it is limited in its extrapolation from animals to humans. More importantly, it does not take into account psychological factors in the stress response, in particular the cognitive appraisal of the situation, emphasised in the transactional model of stress (see Figure 5.3, page 132).

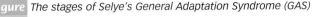

Figure 5.6 *The stages of Selye's General Adaptation Syndrome (GAS)*

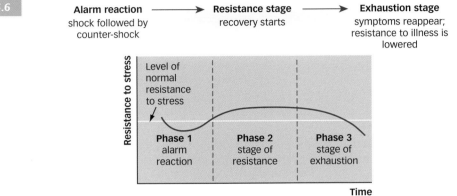

Summary

- The autonomic nervous system, or **ANS**, and in particular the sympathetic branch of the system, is involved in the physiological response to a stressor.
- Selye's **General Adaptation Syndrome (GAS)** describes the stress response in three stages: the **alarm reaction**, the **resistance stage** and the **exhaustion stage**.
- In the first stage, the body prepares itself for the physical response of '**fight or flight**'.
- Prolonged stress is associated with **illness**.
- Selye's model does not take into account **psychological responses** to stress.

Stress-related illness and the immune system

As we saw in the previous section, one of the effects of stress is to suppress the immune system, thus making the stressed individual more vulnerable to illness. However, Evans et al. (1997) found that this vulnerability results only from **chronic stress**, i.e. where stress is prolonged, such as the stress associated with divorce. **Acute stress**, which is short-lived, such as working to a deadline, does not have this effect. It seems that we are able to respond to short-term stressors with few ill effects.

Briefly, the immune system consists of a series of defences that work together to stop infections from spreading. When **antigens** are detected, i.e. dangerous foreign bodies such as bacteria or viruses, the immune system stimulates **leucocytes** (white blood cells), such as natural killer cells, to destroy them. It also produces **antibodies** that bind to antigens and identify them as targets to be destroyed. Antibodies remain in the bloodstream and continue to be effective if the same antigens are present on a later occasion. These processes become less effective when the immune system is damaged.

The physical effects of stress on the immune system have been tested directly, for example in the study by Kiecolt-Glaser et al. (1984) (see Box 5.1).

Box 5.1 Kiecolt-Glaser et al. (1984)

Aims: To investigate whether exam stress is associated with a lower immune response, and to identify other factors that may increase or moderate stress.

Procedure: First-year medical students, 49 males and 26 females, gave blood samples one month before their first-year exams as a baseline measure, and again on the first day of their exams, when exam stress was assumed to be at its peak. They also completed question-naires to assess psychiatric symptoms, loneliness and life events.

Results: Natural killer cell activity decreased between the two samples, indicating a weakening of the immune system. Immune responses were particularly weak in those students who reported feeling most lonely, who were experiencing other stressful life events, and in those reporting psychiatric symptoms, such as depression and anxiety.

Conclusions: Stress is associated with a lowered immune response. This is more extreme when stressors other than the immediate stress of exams are taken into account.

This study highlights the role of life events in the stress response, and this will be examined later in the chapter.

The immune system also plays a role in **inflammation**. If you cut yourself, the blood vessels first of all contract to stop the bleeding and allow clotting. They then dilate, so that more blood can flow to the damaged area. The blood carries leucocytes to combat any foreign bodies that might gain access through the wound, so if your immune system is damaged, you become more vulnerable to the effects of foreign bodies, such as **infection,** and a wound may take longer to heal.

Stress impairs the **healing process**, as demonstrated by Marucha et al. (1998) (see Box 5.2).

Box 5.2 Marucha et al. (1998)

Aims: To investigate the effect of psychological stress on wound healing.

Procedure: Small, 3.5 mm wounds were made on the hard palate of 11 dental students, first during a college vacation and then 3 days before a major examination. Healing of the wound in each case was assessed using two measures: daily photographs and a foaming response to hydrogen peroxide (bubbles of oxygen appear on the wound if healing is incomplete).

Results: Wound healing took on average 3 days longer during the examination period than during the vacation, i.e. 40% longer.

Conclusions: Even something as relatively short-lived and mild such as the stress of an upcoming exam can affect the immune system and delay healing.

Similar effects have been demonstrated for longer-term stressors. Kiecolt-Glaser et al. (1995) investigated 13 women who were highly stressed as a result of looking after relatives with dementia. For them, a small cut took on average 24% longer to heal than for a non-stressed control group.

Cohen et al. (1991) explored the link between stress and vulnerability to infection from cold viruses. Their study is summarised in Box 5.3, and the graph in Figure 5.7 shows the results of their investigation.

Box 5.3	**Cohen et al. (1991)**

Aims: To investigate the relationship between the experience of stressful events and susceptibility to a cold virus.

Procedure: Healthy volunteers were injected with a common cold virus. Volunteers in a similar control group were injected with a harmless salt solution. All participants were also given a stress index, based on the number of stressful events that they had experienced in the past year, the extent to which they felt able to cope, and their experience of negative emotions such as anger and depression.

Results: Almost all of those injected with the cold virus showed signs of infection, although only a third developed colds. Even when other factors were taken into account, such as age, diet, use of tobacco and alcohol, and exercise, there was a positive relationship between the stress index and cold symptoms.

Conclusions: People who are stressed are more vulnerable to infection.

Figure 5.7 *Cohen et al. (1991): the relationship between stress and susceptibility to cold viruses*

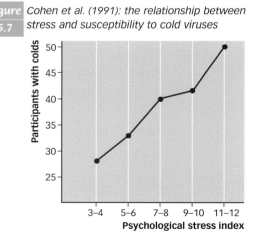

Summary

- **Chronic stress**, rather than acute stress, has been linked to illness.
- Stress impairs the **healing process** and makes people more vulnerable to **infection**.

Stress and serious illness

An early animal study by Brady (1958) demonstrated the link between stress and more serious illness (see Box 5.4).

While this is an animal study, the close similarity between monkeys and humans suggests that the effects of stress may be the same for humans. The use of animals

Box 5.4   Brady (1958)

Aims: To investigate the link between stress and illness in monkeys.

Procedure: Pairs of monkeys were linked to an apparatus that gave electric shocks. Shocks were given every 20 seconds for a period of 6 hours, with the procedure being repeated over several weeks. In each pair, one monkey (the **executive**) could prevent shocks to both monkeys by pressing a lever before the shock was delivered. The other (**yoked**) monkey also had a lever, but pressing it did not prevent shocks.

Results: The executive monkeys developed ulcers; the yoked monkeys did not.

Conclusions: The executive monkeys had to remain constantly vigilant to prevent the shocks, but the yoked monkeys could do nothing to prevent the shocks. Constant vigilance is extremely stressful, and this stress led to the development of ulcers.

in this study allowed researchers to investigate the effects of severe stress in ways that would not have been possible using human participants. However, there was a serious design flaw in the study, in that the monkeys were not randomly allocated to the 'executive' or the 'yoked' condition: only the monkeys who were able to learn that pressing the lever prevented the shock were allocated to the executive condition, so it could be that there were differences between the two groups of monkeys which could account for the differences in outcome for the executive and the yoked monkeys.

There has also been a body of research into a possible link in humans between stress and serious illness, and in particular cancer, coronary heart disease (CHD) and hypertension.

Cancer

Cancer occurs when a body cell begins to replicate out of control, resulting in the presence of many more of this type of cell than there should be. These cells then begin to invade areas of healthy cells, and unless they are destroyed or removed, they eventually cause damage to tissues and organs, and ultimately death. Whenever cancer cells start to multiply, the immune system acts to check their uncontrolled growth, and in a normal healthy person this is successful. However, under stress, resistance to cancer cells may be lowered and cancer more likely to develop because stress suppresses the immune system.

A heightened sensibility to cancer when under stress has been shown in animal research. Visintainer et al. (1983) injected animals with cancer cells. Those that were exposed to stress were more likely to develop tumours than controls that were not stressed. The link between stress and cancer in humans has also been investigated, for example by Jacobs and Charles (1980) (see Box 5.5, page 140).

A meta-analysis of 46 studies, carried out by McKenna et al. (1999), also found an association between the development of breast cancer and stress, while Palesh et al. (2007) found that a history of experiencing stressful life events was associated with the more rapid progression of breast cancer.

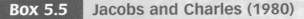

Box 5.5   Jacobs and Charles (1980)

Aims: To investigate a possible association between the development of cancer in children and the experience of stressful life events.

Procedure: The families of 50 children, aged from 3 to 17, were interviewed about the experience of stressful life events during the previous year. Half the children had cancer, while the others were a control group, attending a paediatric clinic for other reasons. Medical records were also consulted to establish the incidence of major stressful life events in the year before the onset of cancer.

Results: Both the interviews and the medical records showed that the cancer group had experienced more frequent stressful life events than controls.

Conclusions: The experience of stressful life events may be linked to the development of cancer in children.

However, stress on its own does not predict the development of cancer. Cancer appears to be caused by an interaction between a number of factors, including hereditary disposition, exposure to environmental factors such as cigarette smoke or asbestos fibres, and changes in the body's immune system. For example, Jacobs and Bovasso (2000) found a stronger association between chronic depression and the development of cancer than between cancer and recent stressful experiences. The role of personality factors in the experience of stress will be examined later in this chapter.

Coronary heart disease

The development of **coronary heart disease (CHD)** has also been linked to stress. There are several factors that make a person more vulnerable to CHD, including smoking, heavy drinking, poor diet, obesity and lack of exercise. CHD is the result of atherosclerosis, a thickening of the walls of the coronary arteries that reduces or blocks the blood supply to the heart. Atherosclerosis can be explained in terms of the fight-or-flight response to stress. This response releases hormones into the bloodstream, raising the heart rate and resulting in stores of fat being released to provide more energy. If physical action is taken, these fat stores are used as energy, but if not, they may be deposited on the walls of blood vessels and create the blockages that restrict the blood supply to the heart, leading to CHD.

In the late 1950s, two cardiologists, Friedman and Rosenman, found that men were much more likely to develop CHD than women, even though there were no real gender differences in predisposing factors to account for their finding. At this time, most men worked and most women did not, so they suggested that work-related stress might account for this difference. They went on to suggest that whether or not a man was vulnerable to developing CHD was related to personality type. They drew a distinction between people with what they called a **Type A** personality, who would be more vulnerable, and those classified as **Type B**, who would be less vulnerable (see Table 5.2).

Friedman and Rosenman investigated the possible role of personality differences in CHD, in a classic study in 1974 (see Box 5.6).

Table 5.2 *Personality: Type A and Type B*

The Type A personality	The Type B personality
Is very competitive	Is less competitive
Is highly motivated to achieve	Is equally ambitious, but not dominated by ambition
Is restless and hyper-alert	Is relaxed
Constantly feels under time pressure	Makes time for leisure activities, family and friends
Is angry	Is not easily angered
Is impatient, hostile, cynical, a perfectionist, and needs to be admired	Is easy-going, forgiving and understanding

Box 5.6 Friedman and Rosenman (1974)

Aims: To investigate a possible correlation between Type A personality and vulnerability to CHD.

Procedure: Several thousand healthy men, aged 39–59, were studied over a period of 9 years. They were interviewed about their eating habits and how they responded in stressful situations, and their behaviour during the interview was also assessed, focusing in particular on impatience, hostility and competitiveness. On the basis of the data gathered during the interview and observation, the participants were divided into two roughly equal groups, Type A and Type B, with sub-groups who were not fully either Type A or Type B. The death rates of the two main groups were compared.

Results: Over the 9 years, 275 participants died from CHD. Nearly 70% of them were in the Type A group. Nearly twice as many Type A as Type B participants died, even when other factors associated with heart disease, such as smoking and obesity, were taken into account. Type A participants also had higher levels of stress hormones, such as adrenaline and noradrenaline, than those who were Type B. There was a moderate but significant correlation between personality type and vulnerability to CHD.

Conclusions: Having a Type A personality predisposes people to CHD.

This research implies that Type A characteristics need to be modified to minimise the risk of developing CHD. It was extremely influential in triggering further research into the effects of stress on the immune system and into the link between stress and illness. However, there are some problems with this study. The division of participants into Type A and Type B was rather crude (even taking the sub-groups into account), in that there are likely to be gradations in the extent to which a person meets the criteria for being assigned to either type. Moreover, the study does not report on which elements of the Type A personality are associated with a vulnerability to CHD. It is also a correlational study, and correlation does not show cause and effect. It may be that rather than the Type A personality leading to higher physiological reactivity, and thus to higher levels of stress and ultimately illness, it might be that genetically determined physiological reactivity is what leads to the development of a Type A personality.

Replications of this research have produced mixed results. While some studies have provided support for the findings of Friedman and Rosenman, Mathews (1984) found a much weaker relationship between Type A personality and CHD, while Ragland and Brand (1988) found no difference between Type A and Type B men in terms of the likelihood of developing CHD. Indeed, their findings suggested that Type A men might in fact be at less risk.

It may be possible to make sense of these rather contradictory findings by differentiating between the various elements of the Type A personality. Dembroski and Costa (1988) suggested that the key factors are hostility, anger and vigorous speech. Williams (1984) found that Type A people with a cynical and hostile outlook on life have an increased risk of developing CHD, while those with a positive outlook actually have a lowered risk. It appears that the hostility component of the Type A personality, rather than the Type A personality itself, might be the risk factor.

Hypertension

Hypertension is a state of chronically high blood pressure. Occasionally it has a physical cause, such as kidney disease, but usually there is no obvious medical cause. Hypertension carries an increased risk of stroke and can lead to CHD, but it has also been linked to stress, for example in a study by Harburg et al. (1973) (see Box 5.7).

Box 5.7	**Harburg et al. (1973)**

Aims: To investigate a possible association between stress and hypertension.

Procedure: Participants living in Denver were divided into 'high stress' and 'low stress' groups, depending on the area in which they lived. A 'high stress' area was one where there was a high crime rate, high population density and high level of poverty. The incidence of hypertension in the two groups was compared.

Results: Participants in the 'high stress' group were more likely to suffer from hypertension than those in the 'low stress' group.

Conclusions: There is some evidence of a link between environmental stressors and hypertension.

Similarly, Cobb and Rose (1973) investigated rates of hypertension in air traffic controllers, whose jobs require constant vigilance because mistakes have potentially very serious consequences, and so are very stressful. The incidence of hypertension among air traffic controllers was compared with that among airmen in a less stressful job. Cobb and Rose found that the incidence of hypertension was several times higher for the air traffic controllers than for the airmen.

These findings need to be interpreted with caution, as there are likely to be many other factors associated with hypertension that could not be controlled for in these studies. Nonetheless, stress may be a factor in the development of hypertension.

Summary

- **Animal studies** have demonstrated a link between stress and the development of **ulcers**.
- While there are many factors in the development of **cancer**, stressful **life events** may lead to a vulnerability to cancer and to its more rapid progression.
- **Coronary heart disease (CHD)** can be linked to the **fight-or-flight response** to stress.
- Vulnerability to CHD has been associated with **Type A personality** characteristics, though the nature of the association is not straightforward.
- **Hypertension** may also be caused by stress.

Life changes and daily hassles

Life changes have already been mentioned in relation to stress. For example, Marucha et al. (1998) showed that exam stress led to slower healing, and Kiecolt-Glaser et al. (1995) found the same for people who experienced the long-term stress of looking after relatives with dementia. The Jacobs and Charles (1980) study suggested a link between stressful life events and the development of cancer in children.

The effects of life changes on levels of stress were investigated systematically by Holmes and Rahe (1967). They developed the **Social Readjustment Rating Scale (SRRS)**, which linked life events to stress and illness. The basic principle was that any life change — whether pleasant or unpleasant — is stressful, because it requires us to adapt to new circumstances. The scale ranked 43 life events in terms of their stressfulness, and was developed using patients' records to identify the life events that the individuals had experienced in the months before they became ill. One hundred independent people were asked to rate each event in terms of how much change it would bring about in a person's life, and these ratings were used to give each event a **LCU (life change unit)** score, using a numerical scale up to 100 (see Table 5.3).

| Table 5.3 | Sample items from the SRRS (from Holmes and Rahe, 1967) |

Life event	LCU
Death of a spouse	100
Divorce	73
Marital separation	65
Death of a close family member	63
Jail sentence	63
Marriage	50
Fired from work	47
Marital reconciliation	45
Gain of new family member	39
Sex difficulties	39
Change in financial state	38
Change in number of arguments with spouse	35
Son or daughter leaves home	29
Outstanding personal achievement	28
Trouble with the boss	23
Change in residence	20
Change in social activities	18
Holiday	13
Christmas	12

Holmes and Rahe claimed that an LCU score of more than 300 for events during the previous year was associated with a range of serious health problems, such as diabetes, stroke and leukaemia, as well as less serious everyday problems, such as headaches and colds. Research conducted by Rahe et al. in 1970 supported this idea (see Box 5.8, page 144).

Similarly, Rahe and Arthur (1977) found that people with high LCU scores were more likely to develop physical and psychological illnesses, more susceptible to sports injuries, and more likely to be involved in traffic accidents.

The SRRS is important in focusing on the idea that life events can have a major effect on our physical and psychological health. It provides a structure that has facilitated research in this area. However, some criticisms can be made of this approach.

First, the evidence is **correlational**, but it is interpreted in terms of the stressors listed on the scale causing illness. In some cases, it could be argued that rather than the stress associated with life events causing illness, illness may instead bring about life events. For example, if people are ill, they may not perform as well as they usually do at work, which could lead to 'trouble with the boss'. Similarly, the early

Box 5.8 **Rahe et al. (1970)**

Aims: To find out whether there is a relationship between the number of LCUs recently experienced and physical illness.

Procedure: Two thousand five hundred naval personnel filled in a questionnaire relating to significant changes in their lives, both positive and negative, in the previous 6 months. An LCU was assigned to each event, and total LCUs were calculated for each person. During the 6-month tour of duty, the ship's doctor kept a health record for each participant. The results were tested for a correlation between illness and LCUs.

Results: There was a small but significant correlation (+0.118) between LCUs and illness.

Conclusions: Life changes, whether positive or negative, have a significant positive relationship with physical illness.

stages of illness could lead to 'change in number of arguments with spouse'. It should also be noted that the correlations found in research using the SRRS, while significant, are usually relatively small.

In addition, the SRRS does not take into account **individual differences** in responses to the listed life events. For example, Christmas could be an extremely stressful time if you are short of money and have several children expecting expensive presents, if you have in-laws coming to stay but you do not get on with them, or if you spend it alone and feel lonely or not valued. On the other hand, Christmas could just be seen as an opportunity for a few days off work and as an event that is not particularly important. The effects of even the most stressful life change — death of a spouse — will also vary according to the individual, depending, for example, on religious beliefs, whether the person died unexpectedly or at the end of a long and painful illness, or indeed one's feelings towards the spouse. Taking these possible variations into consideration, it seems overly simplistic to give a general score to a particular event. Indeed, Lazarus and Folkman (1984) found that how life events are perceived and managed plays a crucial role in their impact.

A further aspect to consider is that the SRRS only looks at **crisis events**, which by definition do not happen often. It does not take into account the effects of longer-term stressors, such as being in a job that you do not like, or looking after a relative with dementia, as in the Kiecolt-Glaser et al. (1995) study. The stress involved here would be long term and gradual. A person could therefore be extremely stressed without having experienced any of the stressors on the SRRS. This supports the findings of Evans et al. (1997), mentioned earlier, which suggested vulnerability to illness results from *chronic* stress rather than short-term acute stress.

Kanner et al. (1981) took a different approach, suggesting that it may not be so much the impact of major life events that leads to stress, but rather the **everyday hassles** that we all experience, such as missing a bus or not being able to find the car keys. They also suggested that, conversely, **uplifts** — minor everyday occurrences, such as someone thanking you for holding a door open for them, or the sun shining — might have a positive effect on our health. Kanner et al. developed a

Hassles and Uplifts Scale, including 117 hassles and 135 uplifts. They used this scale to test their theories, asking respondents to indicate, for each item, how great a particular hassle or uplift was felt to be (see Box 5.9).

Box 5.9 Kanner et al. (1981)

Aims: To investigate a possible association between hassles, uplifts and symptoms of stress, and compare the outcome with the use of the SRRS as a predictor of stress symptoms.

Procedure: One hundred men and women, aged 45–64, were studied. They completed the Hassles and Uplifts Scale once a month for 10 consecutive months. The relationship between hassles and uplifts and stress symptoms, both positive and negative, was investigated. Participants were also assessed each month using the SRRS, and completed a health questionnaire.

Results: Hassles were positively correlated with psychological symptoms associated with stress. There was a negative correlation between uplifts and stress symptoms. The hassles scale was a better predictor of stress symptoms than the SRRS.

Conclusions: Everyday stressors are a better predictor of stress, and therefore vulnerability to illness, than life events.

Much of the research on this subject has focused on the negative effects of hassles. A study by Kanner et al. (1987) found that the experience of uplifts added significantly to the relationship between hassles and stress symptoms in terms of reducing stress symptoms, so a focus on hassles only provides a partial picture.

While this approach makes an important contribution to research in this area, it too can be criticised. Like the SRRS, it does not take into account chronic sources of stress, such as the long-term care of a relative with dementia, or the fact that similar experiences will be interpreted differently by different people and in slightly different situations. For example, losing your car keys when you are not in a hurry to get somewhere may be less of a hassle than when you are late for work. The assessment of the importance of each hassle on the scale goes some way to addressing this, but the ratings provide only a subjective measure, made at the time when the scale is filled in.

Summary

- The **Social Readjustment Rating Scale (SRRS)** is a measure of major **life events** that impact on the experience of stress and illness.
- This approach has been useful in focusing on the role of major life events in the development of stress and illness, and there is research to support the association of life events and **stress-related illness**.
- However, several **criticisms** can be made of the SRRS: it is **correlational**, does not take **individual differences** into account and looks only at **crisis events**.
- An alternative approach has looked at the effect on stress symptoms of everyday **hassles** and **uplifts**.
- While this has extended the life events approach, some of the same **criticisms** can be made of it as of the SRRS.

Workplace stress

People spend a lot of their waking lives at work, so **work-related stress** is an important issue. There are many possible sources of work stress, for example work overload, a noisy environment, overcrowding, poor management, lack of control, lack of support, job insecurity, harassment, bullying and poor relationships with fellow workers. Stress at work not only has the effect of reducing the efficiency of workers, but also makes their working lives unpleasant, and like any experience of stress, can lead to illness. Cox et al. (1981) asked a sample of people what they saw as the main source of stress in their lives. Fifty-four per cent said work, with a further 12% pinpointing trying to balance the demands of work and home.

Work-related stress makes a person's working life unpleasant, and can lead to illness

According to Cherry et al. (2006), work-related stress is a growing problem, with a steep increase in reported cases being found in the 5-year period from 1996 to 2001. While this rise may in part be explained by a greater willingness to seek help, it nonetheless suggests that there is an increasing mismatch between workers' expectations and the actual work environment. A few of the many factors associated with workplace stress will be examined in this section.

Work overload and underload

One source of stress is **work overload**, identified as a major factor in work-related stress by Cherry et al. (2006). This can be **quantitative**, when people feel that they have too much to do or are expected to do it too fast, or **qualitative**, when they find their work too difficult or need more concentration than they are able to give.

However, **work underload** can also be stressful: people may experience stress if they feel that they are not given enough to do or that their skills and abilities are not being fully used.

Lack of control

A major study into stress, related to **characteristics of the job** and the **lack of control** that workers felt they had over their work, was carried out in a Swedish timber mill by Johansson et al. in 1978. Box 5.10 summarises this research.

This is a sound study: it collected a good range of both objective data (hormone levels and absenteeism) and subjective data, in the form of mood ratings, and thus gives more detailed information than one measure alone. It also has high ecological validity because it is a field study, carried out in the workplace, so it provides useful information about some of the causes of work-related stress.

Box 5.10 Johansson et al. (1978)

Aims: To investigate the effect on workers' stress levels of repetitiveness, high attentional demands and lack of control over the pace of work.

Procedure: In a Swedish timber mill, a group of 14 workers was studied. Their work was highly repetitive and demanded a lot of attention, and they had no control over the pace with which their work was carried out. They were compared with a group of ten workers whose working conditions were more flexible. Levels of adrenaline and noradrenaline in their urine were measured both at work and in their free time. The workers also provided ratings of their mood. The frequency of psychosomatic illness and absenteeism in the two groups was also monitored.

Results: At work, the people in the first group showed higher levels of adrenaline and noradrenaline in the urine than those in the control group. Their ratings of mood were more negative, they had more psychosomatic illnesses and they were more often absent from work.

Conclusions: Monotony, vigilance and lack of control are associated with stress. The levels of psychosomatic illness and absenteeism may indicate that stress at work has health implications.

A study by Sundquist et al. (2003) had similar findings: workers whose jobs were very demanding, but who had little control over how their work was carried out, ran an increased risk of long-term illness. Tsutsumi et al. (2007) also identified lack of control in the work situation as a major stressor. In a 9-year longitudinal study, they found that lack of control at work was a significant predictor of suicide among Japanese male workers.

Nature of the job

The nature of the job is also an important source of often unavoidable stress. In a study of New York firefighters, Banauch et al. (2002) found that there was a steep increase in stress-related medical leave during the months following the 11 September attack on the World Trade Center in 2001. They suggest that being frequently at the site of the attack and attending a high number of funerals and memorial services might have contributed to stress-related problems.

Work that requires rotating shifts can by its very nature be a cause of stress. One important source of physiological stress is the disruption of our **circadian rhythms**. Many of our physiological functions, such as heart rate, body temperature and metabolic rate, vary across a 24-hour period. These patterns are known as circadian rhythms and they persist even when our activity pattern is reversed, for example when we work at night and sleep during the day. Reversal of circadian rhythms can take some time, and failure to adapt rapidly may be a source of stress to people on shift work. This is a particular problem when people work rotating shifts, and the circadian rhythms are constantly being called on to adapt to a new pattern, as opposed to when someone is working permanently at night. For example, Gold et al. (1992) found that nurses on rotating shifts made twice as many errors at work as those on permanent day or night shifts. In a study of workers in a chemical factory in Utah, Blakemore (1988) found that lengthening the period between

Mike Abrahams/Amaly

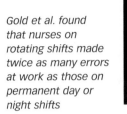

Gold et al. found that nurses on rotating shifts made twice as many errors at work as those on permanent day or night shifts

shift changes from 1 week to 3 weeks, and thus giving the body a longer period in which to adapt to the new shift time, resulted in healthier workers and rising productivity.

Changes in the work environment

Changes in the work environment are also a potential source of work stress, as demonstrated by Verhaeghe et al. (2006) (see Box 5.11).

Box 5.11   Verhaeghe et al. (2006)

Aims: To investigate the effects of recurrent changes in the work environment of hospital nurses on psychological well-being and absence through illness.

Procedure: A questionnaire survey was carried out with 2094 Registered Nurses in ten general hospitals in Belgium, to assess the psychological impact of changes in the work environment over the previous 6 months and rates of absence due to illness.

Results: Nurses who had experienced changes in their work environment scored significantly higher for stress than those who had experienced few changes. They were more likely to have been absent through illness, and for longer periods. While changes that were seen as challenging rather than threatening led to increased job satisfaction, such changes were nonetheless associated with stress and illness.

Conclusions: Changes in the workplace, even when viewed positively, are associated with stress and stress-related illness.

Although this study was carried out in Belgium, the past few years have seen a great number of changes in British hospitals over a short period of time, so these findings may well also be relevant in the UK. This study is also interesting in that it supports the claims of Holmes and Rahe (1967), discussed in the previous section (page 143), that any change, whether negative or positive, is a stressor.

Role strain may be one of the changes in the work environment, where people have difficulty in meeting the fluctuating expectations associated with their roles.

Apker (2005) discusses the changes in the role of hospital nurses in the USA, as a result of attempts to manage health care more efficiently. Nurses continue to fill their traditional roles in providing nursing care, but are frequently required to take on additional roles, such as team leading and administration. In a series of case studies, Apker found that in some instances role strain can cause **burnout**, with nurses leaving their jobs to work in another hospital, or even another field.

Role conflict

Role conflict is also an issue. An early study carried out by Whyte (1948) found that waitresses were under a lot of stress because they were caught between the customers on the one hand, who wanted their food quickly, and the chefs on the other hand, who wanted time to produce the food properly. Similarly, in a study in which 30 police administrators were interviewed, Kroes et al. (1974) found that a major source of reported work stress was the different demands made on them by their superiors (who offered little support), their subordinates, and the community within which they worked.

A waitress in a busy restaurant can experience stress due to role conflict

Tom Craig/Alamy

Summary

- Workplace stress is **widespread** and there is some evidence that it is **increasing**.
- Factors include **lack of control**, the **nature of the job** and the impact of **change**.
- The disruption of **circadian rhythms** in shift work is a source of stress.
- Stress can arise from roles at work, where there is **role strain** or **role conflict**.

Personality factors and stress

In the section on stress and CHD, we looked at research suggesting that someone with a Type A personality may be more vulnerable to stress-related illness, and in particular CHD. A further link between stress and personality has been suggested by Kobasa's concept of the **hardy personality**. Some people seem to cope very well with stressful situations, while others break down under what appears to be very little pressure. In 1979, Kobasa carried out a study to investigate the role of personality in these differences, a summary of which is provided in Box 5.12.

This study was correlational, so it cannot be assumed that personality differences caused the differences in response to stress. For example, it could be that the personality characteristics of those who did not have a hardy personality were the *result* rather than the cause of illness — it would be difficult for a person to become involved in work and social life if they were ill. However, Kobasa et al. (1982)

Box 5.12   Kobasa (1979)

Aims: To identify personality factors that affect an individual's response to stress.

Procedure: Six hundred executives and managers were asked to complete two question-naires. One was a personality questionnaire, and the other asked them to list the illnesses and stressful events that they had experienced in the last 3 years. On the basis of their responses, the participants were divided into two groups: those who had scored above average on illnesses, and those who had scored below average.

Results: For both groups, the scores for stressful events were high. However, in contrast to the high stress/high illness group, those in the high stress/low illness group were more likely to:

● feel more in control of their lives
● have a sense of commitment and purpose in their work and social lives
● welcome change as a challenge

People with these characteristics were defined by Kobasa as having a **hardy personality**.

Conclusions: People with the characteristics that make up a hardy personality are better able to cope with stress.

followed up the 1979 study with longitudinal research, which monitored executives over a 2-year period. This new study found that those who had the positive attitude described by the hardy personality were less likely to become ill, supporting the idea that personality characteristics influence one's response to stress.

Kobasa went on to develop the **Hardiness Scale**, with three individual sub-scales, to assess hardiness (see Figure 5.8).

Figure 5.8   *Components of Kobasa's Hardiness Scale*

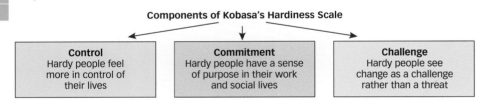

Components of Kobasa's Hardiness Scale

Control	Commitment	Challenge
Hardy people feel more in control of their lives	Hardy people have a sense of purpose in their work and social lives	Hardy people see change as a challenge rather than a threat

Kobasa argued that all three components of hardiness act synergistically (i.e. work together) to produce the effect of moderating stress. However, this idea has been challenged. For example, Pengilly (1997) found that commitment was more important in moderating stress in college students than control or challenge.

Hardiness is also a useful concept in relation to the experience of work stress. In a study of 87 nurses, Turnipseed (1999) found that those nurses who scored high on hardiness were less likely to feel under pressure at work than those with low scores. High-scoring nurses reported a clear understanding of the role of their job and felt that they were part of a team that worked together. In a study of firefighters, Jimenez et al. (2006) found that for people in stressful jobs, a hardy personality reduced the risk of burnout. However, they pointed out that personality factors such as hardiness should not be considered in isolation, but rather in interaction with other aspects of the work situation.

The concepts and links explored in all these studies are interesting because they imply that perhaps people can learn to develop the characteristics of a hardy personality and thus become better able to combat stress. This will be examined later in the chapter. However, Kobasa's participants were involved in the kinds of work that were challenging and stimulating enough to encourage commitment. Hardiness might be more difficult to develop for a person in a monotonous job, or one that is so demanding that he or she is too tired to enjoy a satisfying social life.

Summary

- Kobasa suggested **hardiness** as a personality factor that protects against the effects of stress.
- It can be assessed using the **Hardiness Scale**, with the three components of **commitment**, **control** and **challenge**.
- The concept is useful in understanding **individual differences** in the effects of stress, but it should be seen in relation to other causes of stress.

Emotion-focused and problem-focused ways of coping with stress

The transactional model (which was outlined at the start of the chapter) defines stress as an imbalance between people's perceptions of the demands that a situation makes on them, and their own estimation of their ability to cope with these demands. Folkman and Lazarus (1980) have built on this approach in investigating how we respond to stress. They suggest that we make a two-stage **cognitive appraisal** of a situation. In the **primary appraisal**, the possibility of threat posed by the situation is assessed. In the **secondary appraisal**, coping resources and options for dealing with the situation are evaluated, when the person asks him- or herself: 'What can I do?'

Coping refers to efforts to manage the situation, and Folkman and Lazarus suggest that there are two forms: **emotion-focused** coping and **problem-focused** coping. In emotion-focused (or **palliative**) coping, people attempt to minimise or eliminate unpleasant emotions. This can include thinking about a stressful situation in a different and more positive way, denying that the problem exists, and wishful thinking. In problem-focused (or **instrumental**) coping, people try to avoid negative emotions by taking some action to avoid or minimise the threatening situation: they change their behaviour to cope. For example, an A-level student is taking her exams over the next fortnight, which is potentially a stressful situation. Problem-focused coping would involve taking action to make the situation less stressful, for example by reading over class notes or looking at past exam questions and planning answers to them. Alternatively, using emotion-focused coping, the student could watch television for hours on end, distracting herself from the negative emotions associated with the thought of exams. Emotion-focused coping can be useful as a short-term way of coping with stress. It has the advantage of reducing arousal, which may then make it easier for the person to use a more problem-focused approach, so a third option for the student might be to combine the two coping methods, by watching television for an hour and then doing some structured revision. However, some forms of emotion-focused coping, such as self-blame or wishful thinking, could get in the way of problem-focused coping.

Folkman and Lazarus developed a 68-item **Ways of Coping** check list to measure the extent to which an individual uses each kind of coping strategy. They later revised this to include 42 items, with eight scales: one problem-focused, six emotion-focused and one mixed. They also changed the format from a yes/no answer to a 4-point Likert scale, from 0 = does not apply and/or not used, to 3 = used a great deal (see Box 5.13).

Box 5.13   Folkman and Lazarus (1985): Ways of Coping check list

Problem-focused coping (11 items): for example, 'I try to analyse the problem to understand it better'; 'I'm making a plan of action and following it'.

Emotion-focused coping:
Wishful thinking (five items): for example, 'I wish that I could change what is happening or how I feel'; 'I wish that the situation would go away or somehow be over with'.

Distancing (six items): for example, 'I try to forget the whole thing'; 'I'm waiting to see what will happen before doing anything'.

Emphasising the positive (four items): for example, 'I look for the silver lining'; 'I'm changing or growing as a person in a good way'.

Self-blame (three items): for example, 'I criticise or lecture myself'; 'I realise that I brought the problem on myself'.

Tension reduction (three items): for example, 'I try to make myself feel better by eating, drinking, smoking, using drugs or medications etc.'; 'I jog or exercise'.

Self-isolation (three items): for example, 'I avoid being with people in general'; 'I keep others from knowing how bad things are'.

Mixed (problem-focused and emotion-focused coping):
Seeking social support (seven items): for example, 'I talk to someone to find out more about the situation'; 'I accept sympathy and understanding from someone'.

Quite often, both kinds of coping strategy are used, as demonstrated by Folkman and Lazarus (1980) (see Box 5.14).

The finding that people use a mixture of coping strategies was supported by later research. Folkman and Lazarus (1985) found that, on average, individuals used between six and seven different types of coping, as assessed by their revised check list.

The results of the 1980 study support the idea that a distinction between emotion-focused and problem-focused coping is a useful one. It is perhaps rather limited, however, in that only middle-aged and older participants were tested, so it could be unwise to generalise the findings to younger people. It may well be that our choice of coping strategies changes with age and experience.

Box 5.14 Folkman and Lazarus (1980)

Aims: To assess the kinds of coping strategies used in stressful situations.

Procedure: In this 1-year longitudinal study, 100 participants aged 45–64 years were interviewed once a month and completed self-reporting questionnaires about stressful events that they had experienced. They also completed the *Ways of Coping* check list to indicate how they thought about these stressful events and how they responded to them.

Results: The participants referred to 1332 episodes, and for 98% of these, both problem-focused coping and emotion-focused coping were used. Problem-focused coping was more often used in situations perceived as circumstances that could be changed, and emotion-focused coping when the person believed that there was nothing that he or she could do to bring about change. Participants did not show consistency in the coping methods that they used. Age was not a factor, and gender was only a factor for males in work situations, when they were more likely to use problem-focused coping.

Conclusions: Both emotion-focused coping and problem-focused coping are used in stressful situations, with most people using a mixture of both. The extent to which each is used is influenced by the degree of control that a person believes he or she has over the situation.

A major factor to emerge from these findings is the role of **control** in the choice of coping strategy, as illustrated by the diagram in Figure 5.9.

Figure 5.9 *Control and coping strategies*

Based on this, Lazarus and Folkman (1984) went on to develop the **goodness-of-fit hypothesis**. This suggests that it is adaptive to use emotion-focused coping rather than problem-focused coping in uncontrollable situations. Forsythe and Compas (2005) also conducted research in this area, a summary of which is provided in Box 5.15.

Box 5.15 Forsythe and Compas (2005)

Aims: To assess the 'goodness of fit' between appraisals of the controllability of events and the use of problem- and emotion-focused coping.

Procedure: Participants were assessed on their appraisal of the controllability of major life events and daily hassles, and their use of problem-focused and emotion-focused coping, together with psychological symptoms of stress.

Results: For major life events, the measure of symptoms of stress was high when there was a poor fit between appraisals and coping, for example trying to change a stressor that was appraised as uncontrollable. There were few symptoms of stress when there was a good fit between appraisals and coping, for example using emotion-focused coping when a stressor was perceived as uncontrollable. No effects were found in relation to daily hassles.

Conclusions: The results provide general support for the 'goodness-of-fit' hypothesis.

Park et al. (2004) have also examined the goodness-of-fit hypothesis, providing a little more detail on the relationship between controllability, coping and mood (see Box 5.16).

Box 5.16 | **Park et al. (2004)**

Aims: To test the goodness-of-fit hypothesis in relation to perceived controllability of a stressful event and problem- and emotion-focused coping, and the relationship between controllability, coping strategy and mood.

Procedure: Over a period of 4 weeks, 190 undergraduates were asked to keep an internet daily diary, describing stressful events that they experienced, how controllable these were perceived to be, how they coped, and their daily positive and negative mood.

Results: There was a positive association between participants' appraisals of controllability and the use of problem-focused coping, and a negative association with emotion-focused coping. Participants were also more likely to rate their mood as positive when using problem-focused coping to deal with a stressful event that they perceived as highly controllable than for events over which they perceived themselves as having little control. There were some individual differences in the extent to which participants matched their appraisal of control with a coping strategy.

Conclusions: The results support the goodness-of-fit hypothesis, but there are individual differences in matching perception of control and coping strategies.

This study highlighted the importance of individual differences in the coping strategies used. This suggests that personality factors may also be important in coping with stress. This is what Hosogoshi and Kodama explored in their 2006 study (see Box 5.17).

Box 5.17 | **Hosogoshi and Kodama (2006)**

Aims: To investigate the goodness-of-fit hypothesis in relation to individual personality characteristics.

Procedure: Japanese college students were divided into two groups, based on personality: 61 classified as pessimists and 64 as optimists. They provided information about stressful events that they had experienced, the extent to which they perceived these events as controllable, and their coping strategies. The two groups were compared for their use of problem-focused and emotion-focused coping in situations that they perceived as uncontrollable.

Results: Compared with the group of optimists, the pessimists tended to use neither problem-focused nor emotion-focused coping in uncontrollable situations.

Conclusions: Not using problem-focused coping in uncontrollable situations is consistent with the goodness-of-fit hypothesis, but not using emotion-focused coping challenges it. These findings suggest that, by not using problem-focused coping, pessimists at least do not increase stress in uncontrollable situations and can control their behaviour, but that they may be vulnerable to stress because they cannot use emotion-focused coping effectively. The use of coping strategies needs to be seen in the context of individual personality characteristics.

Summary

- A distinction can be made between **emotion-focused coping** and **problem-focused coping**. People often use both ways of coping with stress.
- The **goodness-of-fit hypothesis** proposes that emotion-focused coping is more adaptive when the source of stress is uncontrollable.
- There is research support for this hypothesis, but **personality differences** may also play a part in the methods of coping used.

Stress management

Stress is not only psychologically damaging but, as was demonstrated above, it is also associated with a risk of developing a serious illness, such as cancer or CHD. It is therefore important to consider ways in which stress may be reduced, and this section will look at how this can be approached. One way is to try to reduce the physiological effects of stress, while others focus on psychological ways of managing stress.

Physiological approaches

One physiological approach to stress management is the use of drugs. Stress is often experienced as anxiety and so may be treated with **anxiolytic drugs**, also known as **minor tranquillisers**. Until fairly recently, barbiturates were widely used, but although they are effective, they are rarely used now for several reasons: they are extremely dangerous in overdose; they are highly addictive; and there might be unwanted interaction with other medications that a person may be taking.

The drugs most commonly used to treat anxiety are **benzodiazepines**, for example **diazepam** (sometimes trade-named Valium or Librium), which regulate the neurotransmitter GABA (gamma-aminobutyric acid). These drugs are prescribed for no longer than 2–4 weeks, where anxiety is severe and the individual is suffering extreme distress. One of the problems with these (or any) drugs is possible side effects. For diazepam these include drowsiness, headache, amnesia, confusion, low blood pressure and occasionally apnoea (the person stops breathing). They are also addictive — hence the relatively brief period for which they should be prescribed — and withdrawal must be gradual.

An alternative anxiolytic drug is **buspirone**, which acts on serotonin receptors. This also has possible side effects, but it is not addictive so withdrawal is not a problem.

Beta blockers may also be used. They treat the physical symptoms of stress, reducing ANS symptoms such as palpitations and tremor. The reduction in physical symptoms may in turn lead to an improvement in the psychological symptoms of anxiety.

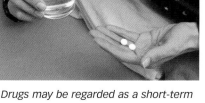

Drugs may be regarded as a short-term method of dealing with stress

A major criticism of the use of drugs to reduce the symptoms of anxiety is that they do not deal with possible environmental factors contributing to the problem, such as looking after a relative with dementia or having a stressful job like firefighting, but only with the physical symptoms. They may therefore best be seen as short-term ways of dealing with stress and may be used in combination with other therapies, such as counselling, if the problem is to be dealt with more radically.

Sometimes people use **alcohol** to reduce stress. It has a sedative effect, slows down neural function and loosens inhibitions. However, the criticisms that can be made of other drugs can also be made of alcohol. Moreover, there is a positive relationship between alcohol consumption and stroke, so the use of alcohol to reduce stress is not to be recommended.

Biofeedback uses psychological means to bring about physiological changes

Biofeedback uses psychological means to bring about physiological changes and is based on the elements of **operant conditioning** (see Chapter 1). Its principles are simple: physiological functions such as heart rate and blood pressure are monitored, the information is then fed back to the patient, who is trained in methods to bring these automatic processes under voluntary control. The training usually involves relaxation techniques.

The feedback provided can take several forms. It can be visual (e.g. a line on a screen that moves up or down as the heart rate changes) or auditory (a tone that changes in pitch). This approach requires specialist equipment, but this is easily available and relatively cheap.

This method has been used with a range of stress-related disorders, such as migraine and tension headaches. Erbeck et al. (1983) found that people could use biofeedback to lower their blood pressure. However, while this approach can be effective, it has the disadvantage of requiring regular practice for the development and maintenance of positive outcomes. Moreover, some people find it hard to acquire the necessary control: it may take many months for the techniques to be developed and benefits to be achieved. A further limitation, as with drugs, is that this approach deals only with the symptoms of stress and does not address the underlying causes.

Earlier in the chapter, it was established that the physiological stress response prepares the individual for 'fight or flight', i.e. physical action. **Exercise** is therefore an appropriate way of responding to stress-related physiological changes. It uses up the blood sugars released by the hormones secreted into the bloodstream when the person is under stress. It also helps to work out tensions that have built up in the muscles and increases strength, flexibility and stamina, making the person better able to combat future stressors. Blumenthal et al. (1987) found that people who exercised were less likely to experience anxiety, depression and tension than those who did not. However, as with all physiological approaches, while exercise may help to ease the symptoms of stress, it does not address the factors that are causing it.

Summary

- There are **physiological** and **psychological** methods of dealing with stress.
- **Drugs** can be effective, but have possible **side effects**.
- In **biofeedback**, functions such as heart rate are brought under voluntary control. This is effective, but the techniques may be difficult to acquire and it may take some time before there are positive results.
- **Exercise** is an appropriate way of dealing with the fight-or-flight stress response.
- The problem with physiological approaches is that they deal only with the **symptoms** of stress and not with the underlying **causes**.

Psychological approaches

Behavioural, cognitive and cognitive-behavioural methods are psychological approaches to stress management that have been shown to be effective. Unlike drugs, these methods have the advantage of having no physical side effects.

The behavioural approach

Behavioural methods have been used to modify **Type A behaviour** (discussed in the section on coronary heart disease in this chapter). There are two approaches that may be considered: the shotgun method and the target behaviour approach.

The **shotgun method** aims to change all the behaviours associated with the Type A personality. In their Recurrent Coronary Prevention Program, Friedman et al. (1986) used a combination of behavioural methods. These included giving advice on diet and exercise, and encouraging people to behave in ways that were incompatible with the Type A personality. For example, they were asked to listen to people without interrupting, or deliberately to stand in the longest queue in a supermarket.

The **target behaviour** approach focuses only on those behaviours that are likely to lead to heart disease. As explained in the section on CHD, Williams (1984) identified cynicism and hostility as the major risk factors for CHD. It is argued that if behaviours associated with these characteristics can be modified, the risk of heart disease will be lowered. Thus, the target behaviour approach concentrates on changing behaviours associated with these characteristics.

The cognitive approach

While these approaches appear to be helpful in addressing stress associated with the Type A personality, they still only deal largely with symptoms. The **cognitive approach** to stress management suggests that people will adapt best to stressful events if they change the way they think about them and if they consciously take control in stressful situations. In the section on personality factors and stress, Kobasa's concept of the **hardy personality** was examined, along with the conclusion that people might be able to develop a more hardy personality and thus protect themselves from the effects of stress. Kobasa has developed hardiness training, which includes three elements:

Kobasa's hardiness training

a **Focusing**: individuals are trained to recognise the physiological signs of stress, such as increased heart rate or sweating. This helps them to recognise sources of stress.

b **Reconstructing stressful situations**: individuals are helped to think about a recent stressful event or situation and consider ways in which it could have turned out better or worse. This helps them to make a realistic appraisal of the stressors that they experience.

c **Compensation through self-improvement**: individuals are encouraged to take on challenges with which they can cope. Through this, they learn that they are capable of coping with stressful situations.

Research by Maddi et al. (1998) suggests that hardiness training can have positive outcomes and be effective in the management of stress (see Box 5.18).

Box 5.18   Maddi et al. (1998)

Aims: To assess the effectiveness of hardiness training.

Procedure: Fifty-four managers in a utilities company were randomly allocated to three conditions: (a) hardiness training, (b) training in relaxation and meditation, and (c) social support, where they discussed the stressors that they experienced. In each condition, participants worked in groups of six, with experienced trainers. There were ten training sessions, which took place once a week, each session lasting $1\frac{1}{2}$ hours. Both before and after training, all participants completed questionnaires, which provided measures of hardiness, job satisfaction, the extent to which they experienced stress, perceived social support and illness. After training, the effects of the three methods of stress management were compared.

Results: After training, relaxation and meditation showed more effect on the measures assessed in the questionnaires compared with the social support group. However, participants in the hardiness training condition showed more improvement than those in the other two conditions on all the measures.

Conclusions: Hardiness can be learned, and hardiness training is a more effective method of addressing stress than relaxation or social support.

Clearly, hardiness training has something to offer. Maddi et al. suggest that future research should aim to identify the essential features that make hardiness training effective, and also to assess its usefulness with people who have specific problems, such as marital difficulties, rather than just the more general stresses of life.

The cognitive behavioural approach

The cognitive approach is combined with behaviour change in **cognitive behavioural therapy (CBT)**. This therapy focuses on current thoughts and gives rather more emphasis to behaviour change than hardiness training. It combines cognitive therapy, to modify or eliminate unwanted and inappropriate thoughts and beliefs, and behavioural therapy, to change behaviour in response to those thoughts. It has been used to help with many disorders, such as phobias and depression, but is also widely used to help combat stress.

The starting point is to help the person make sense of how different aspects of a stressful situation and his or her response to it are linked. A stressful situation or event leads to thoughts, emotions, physical feelings and behaviour, each of which can affect each other. For example, how you think about a problem can affect how you feel physically and emotionally, and vice versa. It can also alter what you do about it. These possible interactions are shown in the diagram in Figure 5.10.

Figure 5.10
The relationship between a stressor, thoughts, emotions and behaviour

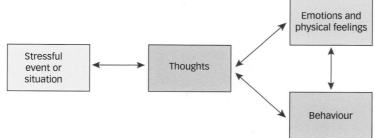

An example could be that of a student who may be stressed because he has an important exam coming up in 2 weeks' time. He can respond to this in helpful or unhelpful ways (see Figure 5.11).

Figure 5.11
Possible responses to exam stress

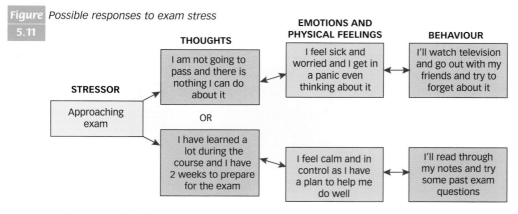

In this example, the same situation has led to two different results. How the student thought about the exam affected his feelings and his behaviour.

The aim of the CBT approach is to change the way we think about a stressful situation, which in turn will affect the way we feel about it and the actions that we take to reduce stress.

CBT can be carried out by clinical psychologists, either on a one-to-one basis or with a group of people. There are even computer programmes that help you to apply the principles yourself. In individual therapy, the client usually meets the therapist once a week or once a fortnight, with each session lasting half an hour to an hour. There are usually between five and 20 sessions, depending on the individual and the nature of the problem.

There is quite a lot of evidence that CBT is helpful when carried out with people on an individual basis. As already mentioned, it is also sometimes done in groups, and Main et al. (2005) found good results from a series of large-scale, one-day workshops in London.

In individual therapy, at the start of each session, the client and the therapist decide on the issue to be addressed. With the help of the therapist, the problem is broken down into its separate parts. The thoughts, feelings and behaviour associated with the problem are discussed, to see if they are unhelpful and how they affect each other, as well as the client's understanding of the stressful event or situation. The role of the therapist is to help the person work out how to change unhelpful thoughts and behaviour. However, talking about the problem is only part of CBT. The client is also given 'homework', i.e. he or she is asked to develop more helpful ways of thinking about a situation and to translate these thoughts into action.

CBT has been widely used and shown to be an especially effective technique for stress management. Indeed, there is evidence that this approach brings about the **physiological changes** necessary to reduce stress. Hammerfald et al. (2006) gave participants a standard stress test and measured cortisol levels before and after the test. They found that those who had taken part in CBT showed a significantly reduced cortisol stress response.

In the earlier discussion of life events, the work of Rahe and Arthur (1977) was mentioned. One of their findings was that people experiencing stress were more susceptible to **sports injuries**. Maddison and Prapavessis (2005) reported similar findings and went on to investigate whether CBT could be an effective way of helping athletes to prevent injury. They randomly allocated 48 rugby players,

Cognitive behavioural therapy has been used to help sports people feel less anxious and be better able to cope

identified as at risk for injury, either to a course of CBT or as controls who received no CBT. They found that compared with controls, those who had taken part in CBT reported missing less time due to injury. This group also reported feeling better able to cope and less anxious.

As discussed earlier, **work-related stress** is a serious problem. Research by Koch et al. (2006) shows that CBT can be successfully applied to this kind of stress (see Box 5.19). Indeed, there is such clear evidence that CBT can be useful in addressing work-related stress that Ross and Altmaier (1994) produced a handbook to facilitate the development of CBT programmes in the workplace.

Box 5.19   **Koch et al. (2006)**

Aims: To evaluate the use of CBT in reducing work-related stress.

Procedure: In a longitudinal study, 133 participants took part in 16 hours of in-patient job-focused group CBT over 3 months. They completed questionnaires when they were admitted to the programme, when they left it, and 3 months later. These provided data on objective measures of stress (such as days off for illness and applications for early retirement), and on subjective measures (such as participants' estimates of the intensity of stressors at work and the extent to which they felt able to cope). The results were compared with those of 156 patients who just received standard treatment for the symptoms of stress (counselling).

Results: After the 3 months of treatment, participants in the intervention group indicated that they were less likely to apply for early retirement than those in the control group. They also felt more in control at work and better able to manage the work-related stressors they encountered.

Conclusions: CBT is an effective way of combating work-related stress.

As it was argued in the section on workplace stress, some kinds of work are more stressful than others. Research has also looked at the use of CBT with individuals whose work is likely to be particularly stressful, for example the work of doctors in general practice (see Box 5.20).

Box 5.20   **Gardiner et al. (2004)**

Aims: To assess the benefits of CBT in reducing stress and improving the psychological well-being of GPs.

Procedure: A group of 85 city GPs in Australia completed a questionnaire before and after a cognitive behavioural stress-management training programme, which lasted 15 hours. A control group of 25 GPs who did not undergo the training programme was also tested. Both groups were also followed up 3 months later.

Results: Compared with the control group, both work-related and more general stress decreased for the CBT group. Their general psychological state and perceived quality of life also improved. These changes were maintained and even increased after 3 months.

Conclusions: CBT is an effective way of helping to reduce work-related stress in people with stressful jobs.

CBT can thus be seen as an effective way of helping people to manage stress. However, it may not be the ideal solution for everyone. If a person is depressed and having difficulty in concentrating, it may be difficult for him or her to get to grips with this approach. People may also find it difficult to talk about their problems and why they are stressed. Nonetheless, one of the advantages of this treatment is that the person is learning skills, so he or she can apply the principles of CBT in new situations without the help of a therapist. The symptoms of stress are less likely to recur, because techniques have been acquired that help the person to cope in future stressful situations. CBT can also be used alongside medication, so the physical symptoms of stress are reduced while more adaptive ways of coping with stress are developed.

Summary

- **Psychological approaches** to stress management include **behavioural**, **cognitive** and **cognitive behavioural** methods.
- **Behavioural methods** are useful but deal largely with **symptoms** rather than the causes of stress.
- **Cognitive methods** aim to change the way people think about stressful situations. An example is **hardiness training**, developed by Kobasa.
- **Cognitive behavioural therapy (CBT)** emphasises the interaction between **thoughts**, **emotions** and **physical feelings** and **behaviour**. It has been shown to be effective in reducing stress in a number of contexts.

Terms explained

burnout: physical and/or emotional exhaustion as the result of long-term stress. It has a negative effect on relationships, the ability to work and resistance to illness.

coronary heart disease (CHD): a narrowing of the small blood vessels that supply blood and oxygen to the heart (coronary arteries), usually resulting from the build-up of fatty material and plaque, i.e. atherosclerosis. This causes the flow of blood to the heart to slow or stop, causing chest pain (**angina**), shortness of breath, and **heart attack**.

goodness-of-fit hypothesis: the suggestion that the best way of coping with a stressful situation will depend on the nature of the situation. If we have some control over the situation, a problem-focused approach makes more sense and is more productive, i.e. is a better fit, than an emotion-focused approach.

immune system: the complex group of specialised cells and organs that protects us against foreign substances, such as bacteria, viruses, parasites and toxins. The system defends the body against infections and other diseases, and is composed of certain white blood cells, antibodies and protein substances that react against bacteria and other harmful material. The system recognises foreign agents or substances, neutralises them and produces a similar response if later confronted with the same challenge.

Social influence

In this chapter, we will be looking at:
- research into conformity
- why do people conform?
- research into obedience
- why do people obey?
- independent behaviour
- the implications for social change of research into social influence

Social psychologists are particularly interested in the effect that other people can have on our behaviour. This field of interest is described as **social influence**. There are many ways in which one's behaviour is affected by others, but only two forms of influence will be examined in this chapter: **conformity** and **obedience**.

Research into conformity

Conformity can be defined as a change in behaviour as a result of group pressure, that is, other people may cause a person to behave differently from the way he or she would if alone. Pressure from others does not necessarily need to be expressed to bring about conformity, it may just be in the mind of the person who experiences it. For example, Lucy may feel that she should choose to study medicine at university because both her parents as well as her older brother are doctors. Of course, pressure from others can also be explicit. In this example, Lucy's parents would suggest that she should study medicine.

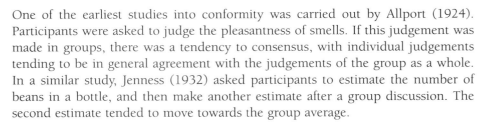

One of the earliest studies into conformity was carried out by Allport (1924). Participants were asked to judge the pleasantness of smells. If this judgement was made in groups, there was a tendency to consensus, with individual judgements tending to be in general agreement with the judgements of the group as a whole. In a similar study, Jenness (1932) asked participants to estimate the number of beans in a bottle, and then make another estimate after a group discussion. The second estimate tended to move towards the group average.

In a further study by Sherif in 1935, a visual illusion called the **autokinetic effect** was used. In this illusion, a static point of light in an otherwise dark room seems to move about and participants are asked to estimate its movement (see Box 6.1).

Box 6.1	Sherif (1935)

Aims: To assess the effect of the judgements of other people on individuals' estimates of the movement of a point of light in the autokinetic effect.

Procedure: Participants were asked to estimate the direction and distance a point of light moved in a dark room. Each participant did this individually over a series of trials so that an average could be calculated for each of them. They were then divided into groups, including people with very different averages, and again asked to make individual judgements in the group situation.

Results: After a few of the trials carried out in groups, individual judgements tended to move towards agreement within the group. This effect was still evident when the tests were repeated later, with participants being tested individually.

Conclusions: When making judgements within a group, there is a tendency to move towards group consensus, i.e. to move towards the average for the group, even when individual judgements are asked for.

These ways of testing conformity have been criticised on the grounds that, in each case, the situation is ambiguous, so there can be no objectively correct judgement. The pleasantness of a smell is a matter of personal opinion, it is not possible to judge with any accuracy the number of beans in a jar, and in the autokinetic effect the light does not actually move at all. Asch argued that for a real understanding of conformity, we need to look at what happens in unambiguous situations, where there is one clearly correct solution. Conformity can be said to have taken place when an individual moves away from a position of certainty in order to conform to obviously incorrect solutions given by others. Asch tested this idea in a classic study in 1951 (see Box 6.2).

Asch (1962) subsequently reported a further series of studies incorporating variations of the original procedure (see Box 6.3).

In a similar study, Allen and Levine (1971) found that conformity dropped when one confederate gave the correct answer, even when this confederate wore glasses with pebble lenses, suggesting unreliable judgement. The effect was similar when the confederate gave a different wrong answer.

Box 6.2 Asch (1951)

Aims: To investigate conformity in an unambiguous situation.

Procedure: Participants were given the simple task of matching a standard line on one card with one of three comparison lines on a separate card. The standard line was always equal in length to one, and only one, of the comparison lines (see Figure 6.1). The participants were tested in groups of between seven and nine, all but one of whom were confederates of the experimenter. The genuine participant believed that he was taking part in a study of perception. The group members sat in a row and were asked to make their judgements in order, with the genuine participant being last but one to be asked. On 12 trials, the confederates were asked to give the same, wrong answer. The answers of the genuine participant were recorded, together with his other behaviour, for example remarks, questions, movements and gestures. A control group, where all were genuine participants, was also tested.

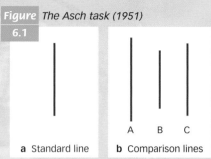

Figure 6.1 *The Asch task (1951)*

a Standard line **b** Comparison lines

A B C

Results: On average, participants in the experimental group conformed to the group's incorrect judgements about 32% of the time. Approximately 25% of the participants never conformed and about one in 20 conformed every time. The remaining participants conformed at least once. Many of those who conformed showed signs of stress, such as nervous laughter and sweating. In the control group, the judgements were virtually 100% correct.

Conclusions: In a group situation, there is a tendency to conform to the judgements of others, even when these judgements are quite clearly incorrect. However, there are considerable individual differences in whether or not people conform.

Box 6.3 Asch (1962): variations of the basic experiment

- One of the confederates — always seated in the fourth position — was instructed to give the correct answer on all trials, including those in which the other confederates gave the same (wrong) answer. The average level of conformity dropped from 32% to just over 5%.

- This procedure was repeated, but the confederate was instructed to switch to the majority (incorrect) opinion halfway through the experiment. Conformity rose from 5% to 28%.

- In a reversal of this, the confederate was instructed to switch halfway through the experiment from giving the majority choice, to the correct answer. The level of conformity to the majority answer of participants who had conformed in the early part of the experiment dropped to just under 9%.

- The experiment was repeated, varying the size of the unanimous majority, using two, three, four, eight and 10–15 confederates. There was virtually no conformity when there was one confederate, and a small effect when there were two confederates. The full effect appeared when there was a majority of three, with no greater effect when there were larger majorities.

- The difference between the lengths of the 'correct answer' line and the line chosen by the confederates was systematically increased and decreased. Conformity fell when the difference was large, though it did not disappear entirely, even when the difference was quite marked. Conformity rose when the discrepancy between the two line lengths was reduced.

It should be noted that there are some ethical concerns with Asch's series of studies. Participants showed clear signs of stress, such as nervous laughter and sweating. However, Asch emphasised the researcher's responsibility to debrief participants fully and claimed that, during the debriefing, most participants expressed interest in the research. Many were glad to have taken part in a study that told them something interesting both about themselves and about people in general. From a cost–benefit point of view, the stress that the participants experienced has to be weighed against the clear demonstration of the effect of social influence on people's public judgements that the research provided, which could not have been achieved if participants had been given full information about the aims and procedures at the outset.

In Asch's research, conformity to facts was investigated. Crutchfield (1954) extended this research in two ways. First, he investigated conformity to opinions, and second, he was interested in whether others had to be physically present for conformity to take place (see Box 6.4).

Box 6.4 **Crutchfield (1954)**

Aims: To investigate conformity to facts and opinions when others are not physically present.

Procedure: More than 600 students and military personnel took part in the study. Each participant worked in a booth on his or her own and was asked to indicate agreement or disagreement using switches that would turn on lights. A display of lights demonstrated what participants believed to be the responses of their fellow participants, but which were in fact manipulated by the experimenter. They believed that their own responses were similarly available to other participants. They were tested on a range of tasks, including clearly incorrect factual statements, and on personal opinions (see Box 6.5).

Results: The degree of conformity varied with the nature of the task. For facts, there was 46% conformity to (c), 30% to (b) and a substantial percentage to (a). For opinions, 37% agreed with (d), none of whom did so when they were asked individually, and again there was substantial agreement with (e). This is surprising in that free speech is enshrined as a right in the American constitution.

Conclusions: The results were in broad agreement with those of Asch. Some participants never conformed, some always conformed and most conformed some of the time. There was conformity both to facts and to opinions, with the extent of conformity depending on the nature of the task. Other people do not have to be physically present for conformity to take place.

Box 6.5 **Sample items from Crutchfield (1954)**

a Agreement with statements such as: '60%–70% of Americans are over 65 years old'; 'On average, Americans sleep 4 to 5 hours a night'.

b An Asch-type task.

c Agreement that a star had a larger surface area than a circle, when in fact it was one-third smaller.

d Agreement with the statement 'I doubt that I would make an effective leader'.

e Agreement with the statement 'Free speech being a privilege rather than a right, it is proper for society to suspend free speech when it feels itself threatened'.

Summary

- **Conformity** refers to behaviour change as a result of explicit or implicit social pressure.
- Early studies used **ambiguous** situations, but **Asch** suggested that conformity could only be established in **unambiguous** situations.
- The series of **line-matching studies** carried out by Asch demonstrated high levels of conformity to clearly wrong answers, where the correct answer was unambiguous.
- **Crutchfield** extended this work by demonstrating conformity to **opinions** and conformity when others were **not physically present**.

Why do people conform?

Informational influence and normative influence

Asch debriefed his participants extensively and in the report of his studies he discussed several reasons why people may conform in unambiguous situations. He identified three main patterns, relating to distortion of perception, judgement and action.

Asch: reasons for conformity

Distortion of perception: a few participants claimed that they believed the majority judgement to be correct and were not aware that their estimates were affected by the majority.

Distortion of judgement: most participants who conformed fell into this category. They came to believe that the judgements of the majority must be correct. These participants lacked confidence in their own judgements and so felt that they should go along with the majority.

Distortion of action: these participants realised that the majority judgements were incorrect, but reported that they agreed with them because they did not want to appear different from, or inferior to, the others in the group.

This suggests that a distinction can be made between **private change**, where people change both their opinion and their behaviour (distortion of perception and judgement), and **public conformity**, where people change their behaviour but not their opinion (distortion of action). For example, some of Asch's 'private change' participants believed that the majority was right, for example they thought that they themselves might be suffering from eyestrain and so were not able to see the stimulus material clearly. Those who showed only public conformity, but no private change, claimed that they had agreed with the majority because they did not want to seem foolish or different from the others, create a bad impression or upset the experiment.

Kelman (1958) picked up on this distinction, using the terms '**internalisation**' to refer to private change, and '**compliance**' to refer to public conformity. These two different kinds of conformity have been related to two sorts of influence, discussed below, which Deutsch and Gerard (1955) called '**informational influence**' and '**normative influence**'. Table 6.1 provides a summary of the terms used by the researchers mentioned so far, and their meanings.

Social psychology

Table 6.1 *Public conformity and private change*

Asch's terms	Kelman's terms	What happens	Influence
Private change	Internalisation	Both behaviour and opinion change	Informational
Public conformity	Compliance	Behaviour changes, but opinion does not	Normative

Informational influence arises from the need to give the correct answer and therefore to be right, when a person feels that others have more relevant information than he or she does. This has been demonstrated clearly in a study by Pincus (1981). In a variation of the Asch study, this time using musical notes, participants were asked to judge which comparison note was the same as a standard note. In this study, there was only one confederate, instructed to give the wrong answer on some trials. When the confederate was introduced as a musical expert there were high levels of conformity. In one of the variations that Asch carried out in his series of studies, there was virtually no conformity with only one confederate. In contrast, in the Pincus study, participants conformed even though they had only heard one person give his opinion before them, and even though that person gave a clearly incorrect answer. Presumably, the participants did not feel confident in their musical judgement when faced with an 'expert' who disagreed with it.

Normative influence refers to the influence of others that may lead a person to conform to **social norms**, and arises from the **need for others' approval**. Norms are unwritten rules that relate to behaviour regarded as appropriate within a particular social group. For example, there are norms about queuing at supermarket checkouts, apologising when we step on someone's toe, not singing during psychology lessons, and so on. These conventions are developed as part of the socialisation process and are picked up by observing the behaviour of others. Respecting these conventions helps to ensure that social interaction runs smoothly, and the consequence of not complying with them is the loss of acceptance and approval by others.

The participants in Asch's study might not be thought of as a group, as they were brought together purely for the purposes of the experiment. However, Tajfel et al. (1971) found that people readily identify themselves as members of a group, even when groups are formed on a completely arbitrary basis, such as on the toss of a coin, and the group members have no direct contact with one another. Some of the participants in Asch's study who conformed to the majority opinion said that they felt it was important to maintain the harmony of the group, which would have been disrupted if they had expressed disagreement with others' judgements. The need for acceptance and approval from others in the group emerges clearly from participants' statements that they did not want to 'be different' from the others, 'look stupid' or 'create a bad impression'.

This kind of concern has been verified using physiological measures. In a study similar to those of Asch, Bogdonoff et al. (1961) measured autonomic arousal in participants. Autonomic arousal is related to anxiety and stress, and blood pressure and heart rate are some of the ways in which it can be measured. They found that arousal was high when participants were faced with an incorrect majority judgement. It dropped if they conformed, but remained high if they did not.

However, the distinction between the two processes of internalisation and compliance may not be clear-cut. It is possible that both may be an influence in a particular situation, as demonstrated by Insko et al. (1983) (see Box 6.6).

Box 6.6 Insko et al. (1983)

Aims: To investigate the role of both normative and informational influence in a colour judgement task.

Procedure: Participants in groups of six were shown a colour slide and asked to decide which of two other slides was more similar in colour. Only one of each group was a genuine participant, with the others being confederates of the experimenter. In a control condition, a different set of participants were tested alone to establish the more frequently given answers. In the study groups, four confederates answered before the genuine participant, giving answers different from those that had been established as most frequent. There were two independent variables:

- public versus private answers
- determined (where the experimenter claimed that it was possible to check independently the accuracy of the judgements made) versus undetermined (where it was claimed that it was purely a matter of opinion, with no way of checking accuracy)

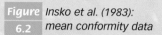 Insko et al. (1983): mean conformity data

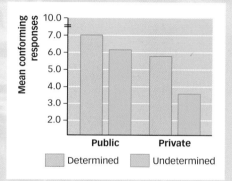

Results: Conformity was more frequent in the 'public' than in the 'private' condition. It was also greater in the 'determined' rather than the 'undetermined' condition. There was greater conformity, both 'public' and private', in the 'determined' condition (see Figure 6.2).

Conclusions: The 'public' versus 'private' comparison showed **normative influence**. The 'determined' versus 'undetermined' comparison showed **informational influence**. Greater conformity, both 'public' and 'private', in the 'determined' condition suggests that informational influence can add to normative influence, so the two can work together to increase conformity.

Summary

- Asch's study showed that people who conform to incorrect judgements do so for different reasons.
- The judgements of others may lead to **internalisation** (or private change), where people change both their opinion and their behaviour. This is the result of **informational influence** and arises from the **need to be right**.
- Others show **compliance** (or public conformity), where people change their behaviour but not their opinion. This is the result of **normative influence** and arises from the **need for approval** from others in the social group.
- Informational and normative influence may **work together** in bringing about conformity.

Social psychology

6

Conformity to social roles

Another reason why people may conform relates to **social roles**. A role is a set of behaviours that are considered appropriate for a person in a particular kind of situation. In Social Identity Theory (SIT), Tajfel (1978) suggested that the social groups to which we belong are an important part of our identities. If people are asked to complete 20 sentences, beginning 'I am…', in quite a lot of the sentences they tend to describe themselves in terms of social categories, such as a mother, a student, a teacher or a rugby player. Group membership shapes our behaviour, and our in-role behaviour is shaped by our beliefs about the demands of the situation and the expectations of others. For example, the role of 'teacher' implies giving students information, setting them tasks, marking their work, going to staff meetings, and so on.

People tend to describe themselves in terms of their social roles, for example as a policeman, a jockey or a student

A seminal study in the area of conformity to social roles was carried out by Zimbardo et al. (1973), a summary of which is presented in Box 6.7.

This study provided a clear demonstration of the readiness with which people may conform to a social role. Participants adopted their roles with relative ease and this is likely to be due, in part at least, to the influence of the media. The prisoners–guards scenario is a standard one in films and on television, and the behaviour of both prisoners and guards reflected rather stereotypical pictures of

Box 6.7   Zimbardo et al. (1973)

Aims: To investigate how people adapt their behaviour to fit roles that they have been asked to take on.

Procedure: Male student volunteers were asked to role-play prisoners and guards in a simulated prison situation, which had been set up in the basement of the Stanford University psychology department. This was made as authentic as possible, for example with individual 'cells', including one for solitary confinement. The students were selected to participate on the basis of tests for emotional stability and physical good health, as well as having clean legal records. They were randomly assigned to be prisoners or guards and were paid for participation. Zimbardo intended the study to last for 2 weeks. He himself took the role of prison superintendent.

'Prisoners' were arrested at home and were charged, finger-printed, strip-searched and deloused. They were given a uniform, a short shift, bearing their prison number. 'Guards' were also given a uniform, together with handcuffs, whistles and dark glasses, to make eye contact with 'prisoners' impossible. In a briefing before the experiment started, they were told that they should not physically harm the 'prisoners', but could use other means to ensure that the 'prisoners' obeyed instructions.

Results: Both 'prisoners' and 'guards' acted out their roles to an extreme degree. The 'guards' became increasingly aggressive, seeming to enjoy the power that they had over the 'prisoners'. They went far beyond the minimum requirements of the role, making 'prisoners' attend endless roll calls, perform long series of press-ups for minor infractions of the rules, take part in humiliating role-play and even clean out toilets with their bare hands. The 'prisoners' became passive and showed extreme stress reactions, such as uncontrolled crying and depression. One 'prisoner' became so disturbed that he had to leave the experiment after 3 days. Because of these extreme reactions, the study was ended after 6 days.

Conclusions: People readily take on roles assigned to them, particularly in an environment that supports these roles. The behaviour of people 'in role' may be very different from their normal behaviour.

how prisoners and guards might be expected to behave. The fact that the students were paid for participation may also have encouraged them to throw themselves wholeheartedly into their roles and may also have made it harder for them to withdraw (the 'prisoner' who left the study early had to be persuaded by Zimbardo that he should leave).

The study was methodologically sound, in that the participants were randomly assigned to be 'prisoners' or 'guards'. If the participants had been allowed to choose which role they preferred — in fact, all the participants had expressed a preference for being a 'prisoner' — it could have been argued that the aggression of the guards was a reflection of individual personality, rather than a demonstration of how ordinary people respond to roles and to the environment in which they find themselves. The screening process ensured that the participants were not unstable and so were not likely to behave in pathological ways. It was also an attempt to make it unlikely that they would become unduly stressed as a result of the study, even though in the event the stress experienced was much greater than had been anticipated. Finally, the participants had no direct experience of the law, which could have distorted their role-play.

However, the study has been widely criticised on ethical grounds. The prisoners were not given full information before the study started, for example, that they would be arrested at home, in full view of their family and neighbours. Some of them suffered extreme stress, and Zimbardo was criticised for not stopping the experiment even earlier than he did, when the full extent of the effects became apparent. In fact, he only stopped it after 6 days when a graduate student pointed out to him that it would be unethical for it to continue. Zimbardo's adoption of the role of prison superintendent was also influenced by the situation and was in conflict with his role as researcher.

Nonetheless, the study provided evidence of the power of conformity to social roles. Zimbardo argued that this information could not have been obtained in any other way and pointed out that the findings can be applied not only to a prisoner–guard scenario, but also to other social relationships where there is a power imbalance, for example parent–child, teacher–student or boss–employee. It also led on to studies into shyness, an area of psychology that had not previously been researched. Zimbardo argued that the shy person acts as his or her own prisoner and own guard, and so prevents him- or herself from taking part in potentially enjoyable and rewarding activities. Perhaps even more importantly, the study was influential in bringing about changes to the prison system in America, and in particular providing support for the notion that an institution can itself have a powerful effect on behaviour.

Summary

- We conform not only to others' opinions but also to **social roles**.
- Zimbardo's prison simulation study demonstrated how **roles** and the **environment** can affect behaviour in situations where there is a power imbalance.

Research into obedience

In contrast to conformity, obedience occurs when a person behaves in a way that he or she would not otherwise behave, as a result of a **direct instruction**.

After the Second World War, German war criminals who had been involved in the Holocaust — the wholesale killing of Jews, together with other 'undesirables' such a gypsies, homosexuals, the mentally ill and people with learning difficulties — were put on trial in Nuremberg for the crimes that they had committed. These trials lasted several years and aroused a great deal of public interest. One of the Nazi high command was Adolf Eichmann, who had escaped to Argentina but was brought to Jerusalem in 1960, where he was later tried and executed for war crimes. Eichmann had been the leading figure in the concentration-camp programme, carrying out Hitler's 'Final Solution' to the Jewish 'problem', which involved the systematic torture and murder of men, women and children. He did not deny his involvement, but his defence against the charges brought against him was that he was only obeying orders that it was impossible for him to refuse — the guilt lay not with him, but with those who gave the orders.

Eichmann did not appear to be a monster. On the contrary, Hannah Arendt, writing about the trial in 1963, was struck by how ordinary he seemed, using the phrase 'the banality of evil'. She argued that attempts to portray him as an evil and sadistic monster were fundamentally misplaced; he was simply an ordinary man who obeyed orders from above, and many people would have acted in the same way in his position.

An American psychologist, Stanley Milgram, was intrigued by the apparent contradiction between the ordinariness of people like Eichmann and the terrible deeds of which they were accused. He was interested in how the idea of obeying orders fitted into the picture, as well as in Arendt's claim that many ordinary people would act in the same way if put in a similar position. He investigated this in a seminal and highly controversial study of obedience in 1963 (see Box 6.8).

Adolf Eichmann on trial, April 1961

Ordinary men who became mass murderers

6

| Box 6.8 | Milgram (1963) |

Aims: To investigate the extent to which ordinary people would obey orders to harm an innocent fellow human being when instructed to do so by an authority figure.

Procedure: Male participants were recruited through a newspaper advertisement to take part in a 'scientific study of memory and learning'. The 40 men selected ranged in age from 20 to 50 years. They had a wide variety of occupations and different levels of education, ranging from those who had manual jobs and only primary school education, to men with doctorates and professional qualifications. Each worked as a pair with a Mr Wallace, an accountant in his fifties, who was a confederate of Milgram but whom the 40 men believed to be a genuine participant.

The experiment was run at Yale University by a young man in a lab coat, who informed Mr Wallace and the genuine participant that the study planned to investigate the effect of punishment on learning. The two men drew lots to decide who was to be the teacher and who the learner, but this was rigged so that the genuine participant was always the teacher. As the learner, Mr Wallace was strapped into a chair and attached to electrodes, linked to a shock generator. At this point, Mr Wallace said that he had a heart condition, but he was assured by the experimenter that although the shocks were painful, they would cause no permanent damage. The teacher's job was to administer a shock every time the learner made a mistake in learning a list of paired associates.

The teacher was then taken into the next room with the shock generator, marked on a 30-point scale with 15-volt intervals from '15 volts — mild shock' up to '450 volts — XXX'. The size of the shock was to be increased by moving one point up the scale each time the learner gave an incorrect answer. Before the study began, the teacher was given a 45-volt shock to make sure that he was convinced the shocks were real. No further shocks were given, although the teacher was unaware of this.

At various points throughout the procedure, the learner complained about his heart bothering him, said that he wanted to stop and that he refused to continue. At 315 volts, he let out a loud scream and at 330 volts there was complete silence from the next room. The teacher was then informed that no answer should count as an incorrect answer and so the teacher should continue to give the shocks. Everything the learner said was scripted and timed to occur when the teacher reached specific shock levels.

Results: All the participants gave increasing shocks in the early part of the experiment; none refused to do so before reaching '300 volts — intense shock'. Some participants expressed unwillingness to continue, but did so when the experimenter said 'Please continue' or 'The experiment requires that you continue' or 'It is absolutely essential that you continue' or 'You have no other choice, you must go on'. This set of four instructions, which Milgram called 'prods', were scripted and used in this set order if the participant was unwilling to continue. If the participant expressed concern for the welfare of Mr Wallace, the experimenter replied: 'Although the shocks may be painful, there is no permanent tissue damage, so please go on'. If the teacher suggested that the learner did not wish to continue, the experimenter replied: 'Whether the learner likes it or not, you must go on until he has learned all the word pairs correctly'. In all, 65% of participants continued to increase the shocks up to the maximum level of 450 volts.

Conclusions: Ordinary people are likely to follow orders given by an authority figure, even to the extent of killing an innocent human being.

Following on from this study, in 1965 Milgram carried out several variations to investigate which aspects of the situation were more important in eliciting obedience (see Box 6.9).

From this series of experiments, the crucial aspects of the situation that promote obedience seem to be the **proximity of the authority figure to the learner**, and the **degree of responsibility** that the 'teacher' needed to take for administering shocks. These issues will be examined later, in the section looking at reasons why people obey others. First, criticisms of Milgram's studies need to be considered, both on methodological and ethical grounds.

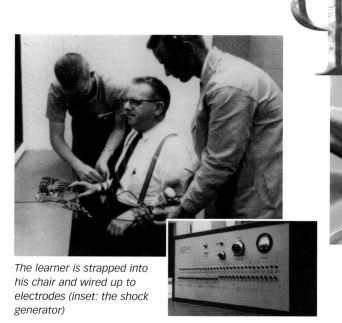

The learner is strapped into his chair and wired up to electrodes (inset: the shock generator)

Box 6.9   Milgram (1965): variations of the initial study

- **Disobedient models**: when the 'teacher' was in the presence of two others (actually confederates of the experimenter) who refused to give shocks, obedience fell from 65% to 10%.

- **Encouragement**: when the participant was not instructed to increase the shocks for each wrong answer, the shock level remained at around 50 volts over the series of trials. However, when two confederates encouraged the participant to increase the shock, the average strength of the shock over 20 trials was 150 volts.

- **Location**: when the study was carried out in a rundown office rather than at Yale University, 50% of participants continued to increase the shocks to the maximum of 450 volts.

- **Proximity of the learner**: when the learner was in the same room as the teacher, the obedience level dropped to 40%. It dropped still further, to 30%, when the teacher had to force the learner's hand on to the shock plate.

- **Proximity of the experimenter**: when the experimenter left the room and gave instructions over the phone, the obedience level dropped to around 20%.

- **Two teachers**: when the participant was paired with another (confederate) teacher who administered the shocks, and the genuine participant only had to read out the words, the obedience level was 92.5%.

The methodology of Milgram's experiments

The methodology of Milgram's studies has attracted several criticisms. Orne and Holland (1968) suggested that the experiments lacked **internal validity**, referring to the extent to which the conclusions drawn from a study are true within the limits of the methods used. They argued that the participants did not believe that they were administering genuine shocks, and therefore the conclusions that Milgram drew about the willingness of people to harm others in obedience to an authority figure were invalid.

Social psychology

To support this, they argued that it is extremely difficult to treat someone you know in the same way as someone who is a complete stranger, so participants may have picked up on the subtle cues provided by the experimenter's behaviour towards Mr Wallace. It must also have seemed odd that the experimenter was completely unperturbed by Mr Wallace's screams and complaints, which could have suggested to the participants that nobody was actually getting hurt. Finally, the set up of the experiment would have seemed odd: why was the 'teacher' required at all, when the experimenter could equally well have given the shocks himself? Orne and Holland suggested that it was Milgram himself, rather than his participants, who was deceived into thinking that the participants accepted the experimental situation at face value.

However, Milgram pointed out that participants completed a questionnaire about a year after the study, in which 56% claimed that they had 'fully believed' that Mr Wallace was receiving painful electric shocks, with a further 24% believing that he was 'probably' receiving them. He also noted the signs of anxiety that participants had shown during the study, for example, nervous laughter, sweating, trembling and stuttering. These obvious signs of stress would not have been shown if participants had not believed that they were administering shocks.

Milgram also suggested two ways of checking whether in fact the participants had been successfully deceived into thinking that they were administering genuine and painful shocks. First, the study could be repeated, eliminating all participants who showed any signs of doubting the cover story. Such a study was carried out by Rosenhan (1969). On the basis of an extensive interview at the end of the study, the data of 30% of participants who had not fully accepted that real shocks were being delivered were eliminated from the analysis. Rosenhan found that 85% of those remaining had continued to deliver shocks up to the maximum level, so the results were even more extreme than those in Milgram's original study.

Milgram's second suggestion, that an experiment should be carried out where participants were their own victims, and could therefore not be in any doubt that they were inflicting harm, was also taken up, by Kudirka this time, in 1965 (see Box 6.10).

Box 6.10   Kudirka (1965)

Aims: To investigate obedience when there is no possibility of participants doubting the negative effects of their behaviour.

Procedure: Participants were instructed to eat 36 quinine-soaked biscuits. These would have had a very unpleasant taste.

Results: Grimaces, moans, expressions of disgust and occasional bouts of nausea demonstrated that this was clearly unpleasant. Nonetheless, virtually all the participants ate all the biscuits.

Conclusions: The suggestion that participants are obedient in experiments such as those of Milgram because they do not accept the experimental situation as real is not supported. There are still high levels of obedience when the reality of the situation is quite unambiguous.

Another study, one with particularly questionable ethics, has also demonstrated obedience when it is quite clear that actual harm is being caused. Sheridan and King (1972) asked participants to give a puppy genuine electric shocks of increasing strength. Even though they could see the puppy yelping, howling and struggling to free itself in response to the shocks, high levels of obedience were found, with every female participant giving the puppy the maximum shock.

Orne and Holland also challenged the **ecological validity** of Milgram's studies, i.e. the extent to which the conclusions can be generalised to relevant naturally occurring situations. They suggested that the obedience shown by Milgram's participants must be seen in the context of the experimental situation. There is an implicit agreement between researcher and participant: the participant agrees to do what the experimenter asks, while the experimenter implicitly promises that no harm will come to the participant in the course of the study. The trust that the participant puts in the experimenter may not apply outside an experimental situation, and therefore the findings of Milgram's experiment cannot validly be generalised outside it.

Milgram suggested that the experimenter–participant relationship is similar to other relationships where there is an imbalance of power. The validity of his research could therefore be tested in a natural situation where this was the case. Hofling et al. did just that in 1966 (see Box 6.11).

Box 6.11   Hofling et al. (1966)

Aims: To investigate obedience where there is an imbalance of power, in a natural setting.

Procedure: A man claiming to be a doctor rang a hospital on 22 separate occasions. Each time, he asked a nurse to give medicine to a patient. This would require the nurse to break three hospital rules:
- Nurses were not allowed to accept instructions over the phone.
- The dose that they were instructed to give was twice the maximum level stated on the box.
- The medicine itself was not authorised, i.e. it was not on the ward stock list.

Results: In reply to questionnaires, most nurses said that they would not obey such an order. In this study, 21 out of 22 nurses followed the orders they were given. When they were debriefed, some of the nurses said that this kind of situation often arose and they followed the instructions because otherwise the doctors would be annoyed.

Conclusions: Where there is an imbalance of power between a person giving instructions and those asked to follow them, a very high proportion of people are prepared to follow unjustified and potentially harmful orders if told to do so by an authority figure.

This study provides some support for the ecological validity of Milgram's research. However, Milgram also claimed his experimental findings to be valid in the context of what had happened in Nazi Germany. There are certainly some similarities between the two situations. Both Milgram's participants and the Nazis who were 'only obeying orders' were put into a situation unlike anything they had ever experienced, and instructed to carry out an extremely distasteful task. In real life, people being given orders to harm or kill others is not an everyday situation.

For example, during the Kosovo conflict, newspapers carried reports of Kosovan men being machine-gunned to death and then set on fire. Presumably, the people who obeyed these orders were not in a normal, everyday situation. It could be that the strangeness of the situation makes obedience more likely, and because Milgram's participants were in an unusual situation, his studies had high ecological validity in this respect.

However, it has been argued that there are also crucial differences between Milgram's experimental situation and obedience in Nazi Germany. First, the experiments were presented to participants in a positive way, i.e. to increase our understanding of human learning, while many Germans recognised the aims of the Nazis as immoral. On the other hand, the Nazi programme, too, was presented positively, in terms of necessary racial purification and the establishment of a Nazi homeland, so perhaps in this respect obedience in Milgram's experiment was not that different from obedience in the 'Final Solution' situation.

Second, Milgram's participants were told that although the shocks were painful, they would not cause any permanent damage, while people like Eichmann knew that they were sending others to their deaths. On the other hand, it is hard to see what other interpretation Milgram's participants could put on Mr Wallace's pleas for the experiment to stop, followed by silence, other than that they were harming him. Indeed, many participants protested at what they were being asked to do, and when they were reunited with Mr Wallace at the end of the experiment, many 'teachers' stated that they thought they had killed him.

Finally, there were no penalties for participants refusing to give shocks in Milgram's experiments, while it would have been dangerous to have refused to obey orders in Nazi Germany: anyone who refused would certainly have been killed. In this respect, there was a notable difference between the situation in Milgram's experiments and the situation in Nazi Germany.

Summary

- The **internal validity** of Milgram's studies has been questioned, but there is evidence from other research that participants accepted that they were harming Mr Wallace.
- Obedience has been demonstrated even when participants are their **own victims**.
- The **ecological validity** of the studies has been questioned, too. However, obedience has also been shown in field experiments, in a natural situation.
- While Milgram's studies in some ways mirror obedience in **Nazi Germany**, there are important **differences**.

The ethics of Milgram's experiments

Milgram's studies have not only been criticised with regard to the methodology used, but also on ethical grounds, in particular by Baumrind (1964), who believed that the experiments should never have taken place. She claimed that the benefits of the research were not enough to justify the distress that participants had

experienced. Certainly, Milgram's research raises a number of ethical issues, in particular the deception of participants and the stress that they experienced as a result of taking part. It is perhaps worth noting that more detailed guidelines were developed as a result of ethical concerns relating to Milgram's research.

First, there was **deception** about the aims of the study: participants were told that it was about the effect of punishment on learning rather than obedience, so they could not give fully informed consent to participate in it. They were also not informed of their right to withdraw at any time. On the contrary, the 'prods' that Milgram used explicitly instructed them to continue and they clearly experienced some pressure to do so. They were also deceived into believing that they were delivering real electric shocks, even though the only shock given in the study was the one delivered to the participant at the outset.

One way of avoiding criticism on these grounds would have been to have given participants full and accurate information about the aims and procedures of the study, and to have asked them to role-play their normal behaviour. However, it seems unlikely that in this case role-play would be a true representation of how they would have behaved if they had not been given this information. Another possibility would have been an observational study of naturally occurring behaviour, but the topic of obedience does not lend itself to this approach. For a valid study to be carried out, deception seems inescapable, and indeed the current BPS guidelines recognise that this may be the case, with deception being avoided wherever possible but not ruled out altogether.

An important way of mitigating this kind of ethical problem, where participants cannot be given full information at the outset, is the use of **debriefing**, and the debriefing that Milgram provided for participants was both thorough and extensive. Debriefing involves giving participants as much information as possible about the study after it has taken place. They are told about the aims of the study, and the reasons behind any deception are explained. They are encouraged to ask questions, and the use to be made of the data is discussed. Participants should also be reassured that the way in which they behaved in the study was perfectly natural in the circumstances, and not in any way unusual or shameful. However, given the nature of Milgram's study, it could be argued that this last aspect of debriefing might be seen as both inappropriate and ineffective. Later research, by Ring et al. in 1970, has looked at the value of debriefing in a replication of Milgram's experiment, a summary of which is provided in Box 6.12, page 180.

The second ethical issue in Milgram's experiment relates to the **stress** that participants undoubtedly experienced as a result of taking part in the study, and it is perhaps even more serious than the deceptions discussed above. This stress had physical effects — at least one participant suffered convulsions — and many would have suffered a loss of self-esteem at the realisation that they had been prepared to harm, and even kill, an innocent person, when told to do so by someone who in fact had no real authority over them. Baumrind (1964) argued that adequate measures had not been taken to protect participants from **psychological harm**.

Box 6.12 Ring et al. (1970)

Aims: To assess the value of debriefing in a replication of Milgram's research.

Procedure: Milgram's research was replicated, but using excruciatingly loud noise (rather than electric shocks), supposedly (but not actually) delivered to the learner's ears. The participants were 57 female students, divided into three groups in the following way:

- They were thanked for participating but not debriefed, and left with the impression that they had really hurt the learner.
- They were thanked and debriefed, and reassured that their behaviour was quite justified. It was also suggested to them that persistence in carrying out the task that they had been given was a more desirable response than leaving before the experiment was over.
- They were debriefed, but not reassured that their behaviour was normal. Instead, they were told that they should have defied the experimenter rather than showing complete obedience.

Results: Those in group 1, who were not debriefed, and those in group 3, who were not reassured about their behaviour, were very upset about the experiment, compared with participants in group 2. However, in follow-up interviews, groups 1 and 3 claimed that they were glad to have taken part and had found it a rewarding and instructive experience. None of them resented being deceived or felt that the study was in any way unethical. Only those in group 1 regretted taking part.

Conclusions: Careful debriefing, which includes both information and reassurance, can go a long way towards overcoming ethical problems. Information appears to be more important than reassurance.

N.B. All participants were fully debriefed when the study had been completed.

In reply to this criticism, Milgram argued that it was not the intention of the study to cause participants stress and that Baumrind was confusing the outcome, i.e. the stress experienced by the participants, with what was expected to happen. He pointed out that before carrying out the study, he had asked many people, including psychiatrists, what they expected the outcome to be. There was general agreement that perhaps fewer than one person in a thousand — someone who was pathologically disturbed — would deliver the 450-volt shock and that most would stop at 150 volts.

However, while the outcome of Milgram's first study may have been extremely unexpected, it cannot have been so for the later studies in the series. He acknowledged that he could have stopped the experiment at a point where it was clear that the participant would continue beyond a particular level of shock, and that as a result some would experience stress, but he did not believe that the brief experience of the experiment was the same as harm. In relation to the issue of the extent to which stress was *caused* to the participants, Milgram argued that it was the way the participants *responded* to the situation that led them to experience stress. He commented that the whole point of the study was that participants had a choice and that most chose obedience.

In relation to the issue of psychological harm, Milgram (1964) carried out a follow-up study, in which those who had taken part in the earlier study were surveyed. He reported that 84% were 'very glad' or 'glad' to have taken part, with 15% feeling neutral and only 1.3% 'sorry' or 'very sorry' to have been part of the experiment. Moreover, nearly three-quarters of participants said that they had learned something of personal importance as a result of participating in the research. Milgram suggested that the ethics of a study are best judged by those who have taken part, rather than in absolute terms.

Baumrind (1964) also suggested that taking part in the research could have led to a **loss of trust in authority**. Milgram agreed that this was possible, but pointed out that to develop distrust of an authority who instructs you to act in an inhumane way towards others was extremely valuable.

Baumrind also claimed that many participants were likely to have suffered long-term harmful effects, including **low self-esteem**. In response, Milgram revealed that all participants had been examined by an impartial psychiatrist 1 year after the study and none showed any sign of suffering lasting harm. It could also be argued that it is not the duty of psychologists to hide from people truths about their own nature, however much they may not wish to know these truths.

It is likely that some participants must have experienced some loss of self-esteem, knowing that they had been prepared to hurt another human being and had been unable to resist an authority figure. This must have been all the more hurtful as the experimenter had no real authority — there was nothing to stop them refusing to continue, as some did. The participants were paid for taking part, but they were paid at the outset and it was made quite clear in the course of the experiment that the money was theirs to keep — they had been paid just for turning up. There was therefore no financial incentive to continue.

Milgram's study continues to be controversial, with many people sharing Baumrind's view that the costs to the participants outweighed the benefits of the study in terms of the information that it provided. It is perhaps worth noting that the American Psychological Association, after an investigation of the study carried out soon after it was published, concluded that it was ethically acceptable, and that in 1965 the American Association for the Advancement of Science awarded Milgram a prize for an outstanding contribution to social psychological research. The study gathered important information about human behaviour that could not really have been established in any other way. Perhaps more than any other experiment, it highlights the capacity for homicidal — even genocidal — behaviour, and not only carries clear implications for international courts, but also changes our perceptions of ourselves. By knowing about this study, we are perhaps ourselves less likely to obey unjustified orders in a similar situation. With this kind of consideration in mind, Elms (1972) judged Milgram's study to be one of the most significant ever carried out in modern psychology, and one of the most moral, both in its attempts to understand important phenomena and in its concern for the welfare of the participants.

6

Summary

- Milgram's studies have been criticised for **deceiving** participants, who could not give their **informed consent** to take part in the study.
- This was at least in part addressed by thorough **debriefing**, which has been shown to be effective.
- Milgram has also been criticised for causing participants **stress** and **psychological harm**. However, Milgram suggested that the ethics of a study should be assessed by participants, most of whom were glad to have taken part.
- The ethics of Milgram's studies continues to be a **controversial** issue.

Other research into obedience

Stimulated by Milgram's research, a more recent series of 19 studies, the **Utrecht Studies of Obedience**, was carried out in Holland during the 1980s by Meeus and Raaijmakers. They suggested that there was an element of ambiguity in Milgram's studies, in that participants could either believe that the shocks given were dangerous, given the labels on the shock generator and the cries of pain coming from the learner, or that they were not, as the experimenter gave repeated assurances that although they were painful, the shocks would cause no lasting harm. The participants might have chosen to accept the experimenter's assurances and so not believed that they were actually causing the learner harm (although, as has been established earlier, there is some evidence that this was not in fact the case). Meeus and Raaijmakers also pointed out that in modern society we are more likely to cause others psychological harm rather than physical harm. Their studies explicitly addressed these points (see Box 6.13).

Box 6.13   Meeus and Raaijmakers (1986)

Aims: To investigate obedience to instructions to cause psychological-administrative harm to others, using a similar paradigm to that used by Milgram.

Procedure: Through a newspaper advertisement, 39 participants, males and females aged 18–55 years were recruited to take part in the study. Each was paired with a job applicant (actually a confederate of the researchers) who was completing a test. If the 'applicant', currently unemployed, passed the test, he would get the job, but he would not be employed if he failed. The participant was asked to make a series of 15 scripted remarks to the applicant while he was completing the test, commenting negatively on his test performance and personality, for example: 'If you continue like this, you will fail the test' and 'This job is much too difficult for you according to the test'. It was made clear to the participants that this commentary was not part of the application process but a separate research project being carried out by the experimenter to investigate a possible link between stress and test achievement. As in Milgram's study, a series of 'prods' was used to encourage the participant to continue with the remarks when they started to refuse to do so. Two variations of the study were also carried out:
- the experimenter was not in the room
- two other participants (actually confederates) refused to continue

Results: In the basic experiment, 90% of participants — a much higher percentage than the 65% in Milgram's study — complied fully with the orders that they had been given, even though they considered them unfair and had protested at continuing to make the negative remarks. As in Milgram's studies, there was a marked drop in obedience in the two variations of the study.

Conclusions: People are willing to inflict psychological harm on others when ordered to do so, even when it is quite clear that actual harm will be caused. It may be easier to cause psychological than physical harm.

Summary

- Meeus and Raaijmakers investigated obedience to orders to inflict **psychological harm**, when it is clear that there has been **actual harm**.
- The obedience rate was **higher** than in Milgram's study.

Why do people obey?

All the studies in the section on research into obedience showed relatively high levels of obedience in people who were instructed to harm others. There may be a number of reasons, some to do with the **situation** and some to do with the **person**, which explain why people do so readily obey in obedience studies.

One situational reason is the **authority of the experimenter**. In Milgram's study, the advertisement used to recruit participants mentioned that it was a 'scientific study'. The experimenter wore a lab coat and the studies took place at Yale University, one of the most prestigious universities in America. All of these aspects of the study would have led to the experimenter being seen as a legitimate authority figure. In one variation, the experimenter was 'called away' and a stand-in (introduced as another participant) suggested the stepwise increase in shocks as his own idea. Obedience was greatly reduced, again suggesting the importance of a recognised authority figure giving the instructions.

Similarly, in Hofling's study of nurses, you will remember that some of the nurses said that they had obeyed the instructions given by doctors over the phone because the doctors would have been annoyed if they had questioned the orders. The nurses obeyed someone whom they saw as a legitimate authority figure.

Further studies have also demonstrated the link between obedience and viewing the person giving the order as an authority figure. For example, Bickman (1974) found that in New York, people were more likely to follow orders to pick up a bag, give someone change for a parking meter or wait for a bus in a different place when the order was given by someone who was dressed in a uniform like that of a police officer, rather than by someone dressed either as a milkman or in an ordinary jacket and trousers. However, these are orders that do not involve harming another person,

Social psychology

6

so while this study shows the influence of authority on obedience, it can only be of limited relevance to the studies that have been examined so far.

Another possible reason for the obedience shown in Milgram's studies is the **gradual increase** in the level of shock, starting at a very mild 15 volts and increasing slowly in 15-volt increments. As each change was so gradual, it would have been difficult to identify the point at which a small and perhaps reasonable punishment became unreasonable. This can be likened to the **foot-in-the-door technique**, where if a person agrees to a small request, he or she is then more likely to respond positively to a larger one. For example, someone on the street might ask for 50p for a cup of coffee, and if this is successful might then ask for £3 to get some food.

Another possible reason for the high rate of obedience in Milgram's studies is being in an **agentic state**. In everyday situations, people are in an autonomous state, i.e. they feel that they are free to make choices in what they do, are aware of the consequences of those choices and accept responsibility for them. In contrast, in an agentic state, the person sees him- or herself as acting as the agent of another person, in this case the individual giving the orders to deliver shocks, who is then seen as bearing the responsibility for his or her behaviour and its outcome. Indeed, in Milgram's study, some participants actually asked who would be responsible if Mr Wallace was harmed, and were assured that the experimenter would take full responsibility, thus explicitly encouraging the agentic state in participants. Similarly, in the Meeus and Raaijmakers study, 45% of participants laid the responsibility for the harm suffered by the job applicant on the experimenter.

There are also reasons to do with the **personal characteristics** of those who readily obey orders. The theory of the **authoritarian personality**, proposed by Adorno et al. (1950), made links between obedience and personality characteristics. **Adorno** himself was a Jewish American at a time when anti-Semitism was widespread in the USA, and was interested in whether prejudice was linked to a particular personality type. He produced scales to measure personality, the most famous of which is the **F-scale**, 'F' standing for 'fascism', in which people indicated whether or not they agreed with a set of statements.

Sample items from the F-scale

- The most important thing to teach children is obedience to their parents.
- Any good leader should be strict with people under him in order to gain respect.
- People can be divided into two distinct classes, the strong and the weak.
- Homosexuals are hardly better than criminals and ought to be severely punished.
- When a person has a problem or worry, it is best for him not to think about it, but to keep busy with more cheerful things.

The scale measures characteristics such as conventionality, submission to those in authority, aggression towards people over whom one is in authority, toughness, destructiveness and superstition, all of which go to make up the authoritarian personality. The scale was successful in identifying people who were likely to be prejudiced: prejudiced people would be likely to show all these characteristics and so agree with all the statements. Adorno's research also showed links between the authoritarian personality and various behaviours, one of which was the likelihood of going to the extreme in a Milgram-type experiment.

Adorno was a **psychodynamic theorist** and, like Freud, believed that personality is developed in childhood. Adults with an authoritarian personality were expected as children to have obeyed their parents immediately and without question, to have been harshly punished for disobedience and to have been shown little affection. As a result of this treatment, they developed unconscious hostile feelings towards their fathers, and as this hostility cannot be expressed directly, it emerges in the way that they treat other people when they are adults. For example, in being aggressive to those over whom they are in authority and submissive towards those who are in authority over them, as well as showing obedience to an authority figure, they are re-enacting symbolically the father–child relationship.

There is some support for the link between the authoritarian personality and obedience. For example, in a replication of Milgram's study, Elms and Milgram (1966) found that people who scored high on the F-scale were more likely to obey orders. Miller (1975) carried out a similar study, but to ensure that the participants were aware that they were genuinely causing harm, asked participants to give themselves electric shocks while working on arithmetic problems. Again, those with authoritarian characteristics were more likely to obey this order.

It would also be expected that someone with an authoritarian personality would be less likely to consider the 'teacher' responsible for giving shocks, as he or she would see unquestioning obedience to authority in a positive way. Blass (1995) presented a short version of Milgram's documentary about his research to students, which showed a 'teacher' administering a 180-volt shock to the 'learner'. The more authoritarian students were less likely than the others to attribute responsibility for giving the shocks to the 'teacher' and to consider the responsibility to be that of the experimenter.

It is possible that individual personality characteristics may have had some influence on the obedience levels found in research. However, given the high levels of obedience found across all the studies discussed above, situational factors would perhaps seem to have more of a part to play.

Summary

- **Situational factors** in obedience studies include the **authority of the experimenter**, the **gradual increase** in punishment and the individual moving from an **autonomous** to an **agentic state**.
- **Personal factors**, such as having an **authoritarian personality**, may also play a part.
- **Situational factors** are likely to have **more influence** than personal factors.

Chapter Social influence

Independent behaviour

All the research that has been examined in this chapter has demonstrated quite high (and in some cases extremely high) levels of conformity and obedience. However, in all the studies looked at, some people did not conform or obey the orders that they were given. Some of the reasons underlying such independent behaviour will now be considered. These reasons can be grouped broadly under three headings: **cultural reasons**, **situational reasons** and **reasons relating to personal characteristics**.

Cultural reasons for independent behaviour

Several researchers have replicated Milgram's study at different times and in different countries. For example, Mantell (1971), using a German sample, found an obedience level of 85%, while Kilham and Mann (1974), using an Australian sample, found somewhat lower obedience levels than those in Milgram's study.

It is difficult to draw any definite conclusions from the results of these studies, because the behaviour of participants in these later studies may well have been affected by knowledge of Milgram's work. The studies were also not exact replications, and small differences in the make-up of the sample, for example in age range or educational level, would make direct comparisons unreliable. Nevertheless, it is possible that differences in the social norms might make it easier for members of some cultures to resist obeying orders.

One broad way in which cultures can be differentiated is in terms of the **individualist/collectivist** distinction (which was outlined in Chapter 3, page 70), based on cultural variation in beliefs, attitudes, norms and values. The emphasis on the needs and goals of the social group in collectivist cultures would suggest that people in these cultures are more likely to conform, while those in an individualist culture, with its emphasis on individual choice and responsibility, are more likely to show independent behaviour. This possible cultural difference has been investigated in research.

Bond and Smith (1996) carried out a meta-analysis of 133 conformity studies carried out in 17 different countries, and which used an Asch-type line-judging task. They found that people from individualist cultures tended to conform less than those from collectivist cultures. Similarly, Sundberg et al. (1970) found that American high school pupils, coming from an individualist culture, showed less conformity than those from an Indian population, with a collectivist culture. Kim and Marcus (1999) had similar findings when comparing European Americans and Asian Americans.

However, the individualist/collectivist distinction is quite broad, and there are variations between different cultures that would all be classified under the same broad heading. Moreover, cultures themselves are not static, and it may be that the general ethos of a country at a particular point in time may lead to a greater or lesser likelihood of people demonstrating independent behaviour. For example, in a replication of Asch's study, Larsen (1974) found much lower levels of conformity among American students than Asch had found 20 years previously. The period when Asch carried out his study was one of low political activity among students, whereas

Larsen's study found that American students were now prepared to question social issues

Larsen's study was done against the background of the Vietnam War, with many American students questioning not only their country's involvement in the war but also other social issues. In a further replication, Larsen et al. (1979) found higher levels of conformity again and argued that this was linked to a drop in student activism, with a return to concerns about jobs and careers.

How individuals are **socialised** within a culture, for example with respect to gender roles, can also influence independent behaviour, as demonstrated by Larsen et al. (1979) (see Box 6.14).

Box 6.14   Larsen et al. (1979)

Aims: To investigate the effect of the status of others in the group on conformity in male and female participants.

Procedure: In a replication of Asch's conformity study, 20 male and 20 female undergraduates were asked to make judgements in groups of seven, six of whom were confederates of the experimenter. The confederates were instructed to give the same wrong answer on 12 of the 18 trials. In the 'high status' condition, the confederates were introduced as graduate assistants or senior students. In the control 'peer' condition, there were no introductions.

Results: Males conformed significantly more often than females in the 'high status' than in the 'peer' condition. Females conformed significantly more often than males in the 'peer' condition. In the debriefing, all the male participants referred to status in the 'high status' condition, while only one of the females did, suggesting that status was more salient for males.

Conclusions: The results can be explained in terms of males learning that power is the crucial factor in achieving goals, whereas females learn the value of interpersonal relationships. The social costs of resisting conformity in the two conditions are therefore different for males and for females.

Social psychology

Situational reasons for independent behaviour

One situational influence affecting conformity is the difficulty of the exercise and how important it is seen to be. In an Asch-type task, Baron et al. (1996) found that people were more likely to show independent behaviour when the task was easy, which would presumably lower informational influence, and when there were no incentives for getting it right.

The nature of the situation affects not only conformity but also **obedience**. For example, Milgram's series of studies showed that independent behaviour was more likely when the experimenter was absent (the 'teacher' would presumably feel less pressure to obey the instructions that he had been given) and when the 'learner' was in the same room as the 'teacher' (the effects of his actions, and therefore of obedience, were then more apparent).

A similar effect was shown when the nature of the task was varied, in the 'two teachers' condition, with more independent behaviour being shown when the participant had to administer the shocks rather than merely playing the more minor role of reading out the word pairs. This finding has also been confirmed in a replication of Milgram's study by Kilham and Mann (1974). It seems that independent behaviour is more likely as distance from the authority figure increases and as the effect of obeying orders is made more immediate.

Summary

- There is some evidence that people from **individualist cultures** are more likely to demonstrate independent behaviour than those from **collectivist cultures**.
- The **general ethos** of a culture at a particular point in time can also be linked to the prevalence of independent behaviour.
- Independent behaviour is related to the **socialisation processes** that a person experiences within his or her culture.
- **Situational influences** on independent behaviour in conformity and obedience studies include **task difficulty** and the **proximity** of both the person giving the order and the victim.

Reasons for independent behaviour relating to personal characteristics

In his debriefing of participants, Asch (1951) distinguished between three different types of response among those who did not conform. Some withdrew emotionally from the situation, while others stuck to their judgement on the basis of feeling a need to cope effectively with the task. In the third group, although the participants were clearly aware of conflict and were sensitive to the group, their **confidence** in their own perceptions allowed them to resist the opposition of the group.

The role of confidence in independent behaviour has also been demonstrated in a replication of Asch's experiment carried out by Perrin and Spencer (1981), in which very few participants conformed. The participants were medical and engineering students. Both these groups deal with physical phenomena, where accurate observation and measurement are crucial. Given the nature of the task in the experiment, their knowledge and skills could have made them more sure of the judgements they were asked to make, and more likely to resist conformity to the group judgement.

A further factor in independent behaviour is previous **life experience**. There is strong evidence of this from one of Milgram's studies, and in particular two participants who refused to follow the experimenter's orders. One of them, Gretchen Brandt, refused to obey when the voltage was raised to 210 volts. It emerged that she had grown up in Nazi Germany. When asked to explain why she had refused to obey the order to give shocks, she replied: 'Perhaps we have seen too much pain'. The other participant, Jan Rensaleer, had lived in Holland during the Second World War. He, too, had had direct experience of the potentially terrible consequences of unquestioning obedience. Both these people accepted responsibility for their behaviour, rather than giving control to the experimenter.

Further evidence for the importance of life experience comes from Burgess (2004). This study asked students to behave in ways that went against their personal attitudes. For example, they were asked to discriminate against a disadvantaged and marginal group, or to write an essay in support of a large increase in student tuition fees. In this study, life experience was again the main factor influencing those who refused to carry out these tasks.

The role of enduring **personality characteristics** in the responses of individuals to social influence has also been investigated. Many current theories of personality, such as the theory of Costa and McCrae (1992), agree about the number and nature of personality factors: there are broadly five factors (or dimensions) of personality, and these are often called the **Big Five**. Each factor is associated with a particular set of traits (see Table 6.2).

Table 6.2 *The Big Five personality factors*

Factor	Characteristics
Extraversion	Assertive, cheerful, excitable, sociable, talkative, daring
Agreeableness	Warm, generous, affectionate, modest, kind, trusting, helpful
Conscientiousness	Organised, reliable, ambitious, decisive, thoughtful
Neuroticism	Emotionally unstable, moody, irritable, insecure
Openness	Imaginative, perceptive, reflective, having many interests

This model was used by DeYoung et al. in 2002 to investigate a possible link between personality and conformity (see Box 6.15).

The researchers suggest that having a tendency to conform has both positive and negative aspects: those who conform will tend to be stable, but also rigid and less able or willing to adjust to novelty and change, because they are likely to have low

6

| **Box 6.15** | **DeYoung et al. (2002)** |

Aims: To investigate the association between personality characteristics and conformity.

Procedure: A sample of 467 participants, aged 15–59 years, completed a personality test and were tested for conformity. The Big Five model of personality was used, with the factors being grouped together into two higher-order factors:
- stability: conscientiousness, agreeableness and emotional stability (i.e. the polar opposite of neuroticism)
- plasticity: extraversion and openness

Results: Stability was a good predictor of conformity, with those scoring high on this factor being likely to conform. Plasticity was negatively associated with conformity.

Conclusions: Relatively stable personality characteristics are associated with conformity. There is an association between the ability to resist pressure to conform and the characteristics of extraversion and openness.

scores on openness. They also suggest that there is a biological basis to these personality characteristics, and therefore willingness to conform, making links to neurotransmitter levels.

Further support for this link between personality and independent behaviour (in this case refusing to obey an unjustified order) comes from Burley and McGuiness (1977). From their study, they concluded that those who were defiant were more socially intelligent, i.e. they had a clearer perception of the social situation of the study and were more able to identify different possible behaviours, such as acting independently, which are characteristics associated with openness.

Rotter (1966) suggested that a personal influence on conformity is **locus of control**. This refers to the extent to which individuals believe they can control events that affect them. Rotter argued that as a result of their experiences, people develop beliefs about what causes events that happen to them. These beliefs guide their attitudes and behaviour. People with a high **internal** locus of control believe that events come about largely from their own actions and efforts. Those with a high **external** locus of control believe that the way events turn out is largely due to other people, fate, chance or luck.

For example, a student with an internal locus of control might attribute getting a good mark for an essay to the result of his or her skill in essay writing, and a poor grade to not having spent enough time in preparing it. A student with an external locus of control might attribute a good grade to luck and a poor grade to the teacher not liking him or her. Locus of control is seen as a continuum along which an individual can be placed at any point.

Rotter (1966) developed a 23-item **forced choice scale** (or Internal-External Locus of Control Scale) to measure locus of control. This consists of pairs of statements, and for each item the respondent is asked to indicate which of the two statements more closely fits his or her views.

Sample items from Rotter's Locus of Control Scale (1966)

a Many of the unhappy things in people's lives are partly due to bad luck.

People's misfortunes result from the mistakes they make.

b Heredity plays the major role in determining one's personality.

It is one's experiences in life which determine what they're like.

c In the case of the well-prepared student there is rarely, if ever, such a thing as an unfair test.

Many times, exam questions tend to be so unrelated to coursework that studying is really useless.

There is some evidence that those with an internal locus of control are less likely to be conformist than those with an external locus of control. Larsen et al. (1979) carried out a study of conformity using a variation of the Asch paradigm. They found that participants who scored high for external locus of control on this scale were more likely to conform to incorrect judgements than those with low scores. However, situational factors were also important, as conformity by those with an external locus of control dropped markedly when others in the group were of low status, whereas those with an internal locus of control were much less affected by status.

A similar interaction between locus of control and situational factors has been shown in a study by Miller (1975), who found that participants with an external locus of control were more obedient than those with an internal locus of control, but only when the person giving the instructions was of high status. Those with an internal locus of control were unaffected by status. Williams and Warchal (1981) suggest that Rotter's internal/external distinction may be insensitive to the variability of different situations.

Evidence to support the suggestion that locus of control on its own is a useful predictor of the response to social influence is relatively weak. For example, in a Milgram-type study, Schurz (1985) found no difference in obedience and independent behaviour between those with an internal and those with an external locus of control. Avtgis (1998), in a meta-analytic review of the relationship between internal and external locus of control and conformity, found only a low, non-significant correlation of 0.37 across studies.

Other personal factors in independent behaviour have also been suggested. For example, in an investigation of associations between personality characteristics and conformity, Heaven (1986) found that there was a significant correlation between conformity and a low **level of education**, suggesting that those with a higher level of education would be more likely to show independent behaviour. Milgram (1974) also reported research carried out by Kohlberg, who found that people who resisted orders to obey had reached a higher stage of **moral development**.

Summary

- **Confidence** has been shown to be an important factor in resisting conformity.
- **Life experience** can lead to independent behaviour in obedience studies.
- The personality factors of **extraversion** and **openness** have been shown to be associated with the ability to resist pressures to conform.
- There is some evidence that people with an **internal locus of control** are more likely to show independent behaviour in conformity studies, but there is considerable variation in the findings.
- In both conformity and obedience studies, the influence of locus of control interacts with **status**.
- **Level of education** and **moral development** have also been suggested as factors in independent behaviour.

The implications for social change of research into social influence

Research into social influence, and in particular conformity and obedience, has much to offer to significant issues outside the laboratory. One subject of specific importance is the role of **conformity to peers**, noted by Dohner (1972), in drug use, truancy, sexual experimentation and other kinds of inappropriate behaviour in adolescents. Lee et al. (2007) found that young people who had recently left high school frequently reported conformity to their peers as a reason for drug use.

Williams et al. (1981) also found that high levels of conformity contributed to alcohol and marijuana use in adolescents. In addition, this study demonstrated a link between conformity and low levels of assertiveness, a finding replicated in a study by Williams and Warchal (1981). These results suggest that showing young people how to be more assertive could help them resist pressure to engage in inappropriate behaviours. Williams (1980) has demonstrated that **assertiveness training** can indeed be effective in reducing substance abuse in young people through lessening conformity to peer pressure.

It should be noted, however, that conformity can also be a positive factor in helping young people to avoid inappropriate behaviour. Mouttapa et al. (2003), on the basis of a study carried out with high school adolescents, found that conformity to authority in the form of parents, teachers and religion was a protective factor against vulnerability to behaviours such as alcohol consumption, drug use and risky sexual behaviours.

Milgram's studies of obedience also have clear relevance to military issues. Blass (1991), himself a Holocaust survivor, believes that we need to learn from the insights provided by Milgram's experiments into the role of obedience to authority. With the rise of revisionism and Holocaust denial, we should raise our consciousness of the effects of unquestioning obedience to unjustified orders from authority figures, to avoid genocide.

This may not be as straightforward as Blass suggests. Minow (2006) points out that studies such as those carried out by Milgram raise serious questions about whether young soldiers can or will use their own sense of moral values to disobey illegal orders. Various legal systems have adopted versions of the rule stating that punishment within the military cannot be avoided using the defence given by Eichmann and others that they were 'only obeying orders'. However, many factors — the stress and fear experienced in wartime, the ambiguities and complexities of the war against terror, together with confusion about what the standards are for interrogation and treatment of civilians by the military — create difficulties for soldiers, who must learn both to obey orders and to resist illegal orders.

There are also implications arising from research looking at obedience to orders to inflict psychological rather than physical harm. Meeus and Raaijmakers stress the need to focus on administrative violence, as it is both much more common and easier to inflict than physical violence, but nonetheless can have negative effects on those who experience it.

Research into both conformity and obedience has highlighted the role of the **hierarchical nature of society**. The influence of an imbalance of power between individuals was demonstrated both in Zimbardo's prison simulation study on conformity to roles and in studies into obedience to authority such as that carried out with nurses by Hofling et al. Clearly, there are times when conformity and obedience are desirable, and indeed necessary, for the smooth functioning of society. However, there also needs to be awareness that both conformity and obedience are at times inappropriate.

Education may have an important part to play. Richey (1976) has suggested that studies such as those of Asch and Milgram are helpful in demonstrating inappropriate conformity and obedience. Given the influence of peer group pressure in adolescence, he suggests that viewing films of these studies and the use of role-play can form a basis for helping young people to find ways to resist conforming to others without antagonising their friends. They could also alert them to the dangers of unquestioningly accepting orders from an authority figure.

Summary

- **Conformity** plays a role in inappropriate behaviours, such as the use of drugs, in young people. **Assertiveness training** can be effective in helping them to **resist** peer pressure. However, conformity may also play a part in helping young people to resist peer pressure.
- Milgram's obedience studies have complex **military implications**.
- There is a need to focus on resisting orders to inflict **psychological harm**.
- Both conformity and obedience studies demonstrate the influence of the **hierarchical nature of society**.
- **Education** has a part to play in raising awareness of the dangers of conformity and unquestioning obedience.

Social psychology

Terms explained

conformity: changing behaviour in response to group pressure, whether or not this pressure is made explicit or is just in the mind of the individual. As a result, the person behaves differently from how they would behave if they were on their own.

debriefing: an interview carried out after a study in which the researcher provides participants with full information about the study, and aims to restore them to the same psychological state they were in before they took part. Participants should be told the aims of the study, if this has not been covered before their participation, and the use to be made of the findings. They should also be reassured that their own behaviour as a participant was perfectly normal. Debriefing is particularly important when participants have been deceived about the nature of the study, as in Milgram's experiments.

independent behaviour: resisting conformity or obedience, i.e. implied or explicit pressure to behave in a particular way, or refusing to respond to a direct instruction.

obedience: as the result of being given a direct instruction, behaving in a way other than a person would choose to behave if not given this instruction.

Psychopathology (abnormality)

In this chapter, we will be looking at:
- definitions of abnormality
- the biological approach to psychopathology
- psychological approaches to psychopathology
- biological therapies
- psychological therapies

Some areas of psychology focus on attempting to establish the **general laws** of human behaviour that can be applied to everyone, such as the nature of short-term memory or the stress response. Other areas are more interested in **individual differences**, for example variations in personality or intelligence. **Psychopathology**, the branch of psychology concerned with psychological disorders, is also an example of this approach. It is an important area in psychology because mental disorders cause a great deal of unhappiness to millions of people, and research in this field aims to help relieve their suffering.

There are a number of controversies within this topic. One important issue is how 'abnormality' might be defined — a crucial question, because if people with a mental disorder are to be helped, we need to establish who falls into this category. There is further controversy about what causes people to develop a mental disorder, and indeed whether we need to concern ourselves with causes. This issue can be important, as what is seen as the cause (the **aetiology**) of a disorder may determine the treatment (**therapy**).

Definitions of abnormality

Several attempts have been made to provide a way of defining an individual as abnormal. Three definitions will be examined here: **deviation from social norms**, **failure to function adequately**, and **deviation from ideal mental health**.

Deviation from social norms

Social norms can be defined as shared expectations within a social group or culture regarding what is considered appropriate behaviour within the group. These norms can apply to different roles, such as the way we might expect a teacher to behave, and to different situations, such as eating in a restaurant or attending a church. Some norms are explicit, such as driving on the left-hand side of the road, but more often they are what Scheff (1966) refers to as **residual rules** — unwritten rules of a social group, of which people are somehow aware and to which they generally conform. For example, you do not stand staring into space in the middle of a busy pavement, or sing rugby songs in a church. The definition of abnormality as deviation from social norms refers to people not observing residual rules, which is seen as both abnormal and undesirable.

However, there are some problems with this definition. One is that we can only make judgements about behaviour in relation to the situation in which the behaviour is shown. For example, singing loudly and tunelessly in the shower would not be seen as abnormal, but the same behaviour in a library would be likely to be viewed as abnormal. Similarly, killing people in wars may be seen as heroic, but as murder at other times.

A further problem is that social norms change over time. For instance, dyeing your hair pink or sunbathing topless would have been regarded as abnormal 50 years ago, but would be seen nowadays as a matter of personal choice. An example of this within the field of mental health is homosexuality. Homosexuality was classified as a mental disorder in the 1973 version of *DSM-II*, the *Diagnostic and Statistical Manual*, which defines and describes mental disorders and which is widely used by psychiatrists. However, it no longer appeared as a listed disorder when the manual was updated in 1980. Most people in the UK now accept homosexuality as falling within social norms, and its acceptance has been ratified by the introduction of civil partnerships between same-sex couples.

It may also be worth noting that some social norms need to be broken. In the 1950s, it was quite common to see notices advertising rooms to let that read 'No coloured, no Irish, no dogs', a practice that has now become not only socially unacceptable, but also illegal.

Nonetheless, the definition of abnormality in terms of deviation from social norms has been applied. Some repressive political regimes, such as that in the former Soviet Union, have classified those who disagreed with the way that the state was run as having a mental disorder, and confined them to psychiatric institutions for challenging the actions of the government.

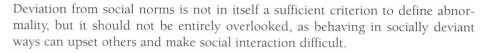

Deviation from social norms is not in itself a sufficient criterion to define abnormality, but it should not be entirely overlooked, as behaving in socially deviant ways can upset others and make social interaction difficult.

Failure to function adequately

Behaviour that is adaptive allows individuals to function well within the social group to which they belong. If a person's behaviour disrupts his or her ability to work or to have rewarding social relationships with others, it can be said to be **maladaptive** and defined as abnormal. Within this general definition, there are several different criteria for defining behaviour as maladaptive.

One criterion is that the individual experiences **personal distress**. For example, symptoms such as loss of appetite, insomnia and general aches and pains may well indicate underlying depression, which — while not uncommon — is classified as a mental disorder. However, there are problems with using this criterion to define abnormality. In some circumstances, for example when someone close has died, distress would be a natural reaction — indeed, lack of distress is likely to be seen as abnormal. Conversely, some people with a mental disorder do not experience distress. For instance, someone with antisocial personality disorder is likely to behave violently and with no concern for the feelings or well-being of others, but does not him- or herself feel distressed.

Another possible criterion is that of **causing distress to others**, as in the above example of antisocial personality disorder, but again there are problems. For instance, someone with an anxiety disorder might be able to hide his or her symptoms from others and so not cause distress to others, but is likely to be very unhappy and to find it difficult to function.

Davison and Neale (1994) have suggested the further criterion of **unexpected behaviour**. Although behaviour inevitably varies a little in different situations, people tend to behave in reasonably predictable ways, and this is one of the factors that allow us to interact appropriately with them. If a person is extremely unpredictable, it is difficult to interact with him or her, and that individual's behaviour would therefore be maladaptive. However, one problem here is the difficulty of where to draw the dividing line between expected variations in behaviour and unexpected behaviour. It may also be the case that someone's behaviour is only unexpected because we are unaware of the reasons behind it.

A final criterion is **bizarre behaviour**. For example, people with obsessive-compulsive disorder (OCD) may feel the need to repeat a behaviour such as washing their hands several hundred times a day, getting extremely sore hands in the process and leaving little time for anything else. However, a lot of mental disorders, such as depression, are seldom associated with bizarre behaviour, so it is not a particularly helpful criterion.

Defining abnormality using the general criterion of failure to function adequately and the idea of deviation from social norms both have something to offer. However, there are also problems with these attempts to identify a single criterion, and in practice, psychologists have often found that it is useful to consider a person's behaviour against several criteria. Rosenhan and Seligman (1969) suggested six criteria, any combination of which could indicate that a person's behaviour is abnormal.

Rosenhan and Seligman's criteria for judging behaviour as abnormal:

- personal distress
- maladaptiveness
- irrationality
- unpredictability
- unconventionality and statistical rarity
- observer discomfort

This list contains all the criteria that have been considered so far and also includes **statistical rarity**, i.e. a behaviour is said to be abnormal if very few people show it. As with the other criteria, this definition has its problems. For example, how rare would a behaviour have to be in order to be classified in this way? Where would the cut-off point be? A mental disorder such as depression, which is relatively common, would not be identified using this criterion. Moreover, some relatively rare characteristics — such as the scientific insight of Stephen Hawking or the creativity of Picasso — would be classified as abnormal, but they are not problematic, so this does not seem to be a helpful criterion. However, like the other suggestions discussed, it may be useful if taken together with additional criteria.

Overall, combining all the criteria seems the best way forward. However, there is still the problem that for each criterion, the person doing the assessment must make a subjective judgement. It could well be that different assessors would disagree about whether a particular criterion had been met or not, particularly with border-line cases.

The conclusion seems inevitable that there is no easy way to define abnormality and that there is no clear-cut dividing line between normality and abnormality. Therefore, it makes sense to see abnormality as a continuum, with 'normal' at one end, 'abnormal' at the other and various degrees of normality in between. This seems a realistic approach, because we have all had irrational thoughts or experienced distress at some time, yet would not necessarily be classified as abnormal or as having a mental disorder.

Deviation from ideal mental health

Because attempts to define abnormality have proved so difficult, it has been suggested that a different approach should be taken: that of defining normality. Anyone who does not meet the criteria for normality would therefore by default be classified as abnormal.

This approach started with Freud, who saw the goal of therapy as a well-balanced individual, able to love and to work, i.e. to lead a productive life and have good and rewarding relationships with others. Other theorists, for example Jahoda in 1958, have built on this approach, suggesting characteristics that describe a mentally healthy person.

Jahoda's characteristics of a well-adjusted person:

- self-acceptance
- potential for growth and development
- autonomy
- accurate perception of reality
- environmental competence
- having positive interpersonal relations

More recently, Atkinson et al. (1983) listed six characteristics that they proposed a normal person would exhibit to a greater extent than someone classified as abnormal, reflecting the idea that mental health and abnormality should be seen as a continuum.

Atkinson et al.'s characteristics of a well-adjusted person:

- efficient perception of reality
- self-knowledge
- ability to control own behaviour
- self-esteem and acceptance
- ability to form affectionate relationships
- productivity

There is considerable overlap between these two lists. Both cover the characteristics that Freud identified as important for good mental health, and in both, the other characteristics refer to having a realistic idea of what you and others are capable of, being able to make sense of what is going on around you, being aware of your own motives and feelings, being able to control to a large extent inappropriate urges, having a sense of self-worth, and feeling comfortable that you are accepted by others.

This approach has intuitive appeal and has the advantage of taking a *positive* approach to mental health, which could be useful, for example, in setting goals within a therapeutic situation. However, it is also not without its problems. As with the other approaches to defining abnormality that have been discussed, judgements are necessarily subjective and there could well be disagreement when different people use these criteria to make an assessment. There is still no clear dividing line between normal and abnormal. These criteria also outline ideal mental health, which raises the question of how many people, who would not be thought of as abnormal, could be said to meet *all* these criteria fully.

Summary

- Controversies in psychopathology include **problems of defining abnormality** and **identifying its causes**.
- One definition is **deviation from social norms**. However, this raises problems of the role of the situation in making judgements, and norms changing across time.
- **Failure to function adequately** is a further basis for definition. This includes the criteria of **personal distress**, **causing distress to others** and exhibiting **unexpected** and **bizarre behaviour**. However, each of these criteria raises problems.

- It has been suggested that different **definitions should be taken together** in making a judgement about abnormality, but this judgement is still **subjective**.
- Abnormality is better seen as a **continuum** from normal to abnormal, with varying degrees of mental health in between.
- An alternative approach to defining abnormality is in terms of **deviation from ideal mental health**. However, assessment is still **subjective**, and the criteria represent an **ideal** that many people may not meet.

The biological approach to psychopathology

There are several models of abnormal behaviour, which vary in terms of what are seen as the **causes** of mental disorders. The perceived causes have implications for what is considered to be appropriate **treatment** or therapy. In this section and the next, the biological model and psychological models will be examined in terms of what each has to offer our understanding of why people develop mental disorders and how they may therefore best be helped.

The biological (or medical) model of mental disorder is the most widely accepted model of psychopathology. A mental disorder is seen as a medical problem, so the term '**mental illness**' is widely used in this context. It is assumed that mental illnesses have a physical cause, and the treatment offered is therefore also physical.

In the medical model of physical illness, symptoms are assumed to be caused by an organic **lesion**, i.e. a change in the structure of body tissue brought about by disease or injury. The symptoms allow **diagnosis**, i.e. identification of the problem, and **prognosis**, i.e. an assessment of the likely outcome of the disorder. Treatment involves treating the lesion by physical means.

For a mental illness, the model is similar. It is often not possible to identify a physical cause for the illness from the symptoms that the patient presents, but it is nonetheless assumed that there is an underlying physical cause. Instead of diagnosis, the disorder will be classified, using one of the **classification systems** such as *DSM*, mentioned in the previous section, as a guide for physical treatment (see Figure 7.1).

Figure 7.1 *The medical model*

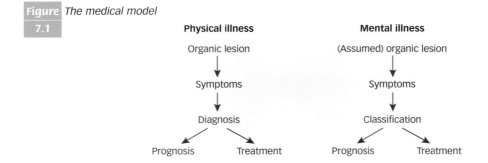

Within the medical model, people are treated by GPs or psychiatrists, who have trained as medical doctors and then carried out further training in mental illness.

The model proposes several possible causes of mental illness. One is **infection** from bacteria or viruses. These cause many physical illnesses, for example measles and flu, and psychological functioning can also be affected in this way. We saw in Chapter 2 how Clive Wearing's memory was affected by a rare viral infection that damaged his brain, and it is possible that some mental illnesses are caused in the same way. For example, there are structural differences between the brains of schizophrenics and those of people who are not schizophrenic. Using MRI scanning, Brown et al. (1986) showed that many schizophrenics have lighter brains, with enlarged ventricles (cavities that hold cerebrospinal fluid). It has been suggested that both these neurological abnormalities and schizophrenia are the result of infection by a virus during foetal development.

Mednick et al. (1988) investigated the incidence of schizophrenia in people who had been exposed, while their mothers were pregnant, to an influenza virus during a 5-week influenza epidemic in Helsinki during 1957. Those exposed during the second trimester of pregnancy were significantly more likely to be schizophrenic than those exposed during the first or third trimesters. As the second trimester is crucial for cortical development, exposure to the virus at this stage could have led to the neurological abnormalities associated with schizophrenia.

However, infection cannot explain most cases of schizophrenia, or the vast majority of cases of mental illness, where there is no evidence of infection, so this explanation is of limited value.

Another explanation is **genetic factors**. Some physical disorders, such as cystic fibrosis and haemophilia, are passed on through the genes, and it is possible that at least some mental illnesses are transmitted from parents to children in the same way. There is quite strong evidence for a genetic basis to bipolar disorder (also known as manic depression) and schizophrenia. For example, the general probability of someone developing schizophrenia is 1 in 100, but Kendler (1983) found that children with a schizophrenic biological parent were 18 times more likely than average to develop the disorder.

However, the evidence is far less strong for other disorders, such as depression. Genetic factors cannot provide a full explanation of abnormality, though they may be a contributing factor. The **diathesis-stress model** of mental illness suggests that genes may create a predisposition to develop certain disorders, which may then be triggered by environmental factors, such as stress.

Mental illnesses are also seen as having a **biochemical cause**. Some have been linked to **hormones**, chemicals produced by the endocrine system. For example, certain disorders of the thyroid gland have been linked to depression. An imbalance of **neurotransmitters** (chemical messengers that carry information between neurones) has also been linked to mental illnesses. For instance, there is evidence that depression is associated with low levels of serotonin and noradrenaline, and schizophrenia with high levels of dopamine. The effect of the drugs used to treat them is to readjust neurotransmitter levels. However, the association between biochemical levels and these illnesses is only correlational: there is not enough evidence to claim that insufficient serotonin *causes* depression, or that too much dopamine *causes* schizophrenia. For example, the neurotransmitter levels and the illness could in both cases be the result of a third factor, such as a genetic predisposition.

Another possible cause of mental illness is **neurological damage**. A famous example of the effect of brain damage on psychological functioning is the case of Phineas Gage, an American railway worker who in 1848 had an iron bar shot into the frontal part of his brain when an explosive charge went off prematurely (see Figure 7.2). As a result of the damage to his brain, he became much less inhibited than previously, swearing, taking his clothes off in public and generally being more impulsive and less conscientious.

Figure 7.2 The case of Phineas Gage

A tamping iron, over 1 metre long and tapering from 1.25 to 0.25 inches in diameter, entered under the left cheekbone and came out through the top of the head.

Another example of mental illness resulting from brain damage is Fregoli's delusion. People with this condition believe that strangers are people they know, even though they do not look like them. They may try to make sense of the mismatch between appearance and identity — as they perceive it — by believing that people they know are going about in disguise (see Box 7.1).

Box 7.1 Ellis and Szulecka (1996): case study of a patient with Fregoli's delusion

Miss C believed that she was being stalked by an ex-lover and his girlfriend, disguised by wigs and wearing dark glasses, who followed her everywhere. She reported them to the police. She would go up to strangers and demand that they took off their disguises, and believed that the gas man who had come to read her meter had adopted this disguise to get into her house.

The false recognition of strangers was eliminated by drugs, but the delusion remained; she merely believed that the police had made the ex-lover and his girlfriend stop harassing her.

Miss C's brain was scanned using a CAT scan, which displays a three-dimensional representation of the brain's structure and is therefore useful for such tasks as locating tumours. The scan showed that as a result of a stroke, there was quite severe damage to the cerebral cortex, which had presumably caused the delusion.

The biological model assumes that the causes of mental illness are **organic**, and therefore the treatment should use **somatic** (physical) therapies. There are three main types of somatic therapy: drugs, ECT (electroconvulsive therapy) and psychosurgery. The use of drugs and ECT will be examined in more detail towards the end of this chapter. Some treatments can be given against the will of the patient by detaining him or her forcibly and providing treatment under the relevant section of the 1983 Mental Health Act — a process known as **sectioning**.

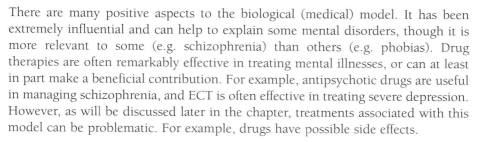

There are many positive aspects to the biological (medical) model. It has been extremely influential and can help to explain some mental disorders, though it is more relevant to some (e.g. schizophrenia) than others (e.g. phobias). Drug therapies are often remarkably effective in treating mental illnesses, or can at least in part make a beneficial contribution. For example, antipsychotic drugs are useful in managing schizophrenia, and ECT is often effective in treating severe depression. However, as will be discussed later in the chapter, treatments associated with this model can be problematic. For example, drugs have possible side effects.

Defining mental disorders as illnesses also means that individuals cannot be blamed for their disorder: they are not 'bad' but 'ill', so hopefully other people will be sympathetic rather than critical of someone who suffers from a mental illness. However, this does not necessarily happen in practice. Jones and Cochrane (1981) found that people's stereotype of a person with a mental illness fitted the symptoms of schizophrenia, where sufferers can be violent and often demonstrate bizarre behaviour, so the response to people with a mental illness may be one of fear rather than sympathy.

One criticism of the biological model is that, with its focus on organic causes, it gives insufficient weight to other factors. For example, depression may be explained partly in terms of physical symptoms, and these may be helped to some extent by medication, but a better understanding of the disorder might well be gained by taking into account environmental factors that may be contributory causes, such as poor housing conditions, financial difficulties or problems at work.

There are also theorists, in particular those known as **anti-psychiatrists**, who are strongly critical of the view of mental disorders proposed by the medical model. In his book *The Myth of Mental Illness* (1972), Szasz challenged the idea that mental illnesses have an organic basis. He argued instead that most such disorders are **functional**: they do not have a physical cause, but are the result of what he called 'problems in living'. For example, Szasz suggested that 'depression' is simply a word used to describe an unhappy person. Treating depression as a medical diagnosis allows us to put in place various practices that we believe will 'cure' the patient, whether or not they wish to be treated. For him, mental disorders are called 'illnesses' because they go against our view of normality, not because they are physical illnesses. He sees psychiatry as a form of **social control**, legitimised by classing abnormal behaviour as an illness, but in reality taking away a person's rights and responsibilities.

This raises an ethical issue. If psychiatrists are justified in believing that a person's abnormal behaviour is the result of an organic problem, which prevents them from functioning adequately, then they are right to treat people, even when treatment is resisted — resistance can be seen as part of the problem. It is the duty of the psychiatrist to act for the person's own good, taking responsibility for the patient's well-being and doing his or her best to relieve the misery of mental illness.

On the other hand, if the anti-psychiatrists are correct, treatment for mental illness can be seen as a violation of a person's human rights. The use of sectioning means that a person who has broken no laws can lose his or her freedom. Unconventional people are being persecuted for behaviour with which society cannot cope. However, these views would also mean that people with mental illnesses would be held responsible for behaviours over which psychiatrists would argue they have no control, and would fail to receive the help that they need.

Summary

- The biological (medical) model views mental illness as having an **organic basis**.
- The causes can be **infection, genetic, biochemical** (i.e. the result of **hormonal factors** or an **imbalance of neurotransmitters**) or **neurological problems**. There is some evidence that these factors play a major role in some disorders.
- As the causes are assumed to be organic, **somatic treatments** are used. These include **drugs, ECT** and **psychosurgery**. These treatments can be effective in dealing with mental illness.
- Using **sectioning**, some treatments can be given against the patient's will.
- **Anti-psychiatrists** believe that the view that there is an organic basis to mental disorders is misplaced and that medical treatments are a form of **social control**.

Psychological approaches to psychopathology

There are several approaches in psychology proposing that the causes of mental disorders are psychological. This section will consider the ideas offered by the **psychodynamic**, **behavioural** and **cognitive** perspectives.

The psychodynamic approach

The psychodynamic account of mental disorders centres around the ideas of Freud, which were discussed briefly in Chapter 1. According to this model, mental disorders are the result of **psychic conflict** and have their roots in childhood experience. The causes lie in the unconscious.

According to Freud, the mind consists of the id, the ego and the superego. In the mentally healthy person, the ego is in control. It finds acceptable ways to express id impulses and it takes into account the requirements of the superego, but without allowing either of these to dominate. Mental disorders arise to a certain extent from conflict between these different parts of the mind, with which we are unable to cope.

Freud believed that our childhood experiences are crucial to our development and what we become as adults. Unresolved issues relating to childhood **psychosexual development** will lead to the development of mental disorders.

For Freud, the **unconscious** was immensely important. The psychic conflict between id, ego and superego, and unresolved issues relating to childhood development, are all unconscious, so our lives are to a large extent controlled by internal forces of which we are mostly unaware. We use **ego defence mechanisms**, such as repression, to prevent the anxiety resulting through psychic conflict from reaching consciousness. However, the use of these defence mechanisms is only effective in the short term, and they also distort our perception of reality. Unconscious issues have not been dealt with, so still continue to affect how we experience the world, as well as our behaviour, leading to mental ill health.

There is some support for the idea that mental disorders, such as depression, may have their roots in childhood experience. As we saw in Chapter 3, Bowlby — himself a Freudian — claimed that failure to form a secure attachment in early childhood could lead to depression in an adult. Kendler et al. (2002) found that maternal separation, and thus a weakening of attachment, was a good predictor of depression in adulthood. Freud also argued that a loss in adulthood, such as the death of someone we love or the loss of a job, causes us to re-experience part of our childhood and show regression. The greater the loss in childhood, the greater the regression and so the greater the likelihood of developing depression. This would suggest that someone whose mother died when he or she was a child would be more likely to develop depression as an adult. However, in this case, research findings are equivocal. Kendler et al. (2002) found that the loss of a parent in childhood was a relatively weak predictor of depression as an adult, while Lewinson and Hoberman (1982) found no link between maternal loss and depression. It should perhaps also be noted that even when an association is found between loss in childhood and later depression, this does not necessarily imply that childhood experiences *cause* later problems.

Since the causes of mental disorders lie in the unconscious, the aim of therapy is to bring unconscious material into consciousness, so the issues that are causing problems can be resolved. The therapy is known as **psychoanalysis**, and is a talking therapy. Using a range of methods, the psychoanalyst will uncover and interpret unconscious material, and so help the patient to 'work through' the underlying problems. The effectiveness of this approach will be examined in more detail later in this chapter.

There are problems with the psychodynamic approach to mental disorders. In particular, many people find the underlying theoretical ideas unconvincing, for example the nature of psychosexual development. The emphasis on sexual factors has also been questioned, with the influence of interpersonal relationships and other social factors being downplayed. There is also criticism of its emphasis on the past, giving relatively little weight to current issues in a person's life, such as relationships within the family and in the workplace, which may be linked to a mental disorder, or to genetic factors. This approach has been accused of being **reductionist** because it sees people as being basically driven by animal instincts over which they have no control.

By their very nature, psychodynamic ideas are difficult to test in an objective and scientific way, with Freud's evidence emerging from the therapy that he carried out with patients, who were relatively few in number and not really representative of people in general. There is also the possibility that Freud's interpretations of this material were biased. There are similar issues in assessing the effectiveness of psychoanalysis.

Summary

- The **psychodynamic approach** believes that mental disorders arise as a result of **psychic conflict**, with their roots in **childhood** experiences, and that their causes lie in the **unconscious**.
- In therapy, **psychoanalysis** aims to bring unconscious material into consciousness.
- There is little **evidence** to support the claims made by this approach, and it relies on **subjective** interpretation.
- This approach has been criticised because the underlying theory is **difficult to test** as it ignores **genetic** and wider **social factors**. It is also seen as **reductionist**.

The behavioural approach

The behavioural approach to mental disorders rests on the principles of behaviourist theory, with its emphasis on learned behaviour. Mental disorders are therefore described in terms of learned inappropriate behaviours, i.e. **maladaptive behaviours**.

In Chapter 1, it was established that both classical and operant **conditioning** suggest that most behaviour is learned and that we learn by **association**. In the case of **classical conditioning**, the association is between a stimulus (an environmental event) and a response (a physiological reaction). This explanation has been widely used to explain the development of phobias. In the same way that Pavlov's dogs learned to salivate to the sound of a bell, individuals may learn to produce a fear response when they see a snake or find themselves in an enclosed space. An example of a phobia developing this way, was described in Chapter 1 in the study of Little Albert carried out by Watson and Rayner (page 13). However, just because Little Albert's rat phobia was developed through learning, it does not necessarily follow that all phobias are developed in this way.

In **operant conditioning**, the association is between a behaviour and its consequences. If a behaviour has a favourable outcome (positive reinforcement), it is likely to be repeated. This principle has been used to contribute towards an explanation for eating disorders, like anorexia nervosa. It may be that admiration for slimness reinforces dieting behaviour, which then becomes a habit.

Social learning theory suggests that we learn behaviours through observation of the behaviour of others and the consequences of their behaviour. For example, a phobia of spiders could be learned through observing a parent showing fear of spiders and modelling this behaviour.

However, while the behavioural approach suggests that learning is the likely cause of mental disorders, identifying a specific cause is not crucial to treatment. The behaviour is the problem, and the aim of treatment is to change behaviour. The theory underlying behavioural therapies is that maladaptive behaviours have been learned and, using the principles of conditioning, new and more adaptive behaviours can be learned in their place. One positive aspect of the behavioural approach to mental disorders is that there are a number of therapies associated with this method, many of which have been shown to be particularly effective (they will be looked at in detail later in this chapter).

The behavioural approach has been criticised for its emphasis on learned behaviour, for example in terms of a phobia arising from a learned association between a traumatic experience and a previously neutral stimulus, as an explanation for the development of mental disorders. In a review of research into phobias, Zinbarg and Mineka (2001) conclude that a traumatic experience does not necessarily lead to a phobia developing, and that phobias can develop without a trauma having been experienced. The research they cite also suggests that the likelihood of a traumatic experience resulting in the development of a phobia depends on the temperament of the person, his or her previous history of exposure to fearful and non-fearful models, and the individual's history of later traumatic experiences.

An evolutionary explanation for phobias, which also challenges the importance of learning, has been proposed by Seligman (1971). We have a **biological preparedness** to develop the common phobias, such as a phobia of heights or spiders, because they were adaptive in our evolutionary past: those who kept away from high places and avoided potentially poisonous spiders were more likely to survive long enough to pass on their genes, and therefore these characteristics, than those who did not. Certainly the more common phobias — heights, spiders, snakes, enclosed spaces and so on — fit well with this explanation, and Öhman (1979), using the techniques of classical conditioning, found that it was more difficult to create phobias (in laboratory conditions) to mushrooms or flowers, which would not be relevant fear objects in evolutionary terms, than to evolutionary fear-relevant stimuli such as snakes or spiders. The role of factors other than learning has also been shown in a large-scale study of twins, carried out by Lichtenstein and Annas (2000). They found that **genetic factors**, as well as environmental factors such as trauma and vicarious learning, are important factors in the development of phobias.

The behavioural approach has been criticised for exaggerating the role of learning in the development of mental disorders, and playing down the influence of genetic factors. There is quite strong evidence for genes having a major role in the development of some disorders, such as schizophrenia.

It has also been criticised as **reductionist**, in that it does not take higher mental processes — such as thoughts, feelings and memories — into account. This makes it less relevant to disorders like generalised anxiety disorder, where the main symptom is excessive worrying and there are no clear behavioural symptoms.

The belief that we do not need to uncover the **causes** of problems for them to be treated has also been challenged, with the suggestion that if the underlying causes of the problems that a person is experiencing are not established, the problems are likely to recur.

Summary

- The **behavioural approach** sees mental disorders as learned **maladaptive behaviours**.
- **Therapies** are based on **conditioning** principles, in which new adaptive behaviours are learned.

Individual differences

- Research suggests that learning is not necessarily central to the development of disorders, especially those like schizophrenia, for which there is strong evidence of a **genetic** basis.
- The approach has been criticised for being **reductionist** and downplaying the importance of establishing **causes**.

The cognitive approach

Cognitive psychologists focus on internal mental processes. In the cognitive model of mental disorders, the causes of disorders are assumed to lie in the way people think about events and experiences, which may be distorted and irrational. This approach has been applied most often to anxiety and depression. For example, Beck related depression to what he called the triad of negative assumptions:

Beck (1987): triad of negative assumptions

- Negative view of **self**: 'I am a worthless person.'
- Negative view of **circumstances**: 'Everything is bleak and I cannot cope with what people expect of me.'
- Negative view of the **future**: 'Things can only get worse and there is nothing I can do to change them.'

The idea of irrational negative thinking as a cause of mental disorder has also been applied to eating disorders. For example, the belief that 'thin' = 'successful, happy and attractive' may influence eating behaviour. There is some evidence supporting a cognitive explanation of bulimia, as demonstrated by Cutts and Barrios (1986) (see Box 7.2).

Because of this kind of faulty thinking, a person is prevented from behaving adaptively.

Box 7.2 Cutts and Barrios (1986)

Aims: To investigate the role of cognitive factors in the development of bulimia by establishing possible cognitive differences between bulimics and non-bulimics.

Procedure: A group of 15 bulimics and a control group of 15 non-bulimics were asked to imagine (a) gaining 5 lb in weight and (b) a neutral scenario, unrelated to weight gain. Participants were matched for age, gender and imagery ability. Their heart rates and muscle tension were monitored as indicators of emotional arousal, and they were also asked to give a verbal response to the activity.

Results: For the 'weight gain' scenario, the bulimics, but not the controls, showed an increase in heart rate and muscle tension, and gave more negative verbal responses. There was no difference between groups for the weight-neutral scenario.

Conclusions: There are cognitive differences between bulimics and non-bulimics in their response to the idea of weight gain. The difference is not general, but specific to weight gain.

The therapies associated with this approach aim to challenge these negative thoughts. The cognitive approach arose out of dissatisfaction with the limitations of the behavioural approach, but as behavioural therapies nonetheless have much to offer, some cognitive therapies have sought to combine the strengths of the two methods in **cognitive behavioural therapy (CBT)**. This approach challenges negative thoughts and also emphasises the importance of behaviour change in response to the more positive thought patterns acquired through therapy. CBT has already been examined in Chapter 5 in relation to stress management, but **rational emotive behaviour therapy (REBT)** will be looked at in detail later in this chapter as an example of this kind of therapy for mental disorders.

While there is some evidence that faulty cognitions are associated with a range of mental disorders, it has been suggested — by Beck (1991) among others — that faulty and irrational thinking may be the *result* rather than the *cause* of mental disorders. However, Lewinsohn et al. (2001) compared a group of adolescents who had unrealistic negative thought patterns with those who did not. A year later, the negative thinkers were statistically more likely to have developed clinical depression than the controls, a finding that is consistent with Beck's idea that patterns of negative thinking lead to depression.

Another possible criticism of the cognitive approach is that it gives little weight to **organic factors**, such as neurotransmitters and genes, and also focuses on the individual, perhaps not giving enough importance to the influence of **environmental factors**, such as poor housing and the characteristics of other family members.

As will be apparent through this account of the different approaches, each method seems to fit better with some disorders than others. For example, there is clear evidence of a biological basis to schizophrenia, while the cognitive approach focuses in particular on depression and anxiety. It seems likely that each approach has something to contribute, so for a full understanding of mental disorders, ideas and information are needed from all of them.

One way in which different approaches can be combined is in the **diathesis-stress model**. As stated earlier, this model suggests that we may have a predisposition to develop a particular disorder, either genetically based or as a result of early life experiences. Whether we go on to develop the disorder will depend on the stress that we experience, which may act as a trigger.

Summary

- The cognitive approach sees mental disorders arising from **faulty thinking**.
- Treatment focuses on developing more **appropriate cognitions**, while **cognitive behavioural therapy (CBT)** builds on this with an emphasis on **behaviour change**.
- This approach may give insufficient weight to **organic** and **environmental factors**.
- The **diathesis-stress model** combines the ideas of predisposition for a disorder, with stress as a trigger.

Biological therapies

Biological therapies are sometimes known as **somatic** therapies (i.e. related to the body): they are physical therapies, resting on the assumption that mental illness has an organic basis. Earlier in the chapter it was mentioned that patients can be given some forms of treatment against their will if they are considered to be a danger to themselves or others. The two kinds of somatic therapy that will be examined in this section, drugs and electroconvulsive therapy, fall into this category.

Drugs

The term '**chemotherapy**' has come to be associated with anti-cancer drugs, but it applies equally to drugs used to treat other illnesses. Drugs are widely used to treat mental illness and can be put into four main groups on the basis of the disorders for which they are used and the effects that they have on behaviour:

- **Minor tranquillisers (anxiolytics)**, such as diazepam (e.g. Valium), which aim to reduce anxiety.
- **Major tranquillisers (antipsychotics)**, such as chlorpromazine (e.g. Largactil), which block the action of dopamine in the brain, and more recently developed drugs, such as clozapine (e.g. Clozaril), which affect both dopamine and serotonin levels.
- **Stimulants**, such as amphetamines. For example, Ritalin is sometimes used to treat hyper-active children.
- **Antidepressants**, which include sub-categories of drugs to treat depression. These include:
  - **tricyclics** (e.g. Amitriptyline), which block the re-uptake of serotonin and noradrenaline, and so prolong the effects of these neurotransmitters.
  - **MAOIs** (monoamine oxidase inhibitors, e.g. Nardil), which can be used for patients resistant to tricyclics. These drugs raise the level of activity of synapses (the gaps between neurones where chemical neurotransmission takes place) and affect serotonin, noradrenaline and dopamine.
  - **SSRIs** (selective serotonin re-uptake inhibitors), such as Prozac and **SNRIs** (serotonin and noradrenaline reuptake inhibitors), such as Venlafaxine. These drugs are more effective and 'cleaner' than other antidepressants.

Drug treatments can be very effective, but are not without their drawbacks. For example, anti-anxiety drugs like Valium have been found to be highly **addictive**, especially if they are used long term. Therefore, there are **withdrawal symptoms** when the patient stops taking them. Patients may also develop a tolerance to anxiolytics, and so need increasingly higher doses, which makes dependency more likely. There are also withdrawal symptoms when a patient stops taking tricyclic antidepressants.

Any drugs, including those used to treat people with a mental illness, can have **side effects**. Traditional antipsychotic drugs, such as chlorpromazine, may lead to epileptic fits. These drugs reduce the availability of dopamine, and so can also lead to symptoms like those in Parkinson's disease, which is characterised by low levels of dopamine and symptoms such as tremors and immobility. Patients who take these drugs also have a 5% chance per year of developing **tardive dyskinesia** — jerky movements of the face, mouth and tongue, and sometimes also the limbs. These side effects have led to a major problem with conventional antipsychotic drugs: because many patients find them difficult to tolerate, they stop taking them and their symptoms reappear.

To overcome this problem, a new generation of antipsychotic drugs — **atypical antipsychotics** — has been developed. The first of these to be used was clozapine, available in the UK and the USA since 1990. Clozapine has been shown to be particularly effective in treating the positive symptoms of schizophrenia, such as hallucinations and delusions, for 30–60% of patients. Because these kinds of drug are easier to tolerate, patients are more likely to continue the treatment.

However, there are also problems with atypical antipsychotics. It is not clear that they are effective in treating the *negative* symptoms of schizophrenia, such as lack of motivation and emotion. Moreover, they have side effects, such as weight gain and excessive salivation. With clozapine, the most serious side effect is an increased likelihood of the patient developing a blood disorder called agranulocytosis, which affects up to 1% of patients, so regular blood monitoring is essential. It is also an expensive drug, and its benefits may not become apparent for many months.

Antipsychotics are not the only kind of drug used to treat mental illness that have potentially serious side effects. MAOIs can cause insomnia, weakness and gastro-intestinal disturbances, and occasionally mania. Tricyclics, according to Spiegel (1989), help 65% of depressed patients and are safer and more effective (but more expensive) than MAOIs. However, the beneficial effects are not usually apparent before 2–3 weeks, and again, there may be serious side effects, including insomnia, heart problems and fatigue. They are also lethal in overdose, and so are dangerous for patients who are at risk of suicide. Prozac was initially hailed as a wonder-drug for treating depression, but it, too, has been found to have a range of side effects, including anxiety and insomnia. It has also been associated with obsessive thoughts of violence and suicide. Doubts have also been raised about its effectiveness.

The **interaction** of drugs used to treat mental illness with other medication also needs to be considered. For example, tricyclics cannot be taken in conjunction with an anti-hypertensive drug for high blood pressure, and cannot be used for at least 2 weeks if the patient has previously been treated with an MAOI. MAOIs also interact with a range of common foods, such as cheese, Marmite and alcohol, occasionally with fatal results.

In addition, there are **ethical issues** surrounding the use of drugs. As was established earlier, patients can be sectioned if they are considered to be a danger to themselves or other people, and may be given drugs without their consent. Do we have the right to insist that drugs are given to an unwilling patient? On the other hand, to what extent is a patient with a mental illness able to give or withhold informed consent, particularly when some of the symptoms of the illness, for example schizophrenia, involve a distortion of reality? It is important to note that there are safeguards in place when a person is sectioned. For example, the person can appeal against sectioning to the **Mental Health Review Tribunal**, and the sectioning is time-limited. Nonetheless, the ethics here are not straightforward.

The use of drugs has also been criticised on the grounds that they merely treat symptoms and do not tackle the root causes of people's problems. For example, in a study of housewives living in Camberwell, Brown and Harris (1978) found that depression was associated with a lack of paid employment, two or more children under the age of 5 years, lack of a close relationship and having lost their own mother in childhood. Antidepressants could offer immediate help, in terms of making the situation more bearable, but at the same time interventions to help change the situation, as in providing social support and helping the individual to explore opportunities for paid employment, would be helpful in the longer term.

Drugs are rarely the whole answer to a mental illness problem, but there is no reason why they should not be used for immediate relief, in parallel with other therapies that may offer more extensive solutions. Many therapists believe that a combination of drugs and psychotherapy is the most effective way of treating patients.

The debate as to whether, or to what extent, drugs should be used to treat mental illness hinges on a cost–benefit analysis. On the benefit side, drugs are readily available, relatively cheap (for example, compared with therapies such as psycho-analysis) and are extremely effective in treating, or at least managing, many mental illnesses. For example, antipsychotic drugs have enabled many people to live relatively normal lives outside an institution. On the cost side, the problems with drug use, and in particular the possibility of side effects, need to be considered. It is by weighing the cost of drug use against its benefits that a conclusion can be reached with respect to whether drugs should be used and which ones, in what quantities and for how long. For example, the side effects of antidepressants may be out-weighed by the benefits of the drugs, given that a severely depressed person is at high risk of suicide.

Electroconvulsive therapy (ECT)

ECT is a treatment for depression, in which an electric current of between 70 volts and 130 volts is passed through a patient's head for a fraction of a second. This induces a **convulsion** or **seizure**.

The idea of using electricity to induce seizures was first proposed in the 1930s by Cerletti, an Italian doctor working in the field of epilepsy. He noticed that epilepsy and schizophrenia never occurred in the same person and reasoned that if he induced a seizure in someone, perhaps their schizophrenia would be cured. Watching procedures in a slaughterhouse, in which animals were made unconscious by passing a current through their heads, gave Cerletti the idea that he could induce a seizure in a patient using this method. This proposal was reported by Bini in 1938.

ECT has had a poor reputation, largely as a result of serious problems with the procedure in the past. For example, physical injury was not uncommon during the convulsion, often leading to broken bones. Nowadays, the technique has been greatly improved. People undergoing ECT are now **anaesthetised** and given a

muscle relaxant to prevent physical injury during the seizure. Because a muscle relaxant has been used, the only sign of the seizure that has been induced is the twitching of the patient's toes. The current is administered by means of electrodes placed on either side of the patient's head. It can also be administered to just one side of the brain (**unilateral ECT**), although bilateral ECT is more common as it is believed to be more effective. In a typical course of treatment, the procedure is repeated three times a week for about a month.

ECT is no longer used for schizophrenia, where chemotherapy can be particularly effective, but is used to treat people whose severe depression has not been helped by drugs. Sackheim (1988) found that between 60% and 70% of people improved with ECT, though the effects tended to disappear within the following year. For this reason, some patients return for **maintenance ECT**, to keep their depression under control.

One ethical issue is that it is not known why ECT is effective or how the therapy works. It has therefore been argued that until this knowledge is gained, ECT should not be used on patients. However, it is worth bearing in mind that this is true of many medical treatments: for example, we do not know how aspirin cures headaches, but this seems a poor reason for not making use of something that can offer real benefits.

It has been suggested that ECT works because of a **placebo effect**. A placebo is an inactive substance or a procedure that is given to a patient who is unaware that it is not expected to have any effect. A placebo is often used as a control, so that a comparison can be made with the effects of a genuine substance or procedure. Often people have a better response to a placebo than they do to no treatment at all. This can be explained in terms of the patient expecting his or her treatment to be effective because of the expert status of the physician. To test for a possible placebo effect for ECT, the patient goes through the entire procedure, including anaesthesia and muscle relaxation, but the electrical current is not strong enough to induce a seizure. There is no evidence that placebo ECT is effective in treating depression, so there must be some aspect of the electrical current to the brain that does help to control depression.

Various other suggestions have been put forward to explain why ECT is effective. One explanation was that it was regarded as a **punishment**. However, for many years now the treatment has been carried out under anaesthetic, so the experience is not unpleasant. Another suggestion was that the **memory loss** experienced following ECT allows patients to restructure their view of life, though given the minimal memory loss associated with unilateral ECT, this, too, seems unlikely. The most likely explanation, accepted by most psychiatrists, is that the shock produces **biochemical changes** in the brain, raising levels of the various neurotransmitters. These changes are stronger than those produced by drugs, which may account for the effectiveness of ECT.

In spite of improvements in the technique, there are still some problems. Patients suffer temporary confusion and memory loss, although Benton (1981) found that this was less likely to occur with unilateral ECT. Memory problems are also minimised if low electrical currents are used — just enough to induce the seizure. According to Friedberg (1977), it takes 5–10 minutes after ECT to remember who you are, where you are and what day it is. In the first few weeks after a full course, there is some **retrograde amnesia** (loss of memories from the period leading up to the treatment) and to a lesser extent **anterograde amnesia** (problems in remembering new information), but subsequently, many patients are not aware of any further memory deficits.

However, some patients have claimed that the memory loss can be much more extensive than this. Early studies report patients who forgot that they had children (Tyler and Lowenbach, 1947), a woman who forgot how to cook familiar dishes (Brody, 1944) and another who could not recognise her own clothing and wanted to know who had put these unfamiliar dresses in her wardrobe (Zubin, 1948). Janis (1950) found that amnesia in ECT patients could extend to childhood events dating back 20–40 years. In 1976, Friedberg quoted a 32-year-old woman, 5 years after she had received 21 ECT treatments:

> One of the results of the whole thing is that I have no memory of what happened in the year to year and a half prior to my shock treatments. The doctor assured me that it was going to come back and it never has. I don't remember a bloody thing. I couldn't even find my way around the town I lived in for 3 years. If I walked into a building, I didn't even know where I was. I could barely find my way around my own house. I could sew and knit before, but afterward I could no more comprehend a pattern to sew than the man on the moon.

It is generally accepted that memory for the period immediately prior to treatment is impaired, but the degree to which there is more extensive retrograde amnesia is a controversial topic because it is difficult to establish what the patient could recall before ECT. However, research by Freeman et al. (1980) has investigated the extent of memory loss using a non-ECT control group (see Box 7.3).

There is further support for the role of depression in amnesia following ECT from Coleman et al. (1996). They found that ECT patients' self-ratings of memory function 2 weeks after treatment were similar to those of non-ECT controls, but that the severity of depressive symptoms was strongly associated with reported memory problems.

Whether amnesia following ECT can be largely attributed to depression or whether it is the direct result of the treatment, there is no doubt that ECT does cause **brain damage**. Friedberg (1977) reported several studies into the effects of electric shocks to the brain, both in animals and in humans, which indicate that haemorrhages and nerve damage are common, while Nagaraja et al. (2007) reported damage to the hippocampus. As this area of the brain plays an important part in memory, this damage is likely to be connected to the amnesia that ECT patients experience. For some patients, relief from crippling depression may outweigh the negative effects of memory loss, while for others this may be too high a price to pay.

Box 7.3 | **Freeman et al. (1980)**

Aims: To investigate the extent of memory loss as a result of ECT.

Procedure: Participants who believed that they had suffered serious memory loss as a result of ECT given between 9 months and 30 years previously, were compared with a matched control group who had not had ECT. All were assessed on a range of tests of cognitive functioning, and also completed scales to measure depression and to provide a self-assessment of memory difficulties.

Results: Of the ECT group, most claimed to have poor memory for the time when they received treatment. Some had retrograde amnesia for the events of several months before ECT. Some also claimed to have anterograde amnesia — for example, one participant claimed to be unable to remember a wedding 6 months after the course of ECT. Overall, the participants in the ECT group were more depressed than the controls. They also scored significantly worse than controls on memories of their own past and on the ability to put names to faces. These deficits corresponded well to the difficulties identified in their self-assessments.

Conclusions: The findings are consistent with the claim that ECT can cause significant memory loss. However, it is also possible that depression leads to poor memory.

It should be noted that the mortality rate for ECT is extremely low, making it one of the safest medical treatments. As ECT is only used for patients whose severe depression means that they may be a danger to themselves — they are at high risk of committing suicide — the possible side effects may be less dangerous than the risks of *not* giving the treatment.

Clare (1980) suggested that ECT is abused by psychiatrists and is used too frequently, merely because it is a fairly quick and straightforward therapy, and therefore relatively cheap. As with chemotherapy, there is also the issue of **informed consent**: should patients who have been sectioned be given this treatment against their will?

Summary

- There are four main groups of **drugs** used to treat mental illness: **minor tranquillisers** (anxiolytics), **major tranquillisers** (antipsychotics), **stimulants** and **antidepressants**.
- While some drug treatments are **effective** for a range of mental disorders, there are issues of **addiction** and **side effects**. **Interaction with other drugs** or foodstuffs can also be a problem.
- Drug treatments have been criticised for treating only **symptoms**, rather than the **causes**, of mental illness.
- **Electroconvulsive therapy (ECT)** involves passing an electric current briefly through the brain.
- It is an effective treatment for **depression** that has not responded to drugs. **Side effects** include temporary **memory loss**, though it is unclear how extensive this is, and **brain damage**.

- It is not understood why ECT works, but it is likely that the shock causes **biochemical changes** in the brain.
- There are issues concerning the use of **sectioning** to treat people without their consent, either with drugs or ECT.

Psychological therapies

There are many other therapies, linked to different approaches to psychopathology, that are used to help people with a mental disorder. Three examples will be discussed here: **psychoanalysis** (associated with the psychodynamic approach), **systematic desensitisation** (associated with the behavioural approach) and **cognitive behavioural therapy (CBT)** which, as mentioned before, brings together the underlying principles of the cognitive and behavioural approaches.

Psychoanalysis

As discussed earlier, according to the psychodynamic approach (associated with Freud), problems lie largely in the unconscious. They arise through psychic conflict and are likely to have their roots in childhood experience. The unconscious holds material that would cause us anxiety. However, although we are not aware of it, this material continues to exert an influence on our lives. For this reason, the aim of psychoanalysis is to bring unconscious material into consciousness during the therapeutic process so that it can be 'worked through', i.e. so that the issues can be dealt with, helped by a therapist.

Psychoanalysis is a talking therapy that lasts a number of years, with several sessions a week. The aim is to make people conscious of their repressed memories, fears, wishes and experiences. To do this, defences against awareness of traumatic unconscious material need to be broken down. With the help of the analyst, the patient can then deal with the repressed material, and so release the power that it has over behaviour. This is called **catharsis**.

Classical psychoanalysis has three stages:

Stages of psychoanalysis

- **Identification** of defence mechanisms — for example, repression, which keeps conflict and sometimes traumatic memories in the unconscious.
- **Release** of this material to consciousness.
- **Redirection** of emotional energy (libido) associated with the defence mechanism, allowing the patient's ego to recognise the conflict and deal with it in relation to current reality. This strengthens the patient's ego and so makes him or her better able to deal with conflicts — both those in the past and those currently experienced.

The main technique by which this is achieved is **free association**, where patients or **analysands** are required to say whatever comes into their mind, however personal, painful or unimportant it seems to be. Freud believed that the thought processes governing what we say are influenced by the unconscious, and therefore what is said is the raw material for analysis. Often the flow of associations will dry up, or there will be odd changes of topic, and these are seen as signs of **resistance**, when the analysand uses tactics to interrupt the session as painful memories are close to coming into the conscious mind. For example, the patient may make a joke, or look out of the window, in an attempt to distract him- or herself and the analyst. This is seen as indicating that important information is near the surface of consciousness, only kept out of consciousness with difficulty, and so is evidence of conflict that can then be explored further by the analyst.

A further part of the process is **transference**, when the analysand's feelings — often repressed hostile feelings towards the parents — are projected onto the analyst. This indicates that repressed feelings are close to the surface of conscious awareness and it allows the analyst to identify the source of the transference, i.e. the person or situation with whom or which the hostile feelings are actually associated, and thus the circumstances that have given rise to these feelings. **Counter-transference** refers to the analyst's feelings about the analysand — for example, his or her dislike of, or attraction to, the analysand. Counter-transference can be used to help the analyst understand the analysand's transference and the defences that he or she uses.

Another technique is **dream analysis**. During sleep, our defences are weakened, so unconscious material is closer to consciousness and may be expressed symbolically in dreams. Part of the analytic process is to interpret the symbols used to express unconscious fears. A dream has both **manifest content** (the story and images of the dream) and **latent content** (the underlying meaning of the dream, residing in the unconscious). The role of the analyst is therefore to interpret the manifest content in terms of the latent content, taking into account factors in the patient's waking life (see Box 7.4).

Box 7.4	Freud's analysis of a dream

One of Freud's patients reported this dream

'I was at home and I was arranging flowers in the centre of a table for a birthday celebration. The flowers were expensive — lilies of the valley, violets and pink carnations. I was decorating them with green paper to hide the untidy parts and make the display more attractive.'

Freud's interpretation

The dream represents the woman's desire to be married, and the birthday mentioned is the birth of a baby. The table is the woman and the flowers are her genitals. The cost of the flowers represents the value that she puts on her virginity, while lilies are the purity it stands for. The pink carnations represent flesh and violets are a symbol for violation. She wishes to make herself look beautiful and hide the parts that she considers ugly.

Behaviour may also have a symbolic meaning that the analyst can interpret. For example, Freud was consulted by a father whose 5-year-old son, known as Little Hans, had a phobia of horses. He was particularly afraid of white horses with black around the mouth and wearing blinkers. According to Freud, Hans was at the age when he would have been going through the Oedipus conflict, when he would desire his mother and wish to destroy his father. The guilt associated with this wish would lead to fear of his father and **castration anxiety**. Because of its threatening nature, this anxiety would remain unconscious but would be expressed indirectly through the ego defence mechanism of **displacement**. Little Hans's phobia of horses therefore expressed his fear of his father. The focus on horses with black around their mouths represented the father's beard and moustache, and the blinkers represented his spectacles.

A final method involves the use of **projective tests**, for example the Rorschach ink blot test and the Thematic Apperception Test (TAT) (see Figure 7.3).

Figure 7.3 *Sample projective test materials*

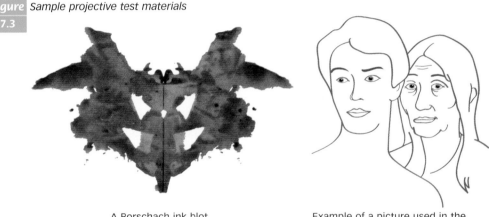

A Rorschach ink blot

Example of a picture used in the Thematic Apperception Test

People are asked to describe what they see in the ink blot, or to tell a story based on the TAT picture. These materials are deliberately ambiguous. The principle underlying these tests is that people will project their own unconscious concerns, fears and wishes on to the material, and thus allow the analyst to start to identify possible problems.

Psychoanalysts consider treatment to have been effective when the patient develops **insight**, i.e. understands the causes of his or her problems and has 'worked through' the issues. The analyst judges when this has been achieved and the conflicts resolved, but the analysand generally also recognises when the process has been completed.

Many people claim that psychoanalysis has helped them. Given its emphasis on past experience, it aims to uncover and deal with the underlying **causes** of people's problems, unlike many other therapies, such as those based on the behavioural approach, which will be discussed in the next section. This means that problems should not recur when psychoanalytical therapy is over.

However, psychoanalysis has been heavily criticised for many reasons. The therapy of psychoanalysis rests on **Freud's theories**, so criticisms of the theories call the therapy into question. The theories have been condemned for being very much of their time, place and culture, developed on the basis of a small sample of neurotic, middle-class Jewish women, living in the essentially patriarchal society of Vienna at the start of the twentieth century. Freud's ideas may therefore be rather culturally limited, though perhaps it should be noted that this criticism could also be made of much of psychology.

The treatment involves a good deal of **interpretation** by the analyst, with no way of independently verifying his or her conclusions. For example, Freud's interpretation of Little Hans's phobia of horses rests on an acceptance of the idea of progression through specific psychosexual stages in childhood, for which there is little evidence. It also seems an overly complex interpretation of Hans's phobia. A similar criticism could be made of the dream interpretation described in Box 7.4.

It has also been suggested that the kind of deep analysis used in psychoanalysis can lead to **false memory syndrome (FMS)**. Many people have gone to therapists with psychological problems whose causes they cannot explain, and in the course of therapy claim to have become aware of repressed memories, i.e. recovered memories, often of childhood sexual abuse, that seem to make sense of the problems that they are currently experiencing. Those they accuse of abusing them often deny that the abuse ever took place and claim that these memories have been implanted during therapy. In many cases, it is impossible to establish whether or not memories recovered during therapy are memories of real events. Such memories relate to the patient's childhood, often many years previously, so there may well not be any supporting evidence.

Psychoanalysis is a distressing process because material that has been pushed into the unconscious is there because it is too painful to acknowledge consciously. It could be argued, though, that this is a price worth paying if the treatment is effective. However, there is considerable dispute over whether the treatment actually works, as evidenced by Eysenck (1952) (see Box 7.5) and Bergin (1971).

Box 7.5 Eysenck (1952)

Aims: To carry out a metastudy (when data from several studies are put together and re-analysed) of research into the effectiveness of various kinds of therapy.

Procedure: A review was carried out of other researchers' published work on the effectiveness of different kinds of therapy. A comparison was made of five studies investigating the effectiveness of psychoanalysis and 19 studies evaluating **eclectic therapies**, where more than one therapeutic approach was used. Rates of recovery were compared with the recovery rates of a control group of patients who had not yet received therapy.

Results: Following therapy, 44% of patients treated with psychoanalysis improved, compared with 65% of those who received eclectic therapy. However, 66% of patients not receiving any therapy improved, a phenomenon known as **spontaneous remission**.

Conclusions: Psychoanalysis is significantly less effective than no treatment.

Although Eysenck's conclusions seem clear cut and well supported, subsequent researchers have criticised his review. For example, he defined people who dropped out of psychoanalysis as 'not cured', which seems a little harsh as they had not completed the treatment.

Bergin (1971) reviewed some of the same papers as Eysenck but did not reach the same conclusion. He defined 'improvement' differently and found that the success rate of psychoanalysis was 83% — much greater than the 44% Eysenck had suggested. He also believed that a 30% spontaneous remission rate was more realistic than the 66% concluded by Eysenck.

So how can these different findings be reconciled? Both studies rest on a subjective definition of what can be classified as 'improvement' or 'cure', and this judgement depends on the beliefs and preconceptions of the person who is providing the definition.

Neither the patient nor the therapist is likely to be an objective judge of whether the patient is 'better' than when he or she started therapy. The judgement of the patients as to whether they are better may well be distorted, perhaps because they are grateful for the care that the therapist has provided, or because they would be unwilling to admit that a lot of time and, in the case of psychoanalysis, money has been wasted on therapy that is of no use. The therapist is unlikely to be willing to judge his or her own therapy as a failure.

A further issue in defining 'improvement' or 'cure' is the point in time when the assessment is made. It may well be that treatment appears to be effective, only for the patient to develop further problems later on. There is really no objective way of assessing the effectiveness of treatment.

There are also practical considerations. Psychoanalysis is time-consuming and expensive, which limits who can benefit from it. However, it may be carried out in a modified form, such as **brief focal therapy**, used by Malan (1973). This cuts down the time required by focusing on specific problems and placing far less emphasis on past experience.

Furthermore, psychoanalysis is a talking therapy, where communication and insight are of utmost importance, so patients need to be of a certain intellectual level. This is reflected in the **YAVIS effect**, which refers to the kind of person who is most likely to benefit from this therapy: **y**oung, **a**ttractive, **v**erbal, **i**ntelligent and **s**uccessful. Since patients must be sufficiently articulate to express their feelings, psycho-analysis has not been seen as a suitable treatment for people with psychotic disorders such as schizophrenia, where patients lack insight into their problems and are more generally out of touch with reality. However, some claims have been made for it, even with this kind of disorder, if it is combined with antipsychotic drugs (e.g. Boker, 1992).

The commitment required to see the psychoanalytical treatment through is also problematic, so it may also not be the best therapy for people who are clinically depressed.

Summary

- **Psychoanalysis** is a therapy associated with **Freud's psychodynamic approach**. It aims to bring unconscious material into consciousness, so that it can be 'worked through' and issues resolved.

- It involves **free association**, the analysis of **transference**, interpretation of **dreams** and **behaviour**, and sometimes the use of **projective tests**.

- It aims to treat **causes**, so problems should not recur.

- It has been criticised as it rests on Freudian theory, which is not widely accepted. It also involves a good deal of **interpretation** and it has been suggested that the analysis may lead to **false memory syndrome (FMS)**.

- There are conflicting views on whether it is **effective**, but this is difficult to assess objectively.

- As psychoanalysis is a lengthy process, shorter forms have been developed, such as **brief focal therapy**.

- It may not be the best choice of therapy for people who are less articulate, for those with psychotic disorders and for patients who suffer from depression.

Systematic desensitisation

Systematic desensitisation is a therapy based on the **behavioural approach**. This approach suggests that maladaptive behaviours are learned and can therefore be unlearned and eliminated, with more adaptive behaviours being learned in their place. Systematic desensitisation is one method, based on the principles of **classical conditioning**, for bringing about new learning. The basic idea was first introduced by Jones (1924) in a study described in Box 7.7, but was popularised by Wolpe (1958).

This technique is primarily used to treat **phobias**, disorders characterised by an extreme irrational fear of an object, activity or situation, and by a powerful urge to avoid the feared stimulus. The fear disrupts the person's life, is out of all proportion to the real danger involved and is recognised as groundless by the person. Systematic desensitisation is based on the idea that it is not possible for two incompatible emotions, such as relaxation and anxiety, to be experienced at the same time. This principle is called **reciprocal inhibition**.

For a person with a phobia who is to be treated using systematic desensitisation, a **hierarchy of fear** is first established, in stages from what the phobic person would find least threatening, up to what would cause him or her the most anxiety. The person is then taught **relaxation techniques**, followed by a **gradual introduction** to the object or situation about which he or she is phobic. This progresses through the hierarchy of fear in a series of small steps, at each of which the person is reminded to apply the relaxation techniques that he or she has acquired. Many studies have shown this to be an effective way of treating phobias, for example the procedure carried out by Newman and Adams (2004) to treat a dog phobic (see Box 7.6).

Box 7.6 Newman and Adams (2004)

Systematic desensitisation was used to treat a 17-year-old boy with a phobia of dogs. A hierarchy of fear was identified (see below). After 28 sessions (just over 16 hours), the boy was able to manage both his behaviour and his anxiety level when in contact with unfamiliar loose dogs.

Hierarchy of fear for a person with a dog phobia

Stage in hierarchy	Description
1	Introduction of pictures and videos
2	Relaxation techniques introduced
3	Dog introduced — no contact/access (dog on other side of window)
4	Access to dog provided (client stood in doorway, leashed dog in courtyard)
5	Dog brought into personal space
6	Contact with dog (petting)
7	Contact with dog (walking alongside)
8	Outdoor contact with dog at park; instructed to stand still and use relaxation techniques when required
9	Introduction of new dog, stages 6 and 7 repeated

This is an example of the technique being carried out **in vivo**, i.e. using live encounters with the feared object or situation. Wolpe suggested that it could also be carried out using the patient's imagination rather than exposing him or her directly to the feared situation or object. However, in vivo exposure is almost always more effective than imaginal exposure.

A slightly modified form of the technique can be used for children who are too young to learn relaxation techniques, as described by Jones (1924) (see Box 7.7).

Box 7.7 Jones (1924)

Little Peter was a 2-year-old child living in an institution. He had an extreme fear of some animals, including rats and rabbits, and this fear had generalised, for example to feathers and cotton wool. In a series of 17 steps, Peter was gradually exposed to a rabbit, using a hierarchy of steps (similar to those outlined in Box 7.6 for a dog phobic). Peter enjoyed food, so this was done while he was eating his lunch; the rabbit was therefore associated with the pleasurable activity of eating. After 40 sessions, Peter ate his lunch while stroking the rabbit on his lap.

A further variant is **vicarious desensitisation**, where models showing or learning appropriate behaviour are used. This is based on the principles of Social Learning Theory (outlined in Chapter 1), which claims that we can learn from observing the behaviour of others and its outcome. For example, Altmaier and Woodward (1981) found that test anxiety was reduced in students who watched videos of a student undergoing systematic desensitisation for a similar problem. Similarly, Bandura and Menlove (1968) showed pre-school children who were afraid of dogs a series of films of children playing with dogs. This experience played a part in helping them to overcome their phobia.

A recent development is the use of **virtual reality (VR)** through 3-D computer simulations. This can considerably simplify the therapeutic process as it avoids having to make complicated arrangements in order to create in vivo circumstances to fit the different stages of exposure. For example, Westerhoff (2007) describes a VR program called SpiderWorld, which has been used successfully with arachnophobes.

One of the advantages of the technique of systematic desensitisation is that it can be used with anyone. Levine et al. (2007) have even shown that a variant of the procedure was effective in treating dogs with a fear of fireworks. Unlike the psychodynamic approach, it does not rely on the person developing insight or having good communication skills. It is also relatively quick, and therefore cheap, and does not require the therapist to undergo years of training in order to carry out the therapy.

Systematic desensitisation can also be used in **combination** with other therapies. For example, Bernstein (1984) reported a case study demonstrating systematic desensitisation being used together with psychodynamic therapy. He describes the treatment of a married graduate student in his mid-30s with a pathological anxiety about studying, fear of criticism and feeling uncomfortable in groups. Systematic desensitisation was used to decrease study anxiety, followed by psychodynamic therapy to address the underlying fears of failure. Similarly, Powell (2004) successfully helped medical students who experienced debilitating anxiety in exams to pass the professional exams that they had previously failed, using a combination of systematic desensitisation, cognitive methods and practice in exam techniques.

Unlike psychoanalysis, this treatment is not interested in the causes of the problem. The behaviour is the issue, so the problem is addressed by changing the behaviour, its cause being seen as irrelevant. Systematic desensitisation has been criticised for not looking at underlying causes, and so not curing the problem but merely dealing with the symptoms. This means that it is possible that **stimulus substitution** can take place, where different symptoms emerge after treatment. However, quite often, information about the cause of the problem may be unimportant. For example, in the case of Little Albert (discussed in Chapter 1, page 13), it is hard to see what contribution to therapy could be made by knowing the procedure of the study in which the phobia was induced. Similarly, is it essential to establish why a person has developed a spider phobia in order to change their response to spiders?

Another issue is the extent to which the new learned behaviour will **generalise** to other situations. This needs to be taken into account by the therapist. A good example is provided by the Newman and Adams study (see Box 7.6): the boy was exposed to different dogs and in different settings, to try to ensure that the behaviour would be generalised to other dogs in other situations. Similarly, the Bandura and Menlove study showed children a series of films of children playing happily with dogs, for the same reason.

The **ethics** of the behavioural approach have also been questioned, and in particular the control exerted over the patient by the therapist. However, when systematic desensitisation is carried out, ideally patients are given control over the situation by constructing their own hierarchy and deciding when they are ready to be exposed to the next stage of the treatment.

Systematic desensitisation clearly has its uses, but at the same time it is limited in its applications. While it may have a part to play in treating disorders other than phobias, it is this kind of disorder for which it is best suited.

Summary

- **Systematic desensitisation** is based on **classical conditioning**. Its main application is in treating **phobias**.
- The person experiences **gradual exposure** to increasingly extreme examples of the object or situation about which he or she is phobic, while practising **relaxation techniques**.
- It is more effective when carried out **in vivo**, but the use of **virtual reality (VR)** can simplify organisation of the stages of exposure.
- It can be applied to **anyone**, and is **relatively quick** and **cheap**. It can also be used in combination with other therapies.
- It has been criticised for not addressing the **causes** of problems. The extent to which learning may **generalise** is also an issue.
- **Ethical concerns** about control need to be addressed in using the technique.

Cognitive behavioural therapy

The cognitive and behavioural approaches are combined in **cognitive behavioural therapy (CBT)**, which has already been looked at briefly in relation to stress management (see Chapter 5). The cognitive aspect of this therapy focuses on modifying faulty thinking, with the behavioural aspect focusing on modifying the behaviour arising from these inappropriate thought processes. It has been used to help with many disorders, in particular anxiety disorders and depression.

There are several variants of CBT, but as an example, **rational-emotive behaviour therapy (REBT)**, the original form of CBT developed by Ellis in 1962, will be examined here The underlying principle — as with any kind of CBT — is that psychological disorders such as depression are caused by irrational beliefs. Beliefs are irrational if they distort reality and involve illogical ways of evaluating yourself, other people and the world around you. These beliefs create persistent and distressing emotions, and block people from achieving their goals. Distorted thinking, emotions and behaviour therefore interact, so the disorder needs to be addressed by changing irrational thinking.

Ellis identified the kinds of irrational ideas often held by his clients:

Sample beliefs underlying undesirable emotions and behaviour

- I need love and approval from those significant to me — and I must avoid disapproval from any source.
- To be worthwhile as a person, I must achieve, succeed at whatever I do and make no mistakes.
- I shouldn't have to feel discomfort and pain — I can't stand them and must avoid them at all costs.
- Every problem should have an ideal solution — and it's intolerable when one can't be found.
- Things must be the way I want them to be, otherwise life will be intolerable.
- My unhappiness is caused by things that are outside my control — so there is little I can do to feel any better.

Ellis pointed out that irrational thinking is often identified by words such as 'should', 'ought' and 'must', whose use he refers to as 'musturbation'. These beliefs control people's emotional responses and make them feel worthless and a failure.

Ellis developed the **ABC model**, referring to **a**ctivating event, **b**eliefs and **c**onsequences, to show how irrational thinking can lead to maladaptive behaviour. An activating event can create rational beliefs about the event, leading to desirable emotions and behaviour, or irrational beliefs, leading to undesirable emotions and behaviour, as shown in Figure 7.4.

Figure 7.4 *Ellis (1955): The ABC model*

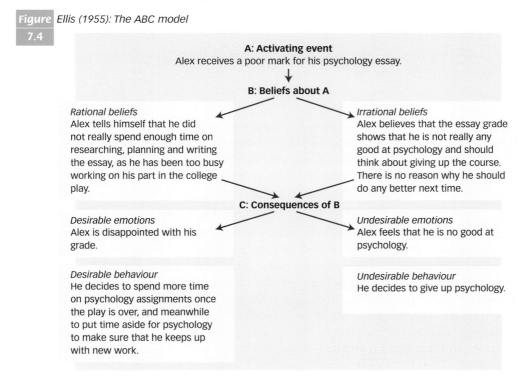

A: Activating event
Alex receives a poor mark for his psychology essay.

B: Beliefs about A

Rational beliefs
Alex tells himself that he did not really spend enough time on researching, planning and writing the essay, as he has been too busy working on his part in the college play.

Irrational beliefs
Alex believes that the essay grade shows that he is not really any good at psychology and should think about giving up the course. There is no reason why he should do any better next time.

C: Consequences of B

Desirable emotions
Alex is disappointed with his grade.

Undesirable emotions
Alex feels that he is no good at psychology.

Desirable behaviour
He decides to spend more time on psychology assignments once the play is over, and meanwhile to put time aside for psychology to make sure that he keeps up with new work.

Undesirable behaviour
He decides to give up psychology.

In therapy, patients are first helped to understand that emotions and behaviours are caused by beliefs and thinking, and then to pinpoint their own irrational beliefs using the ABC format to work on changing their belief systems. In the 'cognitive' part of the therapy, the therapist uses examples from the patient's own recent experience. The therapist notes the **C**, then the **A**. The patient is asked to consider at **B**: 'What was I telling myself about **A**, to feel and behave the way I did at **C**?' As the patient develops understanding of the nature of irrational thinking, this process of 'filling in the gap' becomes easier.

The patient is taught how to challenge his or her irrational beliefs, replacing them with more rational alternatives. The **ABC** format is extended to include **D**: disputing irrational beliefs, **E**: the new effects that the patient wishes to achieve, i.e. new ways of feeling and behaving, and **F**: further action for the patient to take.

For the behavioural part of the therapy, the patient must act against irrational beliefs. For example, to dispute the belief that disapproval is intolerable, he or she is asked to do something deliberately to attract it, and so discover that there are in fact no appalling consequences. Such activities are referred to as **homework**.

REBT is a brief therapy, usually involving between five and 30 sessions over a period of 1–18 months. It is very much task-oriented, focusing on problem solving in the present. The ultimate aim of the therapy is to enable patients to incorporate the new way of thinking into their everyday life, and so to bring about lasting change. Patients will have developed self-help techniques that they will be able to apply in future. They will feel less of a failure, be less likely to self-criticise, develop a more positive sense of their own worth, and so lead a more rewarding life. For this to be achieved, it is important that new ways of thinking should not be imposed on the patients, but rather be developed by them in collaboration with the therapist.

Ellis claimed that this therapy was effective for psychological disorders such as depression, anxiety disorders and sexual problems, though not for more severe mental disorders such as schizophrenia, where talking cures are less effective and medication may be appropriate. However, Ericson (1986) suggests that the principles of CBT may be useful in addressing the symptoms of paranoid schizophrenia. Haaga and Davison (1989) found it to be effective for depression, aggression, anger management and antisocial behaviour. It has also been used in the classroom (e.g. DiGiuseppe, 1999) to improve children's emotional well-being.

A number of case studies have been reported of the successful use of REBT in treating anxiety disorders. For example, Niregi and Uchiyama (2003) used it with a patient suffering from panic disorder, and Gupta (2003) with a man who had a phobia about driving. Ellis himself successfully treated a young man with a phobia about speaking in public (Ellis, 1991), and Savron et al. (2004) report its successful use with 40 patients suffering from obsessive-compulsive disorder (OCD is described earlier in this chapter).

REBT has also been useful in treating eating disorders. Woods and Grieger (1993) used it to treat a young woman suffering from the eating disorder **bulimia nervosa**.

She was taking large doses of laxatives, was alternately binging and starving herself for days on end, and felt depressed, guilty and angry. After REBT, she developed a normal eating pattern, with no recurrence of the disorder 15 months later.

There have also been studies of the effectiveness of REBT in treating depression. Vitiello (2007) found that treating **major depressive disorder (MDD)** with a combination of an SSRI (see page 210) and individual CBT offered advantages over each therapy alone, including overall greater improvement in levels of functioning and measures of quality of life. A similar large-scale project, known as TADS, has also investigated the use of REBT in combination with medication in treating depression in adolescents (see Box 7.8).

Box 7.8	Treatment of Adolescents with Depression Study (TADS) (2007)

Aims: To evaluate the effectiveness of fluoxetine (Prozac), CBT and a combination of the two treatments in treating adolescents with major depressive disorder.

Procedure: Participants were 327 adolescents, aged 12–17 years, who had been diagnosed with MDD. They were treated either with Prozac alone, CBT alone, or a combination of the two therapies. After 12, 18 and 36 weeks, the improvement shown was independently evaluated using rating scales.

Results: The effectiveness of all treatments increased across the period of treatment. After 12 weeks, medication was more effective than CBT, but after 36 weeks, medication and CBT were equally effective. Participants receiving a combination of the two showed the most improvement. Thoughts of suicide and actual suicide attempts were much more common in those treated with medication alone than in those in the CBT and combination groups.

Conclusions: In adolescents with moderate to severe depression, a positive response is faster with drug treatment on its own, or in combination with CBT, than with CBT alone. However, adding CBT to medication improves the safety of medication. The combined treatment of medication and CBT appears to be a better option than either therapy alone.

Moreover, Butler et al. (2006) claim that dropout rates for patients treated with antidepressants are more than twice as high as for those treated with CBT, so including CBT in treatment should help to prevent the problem from recurring. This could be explained in terms of medication suppressing symptoms for as long as it is taken, but CBT providing patients with coping skills that let them deal better with life events. However, there is also some relapse with CBT, so booster sessions may be useful in the period following successful treatment.

Cognitive behavioural therapy has a lot to offer. Unlike drugs, there are no side effects, and as therapy is relatively short term it is practical in terms of both time and cost. The goals of the therapy are clear, in terms of empowering patients to help themselves. It can be used successfully in combination with other therapies, such as medication. However, it is somewhat limited in terms of the disorders for which it is suitable, with little evidence as yet that it has much to offer in the treatment of psychotic disorders like schizophrenia. Evaluation is also problematic as there is no objective measure of improvement.

Summary

- **Cognitive behavioural therapy (CBT)** works on the assumption that mental disorders arise from **faulty thinking**, which leads to **inappropriate emotions** and **behaviour**.
- There are many variations of CBT, of which **rational-emotive behaviour therapy (REBT)**, developed by Ellis, was the original form. The development of mental disorders is described using the **ABC model**, linking **a**ctivating events, **b**eliefs and **c**onsequences.
- CBT challenges inappropriate beliefs, using **behavioural 'homework'** as part of the therapy.
- There is evidence of its effectiveness in treating **anxiety disorders**, **eating disorders** and **depression**. To treat depression, it may usefully be combined with drugs.
- It is **practical** and likely to have **long-lasting effects**, but it is limited in the disorders for which it is appropriate, and objective evaluation is problematic.

Terms explained

biological preparedness: the proposal that animals and humans are innately predisposed to respond more readily to some stimuli than others, particularly where these responses promote survival, or have promoted it in the evolutionary past.

bulimia nervosa: a disorder characterised by episodes of binge eating, followed by self-induced vomiting or other compensatory behaviour, such as the use of laxatives. A person with bulimia is excessively concerned with body size, and has an extreme fear of being, or becoming, fat. It is more often found in females in their late teens or early twenties.

depression: a mood disorder, characterised by feelings of sadness, worthlessness and guilt, and where the normal demands of life are experienced as too much to cope with. A person who is clinically depressed is likely to experience extreme fatigue and difficulty in concentrating, and may suffer from insomnia or a desire to sleep all the time.

informed consent: the ethical requirement that participants in research or clients being offered therapy should be given sufficient information about the procedures before participating, to enable them to decide whether or not they wish to take part.

metastudy: a study that collects and re-analyses the data from several similar studies.

psychotic: describes a mental disorder such as schizophrenia, where a person loses contact with reality. Sufferers may experience delusions or hallucinations, or respond inappropriately to what is going on around them, for example withdrawing into their own private world, or laughing when told that a friend has died.

reductionist: refers to the belief that the subject matter of psychology can be reduced to physical explanations, for example in terms of physiology and biochemistry, with psychological and sociological explanations being seen as unnecessarily complex.

Appendix

References

Abernathy, E. M. (1940) 'The effect of changed environmental conditions upon the results of college examinations', *Journal of Psychology*, Vol. 10, pp. 293–301.

Adorno, T. W. et al. (1950) *The Authoritarian Personality*, Harper and Row.

Allen, V. L. and Levine, J. M. (1971) 'Social support and conformity: the role of independent assessment of reality', *Journal of Experimental Social Psychology*, Vol. 7, pp. 48–58.

Allport, F. H. (1924) *Social Psychology*, Houghton Mifflin.

Altmaier, E. M. and Woodward, M. (1981) 'Group vicarious desensitisation of test anxiety', *Journal of Counseling Psychology*, Vol. 28, No. 5, pp. 467–69.

Andersson, B.-E. (1992) 'Effects of day-care on cognitive and socioemotional competence of thirteen-year-old Swedish schoolchildren', *Child Development*, Vol. 63, pp. 20–36.

Apker, J. (2005) 'Role negotiation, stress, and burnout: a day in the life of a "supernurse"', in E. B. Ray (ed.) *Health Communication in Practice: A Case Study Approach*, Lawrence Erlbaum Associates.

Arendt, H. (1963) *Eichmann in Jerusalem: A Report on the Banality of Evil*, Viking Press.

Aronson, E. (1988) *The Social Animal* (5th edn), Freeman.

Asch, S. E. (1951) 'Effect of group pressure upon the modification and distortion of judgments', in H. Guetzkow (ed.) *Groups, Leadership and Men*, Carnegie Press.

Asch, S. E. (1962) 'Effects of group pressure on the modification and distortion of judgments', in E. E. Maccoby et al. (eds) *Readings in Social Psychology* (3rd edn).

Atkinson, R. C. and Raugh, M. R. (1975) 'An application of the mnemonic keyword method to the acquisition of a Russian vocabulary', *Journal of Experimental Psychology*, Vol. 104, pp. 126–33.

Atkinson, R. C. and Shiffrin, R. M. (1968) 'Human memory: a proposed system and its control processes', in K. W. Spence and J. T. Spence (eds) *The Psychology of Learning and Motivation* (Vol. 2), Academic Press.

Atkinson, R. L. et al. (1983) *Introduction to Psychology* (8th edn), Harcourt Brace Jovanovich.

Avtgis, T. A. (1998) 'Locus of control and persuasion, social influence, and conformity: a meta-analytic review', *Psychological Reports*, Vol. 83, No. 3.1, pp. 899–903.

Baddeley, A. D. (1966) 'The influence of acoustic and semantic similarity on long-term memory for word sequences', *Quarterly Journal of Experimental Psychology*, Vol. 18, pp. 302–09.

Baddeley, A. D. (1996) 'Exploring the central executive', *Quarterly Journal of Experimental Psychology*, Vol. 49 (A), pp. 5–28.

Baddeley, A. D. and Hitch, G. (1974) 'Working memory', in G. A. Bower (ed.) *Recent Advances in Learning and Motivation* (Vol. 8), Academic Press.

Baddeley, A. D., Thomson, N. and Buchanan, M. (1975) 'Word length and the structure of short-term memory', *Journal of Verbal Learning and Verbal Behavior*, Vol. 14, pp. 575–89.

Bales, R. F. (1950) *Interaction Process Analysis: A Method for the Study of Small Groups*, Addison-Wesley.

Banauch, G. et al. (2002) 'Injuries and illness among New York City Fire Department rescue workers after responding to the World Trade Center attacks', *Journal of the American Medical Association*, Vol. 288, No. 13, pp. 1581–84.

Bandura, A. (1965) 'Influence of models' reinforcement contingencies on the acquisition of imitative responses', *Journal of Personality and Social Psychology*, Vol. 1, pp. 589–95.

Bandura, A. and Menlove, F. L. (1968) 'Factors determining vicarious extinction of avoidance behavior through symbolic modeling', *Journal of Personality and Social Psychology*, Vol. 8, pp. 99–108.

Bandura, A., Ross, D. and Ross, S. A. (1963) 'Imitation of film-mediated aggressive models', *Journal of Abnormal and Social Psychology*, Vol. 66, pp. 3–11.

Baron et al. (1996) 'The forgotten variable in conformity research: impact of task importance on social influence', *Journal of Personality and Social Psychology*, Vol. 71, No. 5, pp. 915–27.

Bartlett, F. C. (1932) *Remembering*, Cambridge University Press.

Baumrind, D. (1964) 'Some thoughts on ethics of research: after reading Milgram's behavioral study of obedience', *American Psychologist*, Vol. 19, pp. 421–23.

Beck, A. T. (1987) *Depression: Causes and Treatment*, University of Philadelphia Press.

Belsky, J. (1988) 'The effects of infant day care reconsidered', *Early Child Research Quarterly*, Vol. 3, pp. 235–72.

Benton, D. (1981) 'ECT: can the system take the shock?', *Community Care*, 12 March, pp. 15–17.

Bergin, A. E. (1971) 'The evaluation of therapeutic outcomes', in A. E. Bergin and S. L. Garfield (eds) *Handbook of Psychotherapy and Behavior Change: An Empirical Analysis*, John Wiley.

Berkowitz, L. and La Page, A. (1967) 'Weapons as aggression-eliciting stimuli', *Journal of Personality and Social Psychology*, Vol. 7, pp. 202–07.

Bernstein, S. (1984) 'A case history demonstrating the complementary use of psychodynamic and behavioral techniques in psychotherapy', *Psychotherapy: Theory, Research, Practice, Training*, Vol. 21, No. 3, pp. 402–07.

Bickman, L. (1974) 'Social roles and uniforms: clothes make the person', *Psychology Today*, Vol. 7, No. 11, pp. 49–51.

Bini, L. (1938) 'Experimental researches on epileptic attacks induced by electric current', *American Journal of Psychiatry*, Vol. 32, pp. 297–306.

Blakemore, C. (1988) *The Mind Machine*, BBC Publications.

Blass, T. (1991) 'Understanding behavior in the Milgram obedience experiment: the role of personality, situations, and their interactions', *Journal of Personality and Social Psychology*, Vol. 60, Vol. 3, pp. 398–413.

Blass, T. (1995) 'Right-wing authoritarianism and role as predictors of attributions about obedience to authority', *Personality and Individual Differences*, Vol. 19, No. 1, pp. 99–100.

Blumenthal, J. A. et al. (1987) 'Social support, Type A behavior, and coronary artery disease', *Psychosomatic Medicine*, Vol. 49, pp. 331–39.

Bogdonoff, M. D. et al. (1961) 'The modifying effect of conforming behaviour upon lipid responses accompanying CNS arousal', *Clinical Research*, Vol. 9, pp. 135.

Boker, W. (1992) 'A call for partnership between schizophrenic patients, relatives and professionals', *British Journal of Psychiatry*, Vol. 161 (supplement 18), pp. 10–12.

Bond, R. and Smith, P. B. (1996) 'Culture and conformity: a meta-analysis of studies using Asch's (1952b, 1956) line judgment task', *Psychological Bulletin*, Vol. 119, No. 1, pp. 111–37.

Borge, A. I. H. et al. (2004) 'Early childcare and physical aggression: differentiating social selection and social causation', *Journal of Child Psychology and Psychiatry*, Vol. 45, No. 2, pp. 367–76.

Bousfield, W. A. (1953) 'The occurrence of clustering in the recall of randomly arranged associates', *Journal of General Psychology*, Vol. 49, pp. 229–40.

Bower, G. H. (1972) 'Mental imagery and associative learning', in L. Gregg (ed.) *Cognition in Learning and Memory*, John Wiley.

Bower, G. H. et al. (1969) 'Hierarchical retrieval schemes in recall of categorized word lists', *Journal of Verbal Learning and Verbal Behavior*, Vol. 8, pp. 323–43.

Bowlby, J. (1944) 'Forty-four juvenile thieves: their characters and home life', *International Journal of Psychoanalysis*, Vol. 25, pp. 1–57 and 207–28.

Bowlby, J. (1953) *Child Care and the Growth of Love*, Penguin.

Bowlby, J. (1969) *Attachment and Loss: Attachment* (Vol. 1), Basic Books.

Brady, J. V. (1958) 'Ulcers in "executive monkeys"', *Scientific American*, Vol. 199, pp. 95–100.

Brehm, J. W. (1956) 'Post-decision changes in the desirability of alternatives', *Journal of Abnormal and Social Psychology*, Vol. 52, pp. 384–89.

Brody, M. B. (1944) 'Prolonged memory defects following electro-therapy', *Journal of Mental Science*, Vol. 90, pp. 777–79.

Brown, G. W. and Harris, T. O. (1978) *Social Origins of Depression: A Study of Psychiatric Disorder in Women*, Tavistock.

Brown, R. and Kulick, J. (1977) 'Flashbulb memories', *Cognition*, Vol. 5, pp. 73–99.

Brown, R., Coller, N. and Corsellis, J. A. N. (1986) 'Post-mortem evidence of structural brain changes in schizophrenia: differences in brain weight, temporal brain area, and parahippocampal gyrus compared with affective disorder', *Archives of General Psychiatry*, Vol. 43, pp. 36–42.

Bryant, B., Harris, M. and Newton, D. (1980) *Children and Minders*, Grant McIntyre.

Burgess, J. M. (2004) 'Defiance in obedience research: motivational orientation and refusing to acquiesce', *Dissertation Abstracts International: Section B: The Sciences and Engineering*, Vol. 64 (7–B), p. 3578.

Burley, P. M. and McGuiness, J. (1977) 'Effects of social intelligence on the Milgram paradigm', *Psychological Reports*, Vol. 40, pp. 767–70.

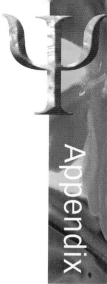

Butler, A. C. et al. (2006) 'The empirical status of cognitive-behavioral therapy: a review of meta-analyses', *Clinical Psychology Review*, Vol. 26, No. 1, pp. 17–31.

Butterworth, B. (1992) 'The man who could only read numbers', in T. Radford (ed.) *Frontiers 01: Science and Technology, 2001–02*, Atlantic Books.

Cannon, W. B. (1929) *Bodily Changes in Pain, Hunger, Fear and Rage*, Appleton-Century-Crofts.

Carter, R. T. and Forsyth, J. M. (2007) 'Examining race and culture in psychology journals: the case of forensic psychology', *Professional Psychology: Research and Practice*, Vol. 38, No. 2, pp. 133–42.

Charlton, T. et al. (2000) 'Children's playground behaviour across five years of broadcast television: a naturalistic study in a remote community', *Emotional and Behavioural Difficulties*, Vol. 5, No. 4, pp. 4–12.

Chermak, S. and Chapman, N. M. (2007) 'Predicting crime story salience: a replication', *Journal of Criminal Justice*, Vol. 35, No. 4, pp. 351–63.

Cherry, N. M., Chen, Y. and McDonald, J. C. (2006) 'Reported incidence and precipitating factors of work-related stress and mental ill-health in the United Kingdom (1996–2001)', *Occupational Medicine*, Vol. 56, No. 6, pp. 414–21.

Clare, A. (1980) *Psychiatry in Dissent*, Tavistock.

Cobb, S. and Rose, R. M. (1973) 'Hypertension, peptic ulcer, and diabetes in air traffic controllers', *Journal of the American Medical Association*, Vol. 224, pp. 489–92.

Cohen, N. J. and Squire, L. R. (1980) 'Preserved learning and retention of pattern-analysing skill in amnesia using perceptual learning', *Cortex*, Vol. 17, pp. 273–78.

Cohen, S., Tyrell, D. A. J. and Smith, A. P. (1991) 'Psychological stress and susceptibility to the common cold', *The New England Journal of Medicine*, Vol. 325, pp. 606–12.

Coleman, E. A. et al. (1996) 'Subjective memory complaints prior to and following electroconvulsive therapy', *Biological Psychiatry*, Vol. 39, No. 5, pp. 346–56.

Collins, A. M. and Loftus, E. F. (1975) 'A spreading-activation theory of semantic processing', *Psychological Review*, Vol. 82, pp. 407–28.

Conrad, R. (1964) 'Acoustic confusion in immediate memory', *British Journal of Psychology*, Vol. 55, pp. 75–84.

Coolican, H. (1990) *Research Methods and Statistics in Psychology*, Hodder and Stoughton.

Costa, P. T. and McCrae, R. R. (1992), *NEO PI-R Professional Manual*, Psychological Assessment Resources.

Cox, T. (1975) 'The nature and management of stress', *New Behaviour*, 25 September, pp. 493–95.

Cox, T., Watts, C. R. and Barnett, A. (1981) 'The experience and effects of task-inherent demand', *Final Technical Report to the US Army Research, Development and Standardisation Group, UK*.

Craik, F. and Lockhart, R. (1972) 'Levels of processing', *Journal of Verbal Learning and Verbal Behavior*, Vol. 11, pp. 671–84.

Craik, F. and Tulving, E. (1975) 'Depth of processing and the retention of words in episodic memory', *Journal of Experimental Psychology: General*, Vol. 104, pp. 268–94.

Craik, F. and Watkins, M. (1973) 'The role of rehearsal in short-term memory', *Journal of Verbal Learning and Verbal Behavior*, Vol. 12, pp. 599–607.

Crutchfield, R. S. (1954) 'A new technique for measuring individual differences in conformity to group judgment', *Proceedings of the Invitational Conference on Testing Problems*, pp. 69–74.

Curtiss, S. (1977) *Genie: A Psycholinguistic Study of a Modern-Day 'Wild Child'*, Academic Press.

Cutts, T. F. and Barrios, B. A. (1986) 'Fear of weight gain among bulimic and non-disturbed females', *Behavior Therapy*, Vol. 17, pp. 626–36.

Davison, G. C. and Neale, J. M. (1994) *Abnormal Psychology* (6th edn), John Wiley.

Dembroski, T. M. and Costa, P. (1988) 'Assessment of coronary-prone behaviour: a current overview', *Annals of Behavioral Medicine*, Vol. 10, pp. 60–63.

Den Heyer, K. and Barrett, B. (1971) 'Selective loss of visual and verbal information in short-term memory by means of visual and verbal interpolated tasks', *Psychonomic Science*, Vol. 25, pp. 100–02.

De Schipper, E. J., Riksen-Walraven, J. M. and Geurts, S. A. E. (2007) 'Multiple determinants of caregiver behavior in child care centers', *Early Childhood Research Quarterly*, Vol. 22, No. 3, pp. 312–26.

Deutsch, M. and Gerard, H. B. (1955) 'A study of normative and informational social influences upon individual judgment', *Journal of Abnormal and Social Psychology*, Vol. 51, pp. 629–36.

DeYoung, C. G., Peterson, J. B. and Higgins, D. M. (2002) 'Higher-order factors of the Big Five predict conformity: are there neuroses of health?', *Personality and Individual Differences*, Vol. 33, No. 4, pp. 533–52.

DiGiuseppe, R. (1999) 'Rational emotive behavior therapy', in H. Thompson and D. T. Brown (eds) *Counseling and Psychotherapy with Children and Adolescents: Theory and Practice for School and Clinical Settings* (3rd edn), John Wiley.

DiLalla, L. F. (1998) 'Daycare, child, and family influences on preschoolers' social behaviors in a peer play setting', *Child Study Journal*, Vol. 28, No. 3, pp. 223–44.

Dohner, J. A. (1972) 'Motives for drug use: adults and adolescents', *Psychosomatics*, Vol. 13, pp. 317–24.

Dollard, J. and Miller, N. E. (1950) *Personality and Psychotherapy*, McGraw-Hill.

Ebbinghaus, H. (1885) *Concerning Memory*, Teachers' College Press (published in 1913).

Ellis, A. (1962) *Reason and Emotion in Psychotherapy*, Lyle Stuart.

Ellis, A. (1991) 'Rational-emotive treatment of simple phobias', *Psychotherapy: Theory, Research, Practice, Training*, Vol. 28, No. 3, pp. 452–56.

Ellis, H. and Szulecka, T. (1996) 'The disguised lover: a case of Fregoli delusion', in P. W. Halligan and J. C. Marshall (eds) *Method in Madness: Case Studies in Cognitive Neuropsychiatry*, Psychology Press.

Elms, A. C. (1972) *Social Psychology and Social Relevance*, Brown.

Elms, A. C. and Milgram, S. (1966) 'Personality characteristics associated with obedience and defiance towards authoritative command', *Journal of Experimental Research in Personality*, Vol. 1, pp. 282–89.

Erbeck, J., Elfner, L. and Driggs, D. (1983) 'Reduction of blood pressure by indirect biofeedback', *Biofeedback and Self Regulation*, Vol. 8, No. 1, pp. 63–72.

Ericson, K. (1986) 'Preventing mental illness: some personal discoveries', *Journal of Humanistic Psychology*, Vol. 26, No. 1, pp. 61–71.

Evans, P., Clow, A. and Hucklebridge, F. (1997) 'Stress and the immune system', *The Psychologist*, Vol. 10, No. 7, pp. 303–07.

Eysenck, H. J. (1952) 'The effects of psychotherapy: an evaluation', *Journal of Consulting Psychology*, Vol. 16, pp. 319–24.

Fisher, R. P., Geiselman, R. E. and Raymond, D. S. (1987) 'Critical analysis of police interview techniques', *Journal of Police Science and Administration*, Vol. 15, pp. 177–85.

Fisher, R. P., Geiselman, R. E. and Amador, M. (1990) 'Field test of the cognitive interior', reported in *The Psychologist*, September 1991.

Flin, R. H. et al. (1992) 'The effect of a five-month delay on children's and adults' eyewitness memory', *British Journal of Psychology*, Vol. 83, pp. 323–25.

Folkman, S. and Lazarus, R. S. (1980) 'An analysis of coping in a middle-aged community sample', *Journal of Health and Social Behavior*, Vol. 21, No. 3, pp. 219–39.

Folkman, S. and Lazarus, R. S. (1985) 'If it changes it must be a process: study of emotion and coping during three stages of a college examination', *Journal of Personality and Social Psychology*, Vol. 48, No. 1, pp. 150–70.

Forsythe, C. J. and Compas, B. E. (1987) 'Interaction of cognitive appraisals of stressful events and coping: testing the goodness of fit hypothesis', *Cognitive Therapy and Research*, Vol. 11, No. 4, pp. 473–85.

Freeman, C. P., Weeks, D. and Kendell, R. E. (1980) 'ECT: II. Patients who complain', *British Journal of Psychiatry*, Vol. 137, pp. 17–25.

Friedberg, J. (1976) *Shock Treatment is Not Good for Your Brain*, Glide.

Friedberg, J. (1977) 'Shock treatment, brain damage, and memory loss: a neurological perspective', *American Journal of Psychiatry*, Vol. 134, No. 9, pp. 1010–14.

Friedman, M. and Rosenman, R. H. (1974) *Type A Behaviour and Your Heart*, Knopf.

Friedman, M. et al. (1986) 'Alteration of Type A behaviour and its effects on cardiac recurrences in postmyocardial infarction patients: summary of the Recurrent Coronary Prevention Project', *American Heart Journal*, Vol. 112, pp. 653–65.

Gardiner, M., Lovell, G. and Williamson, P. (2004) 'Physician you can heal yourself! Cognitive behavioural training reduces stress in GPs', *Family Practice*, Vol. 21, No. 5, pp. 545–51.

Geiselman, R. E. (1999) 'Commentary on recent research with the cognitive interview', *Psychology, Crime & Law*, Vol. 51, Nos 1–2, special issue: 'The cognitive interview: current research and applications', pp. 197–202.

Geiselman, R. E. et al. (1984) 'Enhancement of eyewitness memory: an empirical evaluation of the cognitive interview', *Journal of Police Science and Administration*, Vol. 12, pp. 74–80.

Geiselman, R. E. et al. (1986) 'Enhancement of eyewitness memory with the cognitive interview', *American Journal of Psychology*, Vol. 99, pp. 385–401.

Glanzer, M. and Cunitz, A. R. (1966) 'Two storage mechanisms in free recall', *Journal of Verbal Learning and Verbal Behavior*, Vol. 5, pp. 351–60.

Godden, D. R. and Baddeley, A. D. (1975) 'Context-dependent memory in two natural environments: on land and under water', *British Journal of Psychology*, Vol. 66, pp. 325–31.

Gold, D. et al. (1992) 'Rotating shift work, sleep and accidents related to sleepiness in hospital nurses', *American Journal of Public Health*, Vol. 82, pp. 1011–14.

Goldberg, S., MacKay-Soroka, S. and Rochester, M. (1994) 'Affect, attachment and maternal responsiveness', *Infant Behavior and Development*, Vol. 17, pp. 335–39.

Goldfarb, W. (1943) 'The effects of early institutional care on adolescent personality', *Journal of Experimental Education*, Vol. 12, pp. 106–29.

Grossman, K. et al. (1985) 'Maternal sensitivity and newborn's orientation responses', in I. Bretherton and E. Waters (eds) *Growing Points in Attachment Theory and Research, Monographs of the Society for Research in Child Development*, Vol. 50, Serial no. 209, pp. 3–35.

Gupta, R. (2003) 'Cognitive behavioral treatment on driving phobia for an Asian Indian male', *Clinical Gerontologist*, Vol. 26, Nos 3–4, pp. 165–71.

Haaga, D. A. F. and Davison, G. C. (1989) *Journal of Consulting and Clinical Psychology*, Vol. 61, No. 2, pp. 215–20.

Hamilton, C. E. (1994) 'Continuity and discontinuity of attachment from infancy through adolescence', *Child Development*, Vol. 71, pp. 690–94.

Hammerfald, K. et al. (2006) 'Persistent effects of cognitive-behavioral stress management on cortisol responses to acute stress in healthy subjects — a randomized controlled trial', *Psychoneuroendocrinology*, Vol. 31, No. 3, pp. 333–39.

Harburg, E. et al. (1973) 'Socioecological stress, suppressed hostility, skin colour, and black-white male blood pressure: Detroit', *Psychosomatic Medicine*, Vol. 35, pp. 276–96.

Harlow, H. and Harlow, M. K. (1962) 'Social deprivation in monkeys', *Scientific American*, Vol. 207, pp. 136–44.

Harlow, H. and Zimmerman, R. R. (1959) 'Affectional responses in the infant monkey', *Science*, Vol. 130, pp. 421–32.

Hautamäki, A. (2007) interviewed in *The Psychologist*, Vol. 20, No. 11, pp. 670–71.

Hayes, B. K. and Delamothe, K. (1997) 'Cognitive interviewing procedures and suggestibility in children's recall', *Journal of Applied Psychology*, Vol. 82, No. 4, pp. 562–77.

Hazan, C. and Shaver, P. (1987) 'Romantic love conceptualized as an attachment process', *Journal of Personality and Social Psychology*, Vol. 52, pp. 511–24.

Heaven, P. C. (1986) 'Correlates of conformity in three cultures', *Personality and Individual Differences*, Vol. 7, No. 6, pp. 883–87.

Hegland, S. M. and Rix, M. K. (1990) 'Aggression and assertiveness in kindergarten children differing in day care experiences', *Early Childhood Research Quarterly*, Vol. 5, pp. 105–16.

Hetherington, E. M., Cox, M. J. and Cox, R. (1979) 'Play and social interaction in children following divorce', *Journal of Social Issues*, Vol. 35, pp. 26–49.

Hetherington, E. M., Cox, M. J. and Cox, R. (1982) 'Effects of divorce on parents and children', in M. E. Lamb (ed.) *Non-Traditional Families: Parenting and Child Development*, Lawrence Erlbaum Associates.

Hodges, J. and Tizard, B. (1989) 'Social and family relationships of ex-institutional adolescents', *Journal of Child Psychology and Psychiatry*, Vol. 30, pp. 77–97.

Hofling, K. C. et al. (1966) 'An experimental study in the nurse–physician relationship', *Journal of Nervous and Mental Disorders*, Vol. 143, pp. 171–80.

Holmes, T. H. and Rahe, R. H. (1967) 'The social readjustment rating scale', *Journal of Psychosomatic Research*, Vol. 11, pp. 213–18.

Honig, A. S. and Park, K. J. (1993) 'Effects of day care on preschool sex-role development', *American Journal of Orthopsychiatry*, Vol. 63, pp. 481–86.

Hosogoshi, H. and Kodama, M. (2006) 'Defensive pessimists and coping: the goodness of fit hypothesis', *Japanese Journal of Psychology*, Vol. 77, No. 5, pp. 452–57.

Howes, C. (1990) 'Can the age of entry into child care and the quality of child care predict adjustment in kindergarten?', *Developmental Psychology*, Vol. 26, pp. 292–303.

Humphreys, L. (1970) *Tearoom Trade*, Aldine.

Immelmann, K. (1972) 'Sexual and other long-term aspects of imprinting in birds and other species', in D. S. Lehrmann, R. A. Hinde and E. Shaw (eds) *Advances in the Study of Behavior*, Vol. 4, Academic Press.

Insko, C. A. et al. (1983) 'Conformity as a function of the consistency of positive self-evaluation with being liked and being right', *Journal of Experimental Social Psychology*, Vol. 19, pp. 341–58.

Jacobs, J. R. and Bovasso, G. B. (2000) 'Early and chronic stress and their relation to breast cancer', *Psychological Medicine*, Vol. 30, No. 3, pp. 669–78.

Jacobs, T. J. and Charles, E. (1980) 'Life events and the occurrence of cancer in children', *Psychosomatic Medicine*, Vol. 42, No. 1, pp. 11–24.

Jahoda, M. (1958) *Current Concepts of Positive Mental Health*, Basic Books.

James, W. (1890) *Principles of Psychology*, Holt.

Janis, I. L. (1950) 'Psychological effects of electric convulsive treatments (II. Changes in word association reactions)', *Journal of Nervous and Mental Disease*, Vol. 111, pp. 383–97.

Jimenez, B. M. et al. (2006) 'La personalidad resistente como variable moduladora del síndrome de burnout en una muestra de bomberos' (Hardy personality as moderator variable of burnout syndrome in firefighters), *Psicothema*, Vol. 18, No. 3, pp. 413–18.

Jin, M. K. (2005) 'A cross-cultural study of infant attachment patterns in Korea and the United States: associations among infant temperament, maternal personality, separation anxiety and depression', *Dissertation Abstracts International: Section B: The Sciences and Engineering*, Vol. 66 (5-B), p. 2855.

Johansson, G., Arinsson, G. and Lindström, B. O. (1978) 'Social psychological and neuroendocrine stress reactions in highly mechanised work', *Ergonomics*, Vol. 21, No. 8, pp. 583–99.

Johnson, R., Browne, K. and Hamilton-Giachritsis, C. (2006) 'Young children in institutional care at risk of harm', *Trauma, Violence, and Abuse*, Vol. 7, No. 1, pp. 34–60.

Jones, L. and Cochrane, R. (1981) 'Stereotypes of mental illness: a test of the labelling hypothesis', *International Journal of Social Psychiatry*, Vol. 27, pp. 99–107.

Jones, M. C. (1924) 'The elimination of children's fears', *Journal of Experimental Psychology*, Vol. 7, pp. 382–90.

Kagan, J., Kearsley, R. B. and Zelazo, P. R. (1978) *Infancy: its Place in Human Development*, Harvard University Press.

Kanner, A. D. et al. (1981) 'Comparison of two modes of stress management: daily hassles and uplifts versus major life events', *Journal of Behavioral Medicine*, Vol. 4, pp. 1–39.

Kanner, A. D. et al. (1987) 'Uplifts, hassles, and adaptational outcomes in early adolescents', *Journal of Early Adolescence*, Vol. 7, No. 4, pp. 371–94.

Kant, I. (1991) *Critique of Pure Reason* (trans. N. Kemp) (2nd ed.), Palgrave.

Kelman, H. C. (1958) 'Compliance, identification and internalization: three processes of attitude change', *Journal of Conflict Resolution*, Vol. 2, pp. 51–60.

Kelman, H. C. (1967) 'Human use of human subjects: the problem of deception in social psychological experiments', *Psychological Bulletin*, Vol. 67, pp. 1–11.

Kendler, K. S. (1983) 'Overview: a current perspective on twin studies of schizophrenia', *American Journal of Psychiatry*, Vol. 140, No. 11, pp. 1413–25.

Kendler, K. S. et al. (2002) 'The joint analysis of personal interview and family history diagnoses: evidence for validity of diagnosis and increased heritability estimates', *Psychological Medicine*, Vol. 32, No. 5, pp. 829–42.

Kiecolt-Glaser, J. K. et al. (1984) 'Psychosocial modifiers of immunocompetence in medical students', *Psychosomatic Medicine*, Vol. 46, pp. 1–14.

Kiecolt-Glaser, J. K. et al. (1995) 'Slowing of wound healing by psychological stress', *Lancet*, Vol. 346, pp. 1194–96.

Kilham, W. and Mann, L. (1974) 'Level of destructive obedience as a function of transmitter and executive roles in the Milgram obedience paradigm', *Journal of Personality and Social Psychology*, Vol. 29, pp. 696–702.

Kim, H. and Markus, H. R. (1999) 'Deviance or uniqueness, harmony or conformity? A cultural analysis', *Journal of Personality and Social Psychology*, Vol. 77, No. 4, pp. 785–800.

Kobasa, S. C. (1979) 'Stressful life events, personality, and health: an enquiry into hardiness', *Journal of Personality and Social Psychology*, Vol. 37, pp. 1–11.

Kobasa, S. C., Maddi, S. R. and Kahn, S. (1982) 'Hardiness and health: a prospective study', *Journal of Personality and Social Psychology*, Vol. 42, pp. 168–77.

Koch, S. et al. (2006) 'Stressbewältigung am Arbeitsplatz: ein stationäres Gruppentherapieprogramm' (Occupational stress management: an inpatient group therapy programme), *Verhaltenstherapie*, Vol. 16, No. 1, pp. 7–15.

Koluchova, J. (1976) 'The further development of twins after severe and prolonged deprivation: a second report', *Journal of Child Psychology and Psychiatry*, Vol. 17, pp. 181–88.

Kroes, W. H., Hurrell, J. J. and Margolis, B. (1974) 'Job stress in police administrators', *Journal of Police Science and Administration*, Vol. 2, No. 4, pp. 381–87.

Kudirka, N. K. (1965) 'Defiance of authority under peer influence', unpublished doctoral dissertation, Yale University.

Larsen, K. S. (1974) 'Conformity in the Asch experiment', *Journal of Social Psychology*, Vol. 94, pp. 303–04.

Larsen, K. S. et al. (1979) 'Collaborator status, subject characteristics and conformity in the Asch paradigm', *Journal of Social Psychology*, Vol. 108, pp. 259–63.

Lazarus, R. S. and Folkman, S. (1984) *Stress, Coping and Adaptation*, Springer.

Leach, P. (1979) *Who Cares: A New Deal for Mothers and Their Small Children*, Penguin.

Lee, C. M., Neighbours, C. and Woods, B. A. (2007) 'Marijuana motives: young adults' reasons for using marijuana', *Addictive Behaviors*, Vol. 32, No. 7, pp. 1384–94.

Levine, E. D., Ramos, D. and Mills, D. S. (2007) 'A prospective study of two self-help CD-based desensitization and counter-conditioning programmes with the use of dog appeasing pheromone for the treatment of firework fears in dogs (*Canis familiaris*)', *Applied Animal Behaviour Science*, Vol. 105, No. 4, pp. 311–29.

Lewinsohn, P. M. and Hoberman, H. M. (1982) 'Depression', in A. S. Bellack, M. Hersen and A. E. Kazdin (eds) *International Handbook of Behaviour Modification and Therapy*, Plenum.

Lewinsohn, P. M., Joiner, T. E. and Rohde, P. (2001) 'Evaluation of cognitive diathesis-stress models in predicting major depressive disorder in adolescents', *Journal of Abnormal Psychology*, Vol. 110, No. 2, pp. 203–15.

Lichtenstein, P. and Annas, P. (2000) 'Heritability and prevalence of specific fears and phobias in childhood', *Journal of Child Psychology and Psychiatry*, Vol. 41, No. 7, pp. 927–37.

List, J. (1986) 'Age and schematic differences in the reliability of eyewitness testimony', *Developmental Psychology*, Vol. 22, pp. 50–57.

Loftus, E. F. (1975) 'Leading questions and the eyewitness report', *Cognitive Psychology*, Vol. 7, pp. 560–72.

Loftus, E. F. (1979) 'Reactions to blatantly contradictory information', *Memory and Cognition*, Vol. 7, pp. 368–74.

Loftus, E. F. and Burns, H. J. (1982) 'Mental shock can produce retrograde amnesia', *Memory and Cognition*, Vol. 10, pp. 318–23.

Loftus, E. F. and Palmer, J. C. (1974) 'Reconstruction of automobile destruction: an example of the interaction between language and memory', *Journal of Verbal Learning and Verbal Behavior*, Vol. 13, pp. 585–89.

Loftus, E. F., Levidow, B. and Duensing, S. (1991) 'Who remembers best? Individual differences in memory for events that occurred in a science museum', *Applied Cognitive Psychology*, Vol. 6, No. 2, pp. 93–107.

Loftus, E. F. et al. (1987) 'Time went by so slowly: overestimation of event duration by males and females', *Applied Cognitive Psychology*, Vol. 1, pp. 3–13.

Luria, A. R. (1968) *The Mind of a Mnemonist*, Basic Books.

Maccoby, E. E. (1980) *Social Development*, Harcourt Brace Jovanovich.

Maddi, S. R., Kahn, S. and Maddi, K. L. (1998) 'The effectiveness of hardiness training', *Consulting Psychology Journal: Practice and Research*, Vol. 50, No. 2, pp. 78–86.

Maddison, R. and Prapavessis, H. (2005) 'A psychological approach to the prediction and prevention of athletic injury', *Journal of Sport and Exercise Psychology*, Vol. 27, No. 3, pp. 289–310.

Main, M. and Cassidy, J. (1988) 'Categories of response to reunion with the parent at age 6: predictable from infant classifications and stable over a 1-month period', *Developmental Psychology*, Vol. 24, pp. 415–26.

Main, M. and Goldwyn, R. (1984) 'Predicting rejection of her infant from mother's representation of her own experience: implications for the abused–abusing intergenerational cycle', *Child Abuse and Neglect*, Vol. 8, pp. 203–17.

Main, M. and Solomon, J. (1986) 'Discovery of a disorganised disoriented attachment pattern', in T. B. Brazelton and M. W. Yogman (eds) *Affective Development in Infancy*, Ablex.

Main, N. A., Elliot, S. A. and Brown, J. S. L. (2005) 'Comparison of three different approaches used in large-scale stress workshops for the general public', *Behavioural and Cognitive Psychotherapy*, Vol. 33, No. 3, pp. 299–309.

Malan, D. (1973) 'The outcome problem in psychotherapy research', *Archives of General Psychiatry*, Vol. 32, pp. 995–1008.

Mann, L. (1977) 'The effect of stimulus queues on queue-joining behavior', *Journal of Personality and Social Psychology*, Vol. 35, pp. 437–42.

Mantell, D. M. (1971) 'The potential for violence in Germany', *Journal of Social Issues*, Vol. 27, pp. 101–12.

Marsh, P. et al. (1978) *The Rules of Disorder*, Routledge and Kegan Paul.

Marucha, P. T., Kiecolt-Glaser, J. K. and Favagehi, M. (1998) 'Mucosal wound healing is impaired by examination stress', *Psychosomatic Medicine*, Vol. 60, No. 3, pp. 362–65.

Masling, J. (1966) 'Role-related behavior of the subject and psychologist and its effect upon psychological data', in D. Levine (ed.) *Nebraska Symposium on Motivation*, University of Nebraska Press.

Maslow, A. (1954) *Motivation and Personality*, Harper and Row.

Mathews, K. A. (1984) 'Assessment of type A, anger, and hostility in epidemiological studies of cardiovascular disease', in A. Ostfeld and E. Eaker (eds) *Measuring Psychosocial Variables in Epidemiologic Studies of Cardiovascular Disease*, National Institute for Health.

Mayall, B. and Petrie, P. (1983) *Minder, Mother and Child*, University of London Institute of Education.

McCartney, K. et al. (1985) 'Day care as intervention: comparisons of varying quality programs', *Journal of Applied Developmental Psychology*, Vol. 6, pp. 247–60.

McCloskey, M. and Zaragoza, M. (1985) 'Misleading post-event information and memory for events: arguments and evidence against memory impairment hypotheses', *Journal of Experimental Psychology*, Vol. 114, pp. 1–16.

McKenna, M. C. et al. (1999) 'Psychosocial factors and the development of breast cancer: a meta-analysis', *Health Psychology*, Vol. 18, No. 5, pp. 520–31.

Mednick, S. A. et al. (1988) 'Fetal viral infection and adult schizophrenia', *Archives of General Psychiatry*, Vol. 45, pp. 189–92.

Meeus, W. H. J. and Raaijmakers, Q. A. W. (1986) 'Administrative obedience: carrying out orders to use psychological-administrative violence', *European Journal of Social Psychology*, Vol. 16, pp. 311–24.

Melhuish, E. C. et al. (1990) 'Type of childcare at 18 months–1. Differences in interactional experience', *Journal of Child Psychology and Psychiatry*, Vol. 31, pp. 849–59.

Memon, A. and Bull, R. (1991) 'The cognitive interview: its origins, empirical support, evaluation and practical implications', *Journal of Community and Applied Social Psychology*, Vol. 1, pp. 291–307.

Milgram, S. (1963) 'Behavioral study of obedience', *Journal of Abnormal and Social Psychology*, Vol. 67, pp. 371–78.

Milgram, S. (1964) 'Issues in the study of obedience: a reply to Baumrind', *American Psychologist*, Vol. 19, pp. 848–52.

Milgram, S. (1965) 'Some conditions of obedience and disobedience to authority', *Human Relations*, Vol. 18, pp. 57–76.

Milgram, S. (1974) *Obedience to Authority*, Harper and Row.

Miller, F. D. (1975) 'An experimental study of obedience to authorities of varying legitimacy', unpublished doctoral dissertation, Harvard University.

Miller, G. A. (1956) 'The magical number seven, plus or minus two: some limits on our capacity for processing information', *Psychological Review*, Vol. 63, pp. 81–97.

Milner, B. R. (1966) 'Amnesia following operation on temporal lobes', in C. W. N. Whitty and O. L. Zangwill (eds) *Amnesia*, Butterworth.

Minow, M. (2006) 'What the rule of law should mean in civics education: from the "following orders" defence to the classroom', *Journal of Moral Education*, Vol. 35, No. 2, pp. 137–62.

Mouttapa, M. et al. (2003) 'Authority-related conformity as a protective factor against adolescent health risk behaviors', *Journal of Adolescent Health*, Vol. 33, No. 5, pp. 320–21.

Murdock, B. B. (1962) 'The serial position effect in free recall', *Journal of Verbal Learning and Verbal Behavior*, Vol. 8, pp. 665–76.

Nakagawa, M., Lamb, M. E. and Miyake, K. (1989) 'Psychological experiences of Japanese infants in the Strange Situation', Research and Clinical Center for Child Development, Annual Report, Vol. 11, Nos 87–88, pp. 13–24.

Nakagawa, M., Lamb, M. E. and Miyake, K. (1992) 'Antecedents and correlates of the Strange Situation behavior of Japanese infants', *Journal of Cross-Cultural Psychology*, Vol. 23, No. 3, pp. 300–10.

Nagaraja, N. et al. (2007) 'Glucocorticoid mechanisms may contribute to ECT-induced retrograde amnesia', *Psychopharmacology*, Vol. 190, No. 1, pp. 73–80.

Newman, C. and Adams, K. (2004) 'Dog gone good: managing dog phobia in a teenage boy with a learning disability', *British Journal of Learning Disabilities*, Vol. 32, pp. 35–38.

Niregi, K. and Uchiyama, K. (2003) 'The trial to lead rational-emotive-behavior therapy smoothly for a woman with panic disorder', *Japanese Journal of Counseling Science*, Vol. 36, No. 4, pp. 414–24.

Öhman, A. (1979) 'Fear relevance, autonomic conditioning, and phobias', in P. O. Sjödén, S. Bates and W. S. Dockens (eds) *Trends in Behaviour Therapy*, Academic Press.

Orne, M. T. and Holland, C. C. (1968) 'On the ecological validity of laboratory deceptions', *International Journal of Psychiatry*, Vol. 6, pp. 282–93.

Orne, M. T. et al. (1984) 'Hypnotically induced testimony', in G. Wells and E. Loftus (eds) *Eyewitness Testimony: Psychological Perspectives*, Cambridge University Press.

Page, M. M. and Scheidt, R. J. (1971) 'The elusive weapons effect', *Journal of Personality and Social Psychology*, Vol. 20, pp. 304–18.

Palesh, O. et al. (2007) 'Stress history and breast cancer recurrence', *Journal of Psychosomatic Research*, Vol. 63, No. 3, pp. 233–39.

Papero, A. L. (2005) 'Is early, high-quality daycare an asset for the children of low-income, depressed mothers?', *Developmental Review*, Vol. 25, no. 2, pp. 181–211.

Park, C. L., Armeli, S., and Tennen, H. (2004) 'Appraisal-coping goodness of fit: a daily internet study', *Personality and Social Psychology Bulletin*, Vol. 30, No. 5, pp. 558–69.

Pavlov, I. P. (1927) *Conditioned Reflexes*, Oxford University Press.

Pengilly, J. W. (1997) 'Hardiness and social support as moderators of stress in college students', *Dissertation Abstracts International: Section B: The Sciences and Engineering*, Vol. 58 (3-B), p. 1,583.

Perrin, S. and Spencer, C. (1981) 'Independence or conformity in the Asch experiment as a reflection of cultural and situational factors', *British Journal of Social Psychology*, Vol. 20, pp. 205–09.

Peters, D. P. (1988) 'Eyewitness memory and arousal in a natural setting', in M. M. Gruneberg, P. E. Morris and R. N. Sykes (eds) *Practical Aspects of Memory: Current Research and Issues* (Vol. 1), John Wiley.

Peterson, L. R. and Peterson, M. J. (1959) 'Short term retention of individual items', *Journal of Experimental Psychology*, Vol. 58, pp. 193–98.

Piliavin, I. M. et al. (1975) 'Costs, diffusion and the stigmatised victim', *Journal of Personality and Social Psychology*, Vol. 32, pp. 429–38.

Pincus, J. (1981) 'The Asch effect', *Bulletin of the British Psychological Society*, Vol. 34, p. 39.

Ragland, D. R. and Brand, R. J. (1988) 'Type A behaviour and mortality from coronary heart disease', *New England Journal of Medicine*, Vol. 318, pp. 65–69.

Rahe, R. H. and Arthur, R. J. (1977) 'Life change patterns surrounding illness experience', in A. Monat and R. S. Lazarus (eds) *Stress and Coping*, Columbia University Press.

Rahe, R. H. et al. (1970) 'Prediction of near-future health-change from subjects' preceding life changes', *Journal of Psychosomatic Research*, Vol. 14, pp. 401–06.

Richey, H. W. (1976) 'Teaching techniques of resistance to unwarranted social pressure', *College Student Journal*, Vol. 10, No. 1, pp. 33–39.

Ring, K. et al. (1970) 'Role of debriefing as a factor affecting subjective reaction to a Milgram-type obedience experiment: an ethical enquiry', *Representative Research in Social Psychology*, Vol. 1, pp. 67–88.

Robertson, J. and Bowlby, J. (1952) 'Responses of young children to separation from their mothers', *Courier Centre International de l'Enfance*, Vol. 2, pp. 131–42.

Robinson, J. and Briggs, P. (1997) 'Age trends and eye-witness suggestibility and compliance', *Psychology, Crime & Law*, Vol. 3, No. 3, pp. 187–202.

Robinson, T. et al. (2007) 'The portrayal of older characters in Disney animated films', *Journal of Aging Studies*, Vol. 21, No. 3, pp. 203–13.

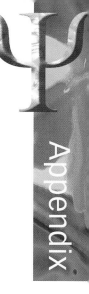

Rosenhan, D. (1969) 'Some origins of concern for others', in P. Mussen, J. Langer and M. Covington (eds) *Trends and Issues in Developmental Psychology*, Holt, Rinehart and Winston.

Rosenhan, D. L. and Seligman, M. E. P. (1969) *Abnormal Psychology* (2nd edn), Norton.

Ross, R. R. and Altmaier, E. M. (1994) *Intervention in Occupational Stress: A Handbook of Counselling for Stress at Work*, Sage Publications.

Rothbaum, F. et al. (2007) 'Attachment and AMAE: parent–child closeness in the United States and Japan', *Journal of Cross-Cultural Psychology*, Vol. 38, No. 4, pp. 465–86.

Rotter, J. B. (1966) 'Generalized expectancies for internal versus external control of reinforcement', *Psychological Monographs*, Vol. 30, No. 1, pp. 1–26.

Rubin, D. C. and Olson, M. J. (1980) 'Recall of semantic domains', *Memory and Cognition*, Vol. 8, pp. 354–66.

Rutter, M. (1972) *Maternal Deprivation Reassessed*, Penguin.

Rutter, M. L., Kreppner, J. M. and O'Connor, T. G. (2001) 'Specificity and heterogeneity in children's responses to profound institutional privation', *British Journal of Psychiatry*, Vol. 179, pp. 97–103.

Sackheim, H. (1988) 'The efficacy of electroconvulsive therapy', *Annals of the New York Academy of Sciences*, Vol. 462, pp. 70–75.

Savron, G., Bartolucci, G. and Pitti, P. (2004) 'Modificazioni psicopatologiche al trattamento cognitivo-comportamentale in 33 soggetti con Disturbo Ossessivo Compulsivo' (Psychopathological modification after cognitive behaviour treatment of obsessive-compulsive patients), *Rivista di Psichiatria*, Vol. 39, No. 3, pp. 171–83.

Schaffer, H. R. and Emerson, P. E. (1964) 'The development of social attachments in infancy', *Monographs of the Society for Research in Child Development*, Vol. 29, No. 3.

Scheff, T. J. (1966) *Being Mentally Ill: A Sociological Theory*, Aldine.

Schindler, P. J., Moely, B. E. and Frank, A. L. (1987) 'Time in day care and social participation of young children', *Developmental Psychology*, Vol. 23, pp. 255–61.

Schurz, G. (1985) 'Experimental examination of the relationships between personality characteristics and the readiness for destructive obedience toward authority', *Zeitschrift für Experimentelle und Angewandte Psychologie*, Vol. 32, pp. 160–77.

Seligman, M. E. P. (1971) 'Phobias and preparedness', *Behavior Therapy*, Vol. 2, pp. 307–20.

Selye, H. (1956) *The Stress of Life*, McGraw-Hill.

Selye, H. (1974) *Stress Without Distress*, Harper and Row.

Shallice, T. and Warrington, E. K. (1972) 'Independent functioning of verbal memory stores: a neuropsychological study', *Quarterly Journal of Experimental Psychology*, Vol. 22, pp. 261–73.

Shapiro, L. (2006) 'Remembering September 11th: the role of retention interval and rehearsal on flashbulb and event memory', *Memory*, Vol. 14, No. 2, pp. 129–47.

Sheridan, C. L. and King, K. G. (1972) 'Obedience to authority with an authentic victim', *Proceedings of the 80th Annual Convention of the American Psychological Association*, Vol. 7, pp. 165–66.

Sherif, M. (1935) 'A study of sane factors in perception', *Archives of Psychology*, Vol. 27, No. 187.

Shinman, S. (1981) *A Choice for Every Child? Access and Response to Pre-school Provision*, Tavistock.

Spiegel, R. (1989) *Psychopharmacology* (2nd edn), John Wiley.

Stacy, M. et al. (1970) *Hospitals, Children and Their Families: The Report of a Pilot Study*, Routledge and Kegan Paul.

Stevenson, C. et al. (2007) 'Adolescents' views of food and eating: identifying barriers to healthy eating', *Journal of Adolescence*, Vol. 30, No. 3, pp. 417–34.

Sundberg, N. D., Rohila, P. K. and Tyler, L. E. (1970) 'Values of Indian and American adolescents', *Journal of Personality and Social Psychology*, Vol. 16, No. 3, pp. 374–97.

Sundquist, J. et al. (2003) 'Psychosocial working conditions and self-reported long-term illness: a population-based study of Swedish-born and foreign-born employed persons', *Ethnicity and Health*, Vol. 8, No. 4, pp. 307–17.

Szasz, T. (1972) *The Myth of Mental Illness*, Paladin.

TADS team (2007) 'The Treatment for Adolescents with Depression Study (TADS): Long-term effectiveness and safety outcomes', *Archives of General Psychiatry*, Vol. 64, No. 10, pp. 1132–44.

Tajfel, H. (ed.) (1978) *Differentiation Between Social Groups: Studies in the Social Psychology of Intergroup Relations*, Academic Press.

Tajfel, H., Billig, M. G. and Bundy, R. P. (1971) 'Social categorization and intergroup behaviour', *European Journal of Social Psychology*, Vol. 1, No. 2, pp. 149–78.

Takahashi, K. (1990) 'Are the key assumptions of the Strange Situation" procedure universal? A view from Japanese research', *Human Development*, Vol. 33, pp. 23–30.

Tizard, B. (1991) 'Working mothers and the care of young children', in M. Woodhead, P. Light and R. Carr (eds) *Growing Up in a Changing Society*, Routledge.

Toyota, H. (2002) 'The bizarreness effect and individual differences in imaging ability', *Perceptual and Motor Skills*, Vol. 94, No. 2, pp. 533–40.

Treatment of Adolescents with Depression Study (2007) 'The Treatment for Adolescents with Depression Study (TADS): long-term effectiveness and safety outcomes', *Archives of General Psychiatry*, Vol. 64, No. 10, pp. 1132–44.

Tremblay, R. E. (2000) 'The development of aggressive behaviour during childhood: what have we learned in the past century?', *International Journal of Behavioral Development*, Vol. 24, No. 2, pp. 129–41.

True, M. M. (1995) 'Mother–infant attachment and communication among the Dogon of Mali', *Dissertation Abstracts International: Section B: The Sciences and Engineering*, Vol. 55 (11-B), p. 5101.

Tsutsumi, A. et al. (2007) 'Low control at work and the risk of suicide in Japanese men: a prospective cohort study', *Psychotherapy and Psychosomatics*, Vol. 76, No. 3, pp. 177–85.

Tulving, E. (1972) 'Episodic and semantic memory', in E. Tulving and W. Donaldson (eds) *Organisation of Memory*, Academic Press.

Tulving, E. (1974) 'Cue-dependent forgetting', *American Scientist*, Vol. 62, pp. 74–82.

Turnipseed, D. L. (1999) 'An exploratory study of the hardy personality at work in the health care industry', *Psychological Reports*, Vol. 85, No. 3, Pt 2 (special issue), pp. 1199–1217.

Tye, M. C. et al. (1999) 'The willingness of children to lie and the assessment of credibility in an ecologically relevant laboratory setting', *Applied Developmental Science*, Vol. 3, pp. 92–109.

Tyler, E. A. and Lowenbach, H. (1947) 'Polydiurnal electric shock treatment in mental disorders', *North Carolina Medical Journal*, Vol. 8, pp. 577–82.

US Bureau of the Census (1994) *Statistical Abstract of the United States* (114th edn), US Government Printing Office.

Van IJzendoorn, M. H. and Kroonenberg, P. M. (1988) 'Cross-cultural patterns of attachment: a meta-analysis of the Strange Situation', *Child Development*, Vol. 59, pp. 147–56.

Verhaeghe, R. et al. (2006) 'Impact of recurrent changes in the work environment on nurses' psychological well-being and sickness absence', *Journal of Advanced Nursing*, Vol. 56, No. 6, pp. 646–56.

Visintainer, M., Seligman, M. and Volpicelli, J. (1983) 'Helplessness, chronic stress and tumor development', *Psychosomatic Medicine*, Vol. 45, pp. 75–76.

Vitiello, B. (2007) 'Combined fluoxetine with cognitive-behavioral therapy vs monotherapy in the treatment of adolescents with major depressive disorder', *Directions in Psychiatry*, Vol. 27, No. 2, pp. 73–82.

Vondra, J. I., Shaw, D. S. and Kevenides, M. C. (1995) 'Predicting infant attachment classification from multiple contemporaneous measures of maternal care', *Infant Behavior and Development*, Vol. 18, pp. 215–25.

Watson, J. B. and Rayner, R. (1920) 'Conditioned emotional response', *Journal of Experimental Psychology*, Vol. 3, pp. 1–14.

Webb, E. J. et al. (1981) *Nonreactive Measures in the Social Sciences* (2nd edn), Houghton Mifflin.

West, S. G., Whitney, G. and Schendler, R. (1975) 'Helping a motorist in distress: the effects of sex, race and neighbourhood', *Journal of Personality and Social Psychology*, Vol. 31, pp. 691–98.

Westerhoff, N. (2007) 'Fantasy therapy', *Scientific American Mind*, October/November, pp. 70–73.

Whyte, W. E. (1948) *Human Relations in the Restaurant Industry*, McGraw-Hill.

Williams, J. M. (1980) 'An experimental investigation of assertiveness training as a drug abuse prevention strategy', unpublished dissertation, Pennsylvania State University.

Williams, J. M. and Warchal, J. (1981) 'The relationship between assertiveness, internal–external locus of control, and overt conformity', *Journal of Psychology*, Vol. 109, pp. 93–96.

Williams, J. M. et al. (1981) 'The relationships between assertiveness, conformity, and drug use', *Journal of Drug Education*, Vol. 11, No. 1, pp. 47–51.

Williams, R. B. (1984) 'Type A behaviour and coronary heart disease: something old, something new', *Behavioural Medicine Update*, Vol. 6, No. 3, pp. 29–33.

Wollen, K. A., Weber, A. and Lowry, D. H. (1972) 'Bizarreness versus interaction of mental images as determinants of learning', *Cognitive Psychology*, Vol. 3, No. 3, pp. 518–23.

Wolpe, J. (1958) *Psychotherapy by Reciprocal Inhibition*, Stanford University Press.

Woods, P. J. and Grieger, R. M. (1993) 'Bulimia: a case study with mediating cognitions and notes on a cognitive-behavioral analysis of eating disorders', *Journal of Rational-Emotive and Cognitive Behavior Therapy*, Vol. 11, No. 3, pp. 159–72.

Wyra, M., Lawson, M. J. and Hungi, N. (2007) 'The mnemonic keyword method: the effects of bidirectional retrieval training and of ability to image on foreign language vocabulary recall', *Learning and Instruction*, Vol. 17, No. 3, pp. 360–71.

Yuille, J. C. and Cutshall, J. L. (1986) 'A case study of eyewitness memory of a crime', *Journal of Applied Psychology*, Vol. 71, pp. 291–301.

Zechmeister, E. B. and Nyberg, S. E. (1982) *Human Memory*, Brooks/Cole.

Zimbardo, P. G. et al. (1973) 'A Pirandellian prison: the mind is a formidable jailor', *New York Times Magazine*, 8 April, pp. 38–60.

Zimmermann, P. et al. (2000) 'Longitudinal attachment development from infancy through adolescence', *Psychologie in Erziehung und Unterricht*, Vol. 47, pp. 99–117.

Zinbarg, R. E. and Mineka, S. (2001) 'Understanding, treating, and preventing anxiety, phobias, and anxiety disorders', in M. E. Carroll and B. Overmier (eds) *Animal Research and Human Health: Advancing Human Welfare Through Behavioral Science*, American Psychological Association.

Zubin, J. 1948) 'Memory functioning in patients treated with electric shock therapy', *Journal of Personality*, Vol. 17, pp. 33–41.

Sample questions

Memory

(1) Identify **two** differences between the working memory model and the STM component of the multi-store model of memory. *(4 marks)*

(2) Explain **one** criticism of the multi-store model of memory. *(4 marks)*

(3) Describe **two** factors that can lead to distortion in eye-witness testimony *(4 marks)*

(4) Outline the principles of the cognitive interview, and explain how they link to what we know about how memory works. *(8 marks)*

(5) Identify the three main components of working memory. *(3 marks)*

(6) Give an example of research findings that show the effect of leading questions on eye-witness testimony. *(2 marks)*

(7) Marie has to learn a list of French words and their English equivalents. Outline **one** possible strategy she could use to help her, and explain why it might be useful. *(4 marks)*

(8) Outline and evaluate research into the effectiveness of strategies used to improve memory. *(12 marks)*

(9) A researcher is interested in the effect of the method of loci strategy on memory for a list of words. This involves mentally placing each item to be remembered in a familiar place, such as your own house, and then mentally 'collecting' the items at the recall stage.

One group of psychology students is given a list of items and asked to use the method of loci to remember them. This method is explained to them. A second group of students is given the same list, and just asked to try to remember the items. The number of items remembered by each group is compared.
(a) The design of this study is:
  ● repeated measures
  ● independent groups
  ● matched participants *(1 mark)*
(b) Identify **two** possible confounding variables, and suggest how they might be overcome. *(6 marks)*

(10) Identify and explain **one** strength and **one** weakness of the multi-store model of memory. *(8 marks)*

Attachment

(1) Using the list below, complete the table by writing the letter under the appropriate heading, to distinguish between the responses of children with different attachment types to separation from the mother and reunion with her:

A The child is distressed when the mother leaves the room.
B The child avoids interaction with the mother when she returns.
C The child is easily comforted when reunited with the mother.
D The child is extremely distressed when the mother leaves the room.
E The child is not distressed when the mother leaves the room.
F The child seeks to be with the mother when she returns, but is not easily soothed.

	Response to separation	Response to reunion
Type A (anxious-avoidant)		
Type A (anxious-avoidant)		
Type C (anxious-ambivalent or resistant)		

(6 marks)

(2) Outline Bowlby's attachment theory. (4 marks)

(3) Describe some of the variations of patterns of attachment between cultures. (4 marks)

(4) Discuss the effects of institutionalisation on attachment. (12 marks)

(5) A researcher is interested in mothers' beliefs about the importance of early mother–infant attachment. She hands out a questionnaire, with open-ended questions, to all the mothers who attend a mother-and-baby clinic on a particular day, with a stamped addressed envelope for their return.

(a) Identify **one** advantage and **one** drawback of using questionnaires in this way. (2 marks)

(b) What is meant by 'open-ended questions'? (1 mark)

(c) Identify **one** advantage and **one** drawback of using this kind of question. (2 marks)

(d) Outline the steps the researcher should take to make the investigation as ethical as possible. (4 marks)

(6) Identify **three** aspects of day care that are associated with the care offered being of high quality. (3 marks)

(7) In what ways might day care contribute to children's social development? (2 marks)

(8) Summarise research findings on the effect of day care on aggression. (4 marks)

(9) A researcher is planning an observational study of aggression shown by young children in a day care centre. Describe **two** ways in which levels of aggression could be measured. (4 marks)

(10) What ethical problems might arise in carrying out this study, and how
could the researcher deal with them? *(6 marks)*

Stress

(1) Identify **two** illnesses associated with stress. *(2 marks)*

(2) A researcher is interested in the relationship between stress and illness. Participants
complete a questionnaire aiming to measure the current level of stress they are
experiencing. A further questionnaire assesses recent experience of illness on
several measures, e.g. the number of days taken off work with stress over the past
6 months. The two measures are plotted on a scattergraph:

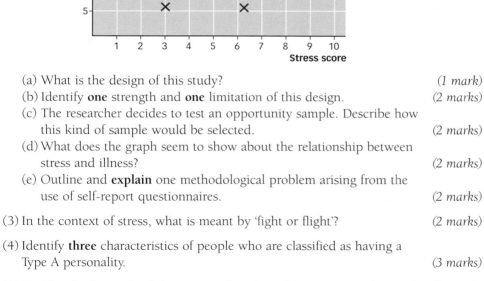

(a) What is the design of this study? *(1 mark)*
(b) Identify **one** strength and **one** limitation of this design. *(2 marks)*
(c) The researcher decides to test an opportunity sample. Describe how
this kind of sample would be selected. *(2 marks)*
(d) What does the graph seem to show about the relationship between
stress and illness? *(2 marks)*
(e) Outline and **explain** one methodological problem arising from the
use of self-report questionnaires. *(2 marks)*

(3) In the context of stress, what is meant by 'fight or flight'? *(2 marks)*

(4) Identify **three** characteristics of people who are classified as having a
Type A personality. *(3 marks)*

(5) Decide whether each of these ways of coping with exam stress is emotion-focused
or problem-focused and write the letter under the appropriate heading in the table:
A   planning a revision timetable
B   going out with friends for an evening
C   practising answering possible questions
D   going to the gym

E thinking that the exam will soon be over

F going over class notes

Problem-focused coping	Emotion-focused coping

(6 marks)

(6) Outline the aims of CBT, and give a brief account of how it is carried out. (6 marks)

(7) Holmes and Rahe suggested that the findings of research using the social readjustment rating scale (SRRS) demonstrate that life changes are an important source of stress. Give **two** criticisms of this interpretation of the findings. (2 marks)

(8) Outline **one** advantage and **one** drawback of using drugs to deal with stress. (2 marks)

(9) Give **two** examples of the kinds of hassles found in scales such as the Hassles and Uplifts Scale developed by Kanner. (2 marks)

(10) Discuss the effectiveness of CBT as a way of dealing with stress. (12 marks)

Social Influence

(1) Give an account of **two** explanations as to why people might obey an order given by an authority figure, as in Milgram's experiments. (4 marks)

(2) Summarise the findings of Milgram's studies of obedience. (4 marks)

(3) In Asch's study of conformity using a line-matching task, a genuine participant agreed with the clearly wrong judgements of Asch's confederates. Which kind of influence — normative or informational — is likely to have been stronger here? Explain your choice. (2 marks)

(4) In a conformity study, a participant agrees with the clearly wrong opinions of the other group members, but does not change her opinion. Which term is used to describe this change in behaviour but not opinion? (1 mark)

(5) For each of the following statements, tick the correct alternative:
Normative social influence:
(a) is more likely when the situation is:
ambiguous ☐
unambiguous ☐
(b) arises from:
the need to be right ☐
the need to be accepted by the group ☐ (2 marks)

(6) Identify **two** factors that are associated with independent behaviour.   *(2 marks)*

(7) Milgram's studies have been criticised on the grounds that they have low ecological validity. What is meant by ecological validity?   *(1 mark)*

(8) Explain how Milgram's studies could be considered to have low ecological validity.   *(4 marks)*

(9) Maria fails her driving test. Decide whether each of the reasons she gives to explain this is associated with an internal or an external locus of control, and write the letter under the appropriate heading in the table:
   A   The examiner didn't like me.
   B   I didn't practise enough before the test.
   C   I was just unlucky.
   D   The cyclist who swerved into my path put me off.
   E   The examiner's attitude made me nervous.
   F   I made some silly mistakes because I was not concentrating.
   G   I didn't listen to my instructor's advice.

Locus of control	
Internal	External

   (6 marks)

(10) Discuss the ethical issues arising in Milgram's research into obedience.   *(12 marks)*

Psychopathology

(1) Explain what is meant by the definition of abnormality as 'deviation from social norms'.   *(2 marks)*

(2) Outline **two** limitations of this definition.   *(4 marks)*

(3) Describe the key features of the behaviourist approach to psychopathology.   *(6 marks)*

(4) Give **one** strength and **one** limitation of the use of ECT as a therapy.   *(4 marks)*

(5) Identify which **three** of the following statements relate to the psychodynamic approach to psychopathology, and write the letters in the boxes below:
   A   Mental health problems are the result of maladaptive thinking.
   B   Childhood experience is a critical factor in the development of mental disorders.
   C   To a large extent, the causes of mental health problems lie in the unconscious.
   D   There is a physical basis to psychological problems.
   E   We do not need to understand the cause of a psychological disorder in order to be able to treat it.

F   We use defence mechanisms to protect ourselves from the anxiety caused by painful experiences.

(6) Emma has developed the eating disorder bulimia nervosa. She takes large doses of laxatives, and alternately binges and starves herself for days on end. She constantly feels depressed, guilty and angry. She has been referred for treatment to a cognitive behavioural therapist. What are the aims of CBT in treating a person like Emma? *(2 marks)*

(7) Outline how CBT might be carried out to help Emma with her problems. *(6 marks)*

(8) Jenny has a spider phobia. She panics whenever she sees even the smallest spider, and her phobia restricts what she is able to do. For example, she can't go camping with her friends because she is afraid of a spider getting into the tent. How could systematic desensitisation be carried out to help Jenny overcome her phobia? *(6 marks)*

(9) Identify the aims of psychoanalysis, and describe one of the methods that might be used to achieve these aims. *(4 marks)*

(10) Describe and evaluate the use of drugs to treat mental disorders. *(12 marks)*

Index

Bold page numbers indicate definitions of terms.

B

Bandura, Albert, social learning theory **15–16**
bar chart **124**, 125, **126**
behaviour 58, **199**, **209**, **218**, **221**, **228**
behavioural approach **157**, **162**, **204**, 206–08
behaviourism 3, **5**, **6**,12, **17**, **23**
'being' need **21**, **22**
Belsky case study, on day care 83
benzodiazepines **155**
beta blockers **155**
between-groups design **104**
bias **112**
Bielefeld longitudinal study 68
Big Five, personality factors **189**
bimodal values **123**
biochemical changes in brain (ECT) **201**, **213**, **216**
biofeedback **156**, **157**
biological approach to psychopathology 200–07, 210–16, **228**
biopsychologists **2**, **24**
bipolar disorder 201
bizarre behaviour **197**, **199**
blood 134, 156, 211
Bobo doll study 90, 91
Borge et al. case study on day care and aggression 85
Bowlby, John **60–63**, 61, 62, 73–74
  on day care 81, 87–88
  theory of attachment 60, 61, 87
Brady case study, stress in monkeys 139
brain damage 18, 201, 202, **215**
  and electro-convulsive therapy (ECT) **214**
  scanning techniques 3, 17
brief focal therapy (Malan) **220**, **221**
British Psychological Society (BPS) **114**, **121**
broken home and delinquency 75
bulimia nervosa 208, **226**, **228**
burnout **135**, **149**, 150, **162**
buspirone drug **155**

C

cancer **139**
care, non-maternal 83

case-study method, Freud **6**
castration anxiety 10, **218**
catharsis **216**
cause-and-effect relationship 90, **94**
causes of stress/mental disorders **157**, 200, 207, **221**
chemotherapy **210**
children **7**, 9–10, 82, 87, 204, 205, **206**
  development of 2, 4
  experience of emotion **69**
  in Sweden 86
  temperament **84**, 85
  watching TV 108, 109
chronic stress **136**, **138**
circadian rhythms **147**, **149**
classical conditioning **12**, 14, **17**, **23**, 58, **206**, **221**
clinical interview **99**–100
closed-ended questions **98**, **100**
clozapine 211
coding units **128**
cognitive approach 80, **157**, 204, 208–10
cognitive behavioural therapy (CBT) **158–62**, **209**, **216**, **224**, 226–28
  stress **151**
cognitive psychologists **2**, 19–21, **23**, 90
Cohen case study, stress 138
collectivist culture **70**, 71, **73**, **188**
combination with other therapies **223**
comparative psychology **2**, **23**
compliance **167**, **169**
conditioned emotional response **13**, **206**, 207
conduct problems **80**
confidence **188–89**, **192**
confidentiality **119**, **121**
conformity 163–67, 170–72, **192**, 193
connectionism 20,23
conscious awareness **21**
consent, fully informed **117–18**, **121**
consequences **17**
consistency **110**, **112**
constructivism 4, **24**
construct validity **112**
contact comfort **59**
content analysis **112**, **127–28**

Q

qualitative analysis **128**
qualitative data, presentation **100**, 107–08, 126–28
quality of care **82**, **86**, **87**
quantitative data collection **100**, **107**, **108**, **128**
quasi-autistic features **79**
quasi-experiments **91**, **94**
quasi-random sample **113**
questionnaires **98–99**, **100**, 108–110

R

Rahe et al. case study, stress **144**
random allocation **91**, **94**, **105**
random sampling **113**, **114**
range of scores **123**, **124**
ranking items **128**
rational emotive behaviour therapy (REBT) **209**, **224–28**
rationalism (or nativism) **3**, **24**
reality principle **8**
reciprocal attachment in infants **61**
reciprocal inhibition **221**
Recurrent Coronary Prevention Program **157**
redirection of emotional energy (libido) **216**
reductionist approach **106**, **205**, 207–08, **228**
reflexive analysis **108**, **127**
reinforcement **14**, **17**
relaxation techniques **221**, **224**
release of defence mechanisms **216**
reliability **95**, 110–12
repeated measures design **104–05**
replication **91**, **98**, **128**
repression **9**, **12**
researcher bias **99**, **101**
research methods 89–129
resistance **134**, **136**, **217**
  to peer pressure **193**
response set **109**

retrograde amnesia (ECT) **214**
retrospective study 75
return rate, postal questionnaires **100**
reunion with mother **65**
reverse engineering **19**
rhesus monkeys, attachment to mother 59, 62
Rogers, Carl, humanistic psychologist **22**, **23**
role conflict at work 148–49, **149**
Romanian children, adoption 79, 80
Rorschach inkblot test 218
Rosenheim and Seligman, criteria for abnormality 198
Rothbaum, case study, on attachment 71
Rotter, Locus of Control Scale 190, 191
Rutter case study, institutionalisation 79–80

S

safety, need for **21**, **61**
sampling **112**, **127**, **128**
scattergraphs **126**
schizophrenia 18, 201, 203, 207, 211–12
scientific methods **19**, **21**
'screw you' effect **92**
secondary appraisal **151**
secondary drive hypothesis **59**
sectioning **202**, **203**, **204**, **216**
secure attachments, failure in childhood 205
seizure **212**
selective serotonin re-uptake inhibitors (SSRIs) **210**
self, negative view **208**
self, sense of **22**
self-actualisation **21**, **22**, **23**
self-report techniques 98–100
self-selected sample **99**
sensations 5
sensitive measure **122**, **124**
sensitive period 60, 63
separation anxiety 58, **61–63**, **65**, 73–75
serotonin 18, 201, 202
serotonin/noradrenaline reuptake inhibitors (SNRIs) **210**